CREATING LOCAL ARTS TOGETHER

Those of us who teach Music in Missions, Multicultural and Global Worship, or Arts in Worship courses in theological training institutions welcome the publication of the manual, *Creating Local Arts Together*. This volume contains specific and clear steps to lead the reader to explore local art forms and to encourage local artists to use them to advance kingdom goals. It also contains many resources for students doing internships in arts in cross-cultural settings. The manual provides a long-needed "how-to" guide built on a fundamental truth, that God is the Supreme Creator, and that since we are created in his image we can inspire and motivate others to use their creativity for his glory throughout his world.

Edgar Cajas, PhD
associate professor of Church Music, Southwestern Baptist Theological Seminary
director-founder of Alfredo Colom, a Christian school for Guatemalan music teachers

Creating Local Arts Together combines intellectual rigor with a loving sensitivity toward local communities, and it's all informed by a great breadth of experience. In this age of the endangerment of so many of the world's distinctive artistic traditions—and with the expansion of Christianity often blamed for it—I'm excited by the potential effects of this thoughtful guide. I hope Schrag's encouragement through the manual will bear fruit in a new flourishing of arts and creativity throughout the Christian church.

Neil R. Coulter, PhD
senior editor of the journal *Global Forum on Arts and Christian Faith*

In 2012 I found my wife and myself up in the mountains of northern Philippines conversing with the believers of a tribal group, introducing them to the possibility of using their indigenous musical forms and instruments in their worship. When they said yes to the idea, I began wondering, "How do I start the process?" *Creating Local Arts Together* is God's answer to that prayer. I am a musician with no training in ethnoarts, but this material empowers me to do the work of the Lord in ways that will be meaningful and productive.

Roy Fabella
Philippine Ethnoarts Community of Practice
ministry director and missionary, Windsong Christian Music Ministries, Inc.

The book you hold in your hands is the result of great effort by many people who have worked in the area that most deeply touches the heart of a people—the arts. Its seven steps allow anyone, beginner or not, working in a cross-cultural context to integrate arts into his or her ministry. The gospel message is too important to be misunderstood; local arts allow everyone to hear God speaking directly to them. Studying and applying the manual will help you tap into this powerful component of the spread of the kingdom of God.

Héber Negrão
Missão Evangélica aos Indios do Brasil, Evangelical Mission to Brazilian Indians

The sheer breadth of this project speaks of the multitudes of peoples around the world longing to offer worship and witness drawing from their cultural wealth in ways that bring glory to God. Especially significant is how the dual volumes, a textbook and a companion "make-it-happen" practical guide, offer opportunities for continued growth in the ministry of the church worldwide.

Roberta R. King, PhD
director, Global Christian Worship program, Fuller Theological Seminary

I have known Dr. Schrag for years. His love for people in general and Africa in particular has always touched me. This love is so intense that it pushes him to share all that he receives from the Lord. In this season—characterized by a growing awareness of African identity in African churches and in Cameroon in particular—this book is like a bulldozer, paving the way for the enrichment of our arts. I strongly recommend *Creating Local Arts Together* to worship leaders, theology professors, musicians, and all who crave to see peoples of all cultures give the best of themselves to the Lord.

Pastor Roch Ntankeh
worship leader, Yaoundé, Cameroon

Creating Local Arts Together is the perfect companion to field workers wishing to encourage a community in reaching their kingdom goals through the exploration and power of local arts. The painstaking efforts of the authors combined with their years of field experience provide one with practical tools to apply in research, analysis, and "sparking" of indigenous art for the glory of God and the blessing of his people. This manual is number one on our resource list as it contains in one thorough, yet convenient place so much of the practical wisdom we've received from various books, lectures, and presentations.

Justin and Bethany Randolph
arts specialists, Wycliffe Bible Translators, Eastern Europe

As soon as you get ready to open this book, put everything else aside and read it carefully. In the past, Mono traditional instruments were used only for ceremonial rituals honoring ancestral deities. But in 1992 Brian Schrag moved to my village as a Bible translator and started learning to play traditional Mono songs on the *kundi*—a local harp. Eventually a small group joined him and began composing Scripture-based songs. Today, in all of the Mono churches, we see a radical change in how Christians live, because God's message communicated through *kundi* songs directly touches their hearts. Many declare by their actions that the Spirit has used this to bring them back to the foot of the cross of Jesus Christ. We hope this manual will inspire those who read it. Even more, we declare to our Christian brothers and all of God's servants in other places that the manual is truly useful in bringing people back to God.

Rev. Gaspard Yalemoto
director, Mono Bible Translation Program, Democratic Republic of the Congo

CREATING LOCAL ARTS TOGETHER

A MANUAL TO HELP COMMUNITIES REACH THEIR KINGDOM GOALS

Brian Schrag

James R. Krabill
GENERAL EDITOR

www.ethnodoxologyhandbook.com/manual

WILLIAM CAREY
LIBRARY

Published by William Carey Library
1605 E. Elizabeth Street
Pasadena, CA 91104 | www.missionbooks.org

Brian Schrag, author
James R. Krabill, general editor
Melissa Hicks, production editor
Brad Koenig, copyeditor
Hugh Pindur, graphic design
Josie Leung, graphic assistant
Rose Lee-Norman, indexer

William Carey Library is a ministry of the
U.S. Center for World Mission
Pasadena, CA | www.uscwm.org

Printed in the United States of America

16 15 14 13 12   5 4 3 2 1 COU 2000

Front cover photos courtesy of The Lausanne Movement ©, Cape Town 2010; photos by James R. Krabill, used by permission.

Section divider photo, "The Dancing Feet," courtesy of Leo Vartanian
Nadëb NT Celebration, July 2012, Wycliffe Global Alliance ©
http://www.wycliffe.net

All other section divider photos courtesy of James R. Krabill.

Library of Congress Cataloging-in-Publication Data

Schrag, Brian.
  Creating local arts together : a manual to help communities reach their kingdom goals / Brian Schrag, author ; James R. Krabill, general editor.
    p. cm.
  Includes bibliographical references.
  ISBN 978-0-87808-494-4
1. Christianity and the arts. 2. Evangelistic work. I. Krabill, James R. II. Title.
  BR115.A8S37 2012
  261.5'7--dc23
                    2012019777

CONTENTS

CLOSING MATTER

FIGURES

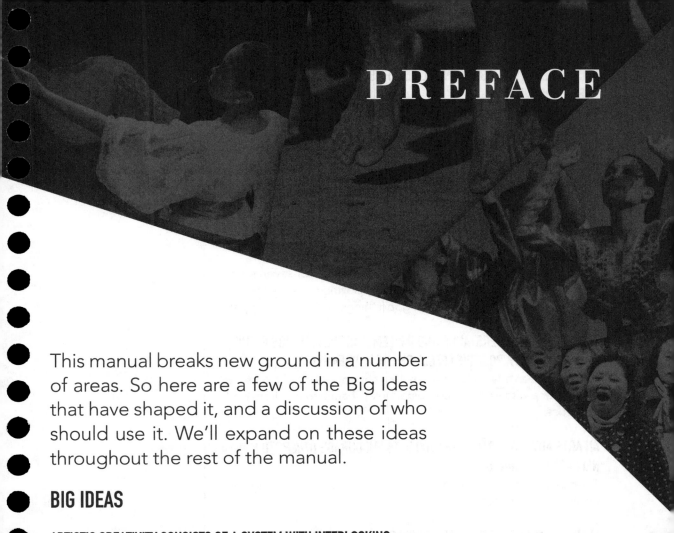

This manual breaks new ground in a number of areas. So here are a few of the Big Ideas that have shaped it, and a discussion of who should use it. We'll expand on these ideas throughout the rest of the manual.

BIG IDEAS

ARTISTIC CREATIVITY CONSISTS OF A SYSTEM WITH INTERLOCKING COMPONENTS: KNOWLEDGE, SKILLS, PHYSICAL RESOURCES, SOCIAL PATTERNS, AND PEOPLE IN VARIOUS ROLES.

It's rare for someone in *any* community to have the perspective to describe their creative system. The process in this manual helps reveal the dynamics and details of such systems.

THERE IS NO ARTISTIC FORM THAT COMMUNICATES INTENDED MESSAGES UNIVERSALLY.

We often hear the phrase, "Music is a universal language, " presented as an axiom. This likely results from a misreading of American poet Henry Wadsworth Longfellow. Longfellow does indeed state that "[m]usic is the universal language of mankind— poetry their universal pastime and delight." In the preceding sentences, however, he celebrates the variety displayed in Italian, Swiss, Scotch, English, and Spanish songs. Examples in the Manual support the assertion that music exists univerally, but takes forms and meanings particular to each community. The same is true of every form of artistic communication.

PREFACE

PREPARE

STEP 1

STEP 2

STEP 3

STEP 4

STEP 5

STEP 6

STEP 7

CLOSING

LOCAL CREATIVITY HAS ESSENTIAL BENEFITS THAT OUTSIDE CREATIVITY DOESN'T PROVIDE.

These benefits include more penetrating, relevant, memorable, and engaging communication for education and motivation.

EVERY COMMUNITY CAN BENEFIT FROM MORE LOCAL CREATIVITY.

The need is sometimes urgent, especially in ethnolinguistic minorities whose arts are stagnant or dying.

SPECIFIC KINDS OF CREATIVITY CAN BE ENCOURAGED THAT WILL HELP A COMMUNITY REACH GOALS THEY EXPLICITLY CHOOSE.

This field manual describes a method, composed of seven steps, called Create Local Arts Together (CLAT; also known as *cocreation*). If a community follows the steps, good things are likely to happen.

SOMEONE WHO UNDERSTANDS AND IMPLEMENTS THE METHODS IN THIS BOOK CAN HAVE A POSITIVE EFFECT ON LOCAL CREATIVITY.

This person—an arts advocate—may be a community insider, outsider, or someone with a unique combination of characteristics from both identities.

AN ARTS ADVOCATE'S PRIMARY JOB IS TO ENCOURAGE *OTHERS* TO MAKE NEW ARTISTIC THINGS.

Their posture toward a community is one of learning, dialoguing, facilitating, and encouraging.

LEARNING ABOUT INSIDER CATEGORIES OF ARTISTIC COMMUNICATION FIRST—THAT IS, A COMMUNITY'S ARTISTIC GENRES—PROVIDES MORE INSIGHTS USEFUL FOR THE CLAT PROCESS THAN STARTING WITH OUTSIDE CATEGORIES.

You'll notice that one of the first research activities we describe is to make a list of local artistic genres ("Take a First Glance at a Community's Arts," Step 1). Exploring how the Euro-American artistic domains of music, dance, drama, oral verbal arts, and visual arts relate to local genres is buried in Step 4. Because every community divides its artistry in different ways, starting with the outside categories can lead to confusion and wasted time.

THE CHURCH'S CURRENT MISSION ON EARTH IS BEST UNDERSTOOD IN RELATIONSHIP TO PRIOR EVENTS: GOD'S CREATION OF THE UNIVERSE, THE FALL, AND JESUS' BRINGING OF THE KINGDOM OF HEAVEN.

It is not enough for a group of Christians to develop the arts that their particular history has produced. Rather, we must also be aware of God's artistry and its purposes in the rest of his creation and in heaven.

PREFACE

PREPARE

STEP 1

STEP 2

STEP 3

STEP 4

STEP 5

STEP 6

STEP 7

CLOSING

WHO SHOULD USE THE MANUAL?

We originally envisioned the manual as a tool for Christians working professionally in cultural contexts very different from their own. This could include missionaries, international aid workers, and others. As we taught the method to diverse groups, however, we found that people could apply it to many situations that we wouldn't normally label cross-cultural. A worship leader in a local church, for example, said "I need to do this. I need to first get to know my congregation and encourage different kinds of artists to create new things for God's purposes."

This makes sense. Every individual human represents a package of experiences, ideas, neurological connections, physical qualities, emotions, and other characteristics that can never be known entirely by someone else. Of course, if you want to engage with people that group themselves around a language, worldview, geography, diet, and social patterns very different from yours, you will need to expend much effort and use many skills; we provide rigorous research and other activities that will help those of you in this situation. But you could also apply the approach to people who are very much like you, your best friend, or your spouse. In fact, you could follow the CLAT process to learn something new about your own artistic gifts and life goals, and create something artistic that would improve your own future.

So though we mostly use examples where people are crossing large cultural barriers, don't let that stop you from finding other applications.

HISTORY AND ACKNOWLEDGMENTS

This manual beautifully exemplifies its content. Each member of a crowd contributed their gifts to a common goal: a friendly, useful, aesthetically-crafted compendium of wisdom steeped in centuries of ideas and events, geared toward understanding the present, and directed by a vision of a better future. Contributors drew on the historically robust discoveries and methods of academic disciplines like ethnomusicology, folklore, performance studies, anthropology, biblical studies, and missiology. Interactions with colleagues in the Applied Ethnomusicology sub-groups of the Society for Ethnomusicology and the International Council of Traditional Music were especially helpful.

We were inspired by examples of artistic contributions to the spreading church throughout its 2,000-year history. We founded many of our approaches on the thoughts of pioneers in the application of ethnomusicology to Christian aims like Drs. Vida Chenoweth, Roberta King, Tom Avery, John Benham, Arthur Morris Jones, Professor Kwabena Nketia, and David Dargie, and

PREFACE

PREPARE

STEP 1

STEP 2

STEP 3

STEP 4

STEP 5

STEP 6

STEP 7

CLOSING

educational institutions like Wheaton College, Daystar University, Fuller Seminary, Bethel University, Southwestern Baptist Theological Seminary, European Training Programme, Payap University, and the Graduate Institute of Applied Linguistics (GIAL). Publications like *All the World Will Worship*, *All the World is Singing*, *EM News*, and *EthnoDoxology* were also important to the expansion of knowledge in this domain. Professor Paul Neeley has been a strong force in much of this milieu.

The nascent form of this manual consisted of the limited resources we garnered and produced to teach a new curriculum at GIAL in 2008. A core of SIL International ethnomusicologists was responding to two realities. First, many of us were frustrated by our incompetence in interacting with the elements of dance, visual, drama, verbal, and other arts that almost invariably went hand-in-hand with communities' music. Second, we realized that artistic forms of communication have a much wider range of benefits than the kinds of church-based song-writing workshops that constituted the majority of our work. So we read experts in other domains, sometimes gathering them for discussion and debate, taught classes at GIAL, asked for feedback from our patient students, and the material matured. GIAL now offers an MA in World Arts based on this curriculum.

In the meantime, the International Council of Ethnodoxologists (ICE, founded 2003) had been noticing and nurturing interest in this new approach in other Christian organizations. William Carey Library agreed to publish a two-volume project coordinated by ICE: a handbook and a manual. I was in charge of the manual and soon realized I needed lots of help. I asked a few dozen people to contribute, using a complicated, web-based process that often stifled their creative output rather than releasing it.

In the end, I wrote or edited most of what you'll read in this volume. But I integrated contributions and feedback from dozens of people, trying to create an organic, one-voiced whole. So instead of trying to cite the source of each idea in the text, creating a nightmarish web of footnotes, I'll identify contributions here (all published sources are cited in the text, of course). Some acknowledgements will contain some detail, others will be more general. Please forgive my lapses of memory or attribution. A community truly produced this bit of written artistry.

Our community's deepest gratitude to each of you for these contributions (in alphabetical order):

- Wendy Atkins (ATS ICE certified)—activities related to worldview and baptism rites
- Dr. Tom Avery—identifying arts, analyzing music, and the unfettered encouragement to follow this multiartistic path
- Ian Collinge (MA)—activities to research and encourage multicultural worship

PREFACE

PREPARE

STEP 1

STEP 2

STEP 3

STEP 4

STEP 5

STEP 6

STEP 7

CLOSING

- Dr. Neil Coulter–descriptions of research methods
- Cory Cummins–modification of the cocreation graphic, and sports-related content
- Lydia Duggins–an activity to encourage multi-sensory communion with God
- Dr. Dan Fitzgerald–music and oral verbal arts, and activities related to translation
- Dr. Sue Hall-Heimbecker–various Glimpses, research, and input into categories of signs of the kingdom
- Brad Keating (MA)–hours of detailed, frank discussion of applying a common method to analyzing all artistic genres, and original design of the cocreation graphic
- Matt Menger (MM)–activities and general comments
- Michelle Petersen (MA)–evaluation methods, Scripture interpretation, multiple activities, Glimpses, Results Based Management, and foundational work in everything related to drama
- Dr. Robert Reed and Michael Harrar–content related to visual arts
- Dr. Julisa Rowe–content related to drama
- Mary Beth Saurman (MA)–Glimpses, evaluation methods, multiple activities, and glossary items
- Amy Schmidt (MFA)–content related to dance
- Glenn Stallsmith (MA)–content related to basic research
- Dr. Pete Unseth–content related to proverbs

Another special category of gratitude goes to Dr. Julie Taylor for her insistent calls for simplicity, practicality, and completion, and Dr. Robin Harris, for her constant, sparkly encouragement.

Finally, all of these people (and more I've undoubtedly left out) evaluated, improved, suggested, or encouraged the process in other ways: Harold Best, Kevin Calcote, Duane Clouse, Peggy Connett, Frank Fortunato, James Harris, Mary Hendershott, Valerie Henry, Harriet Hill, Margaret Hill, Ken Hollingsworth, Debbi Hosken, Laura Huggins, Eric Jones, Pat Kelley, James R. Krabill, Megan Larson, April Longenecker, Paul McAndrew, Roch Ntankeh, Jonathan and Quynh Parlane, Evy Pun, Justin Randolph, Scott Rayl, Todd Saurman, D. P. Smith, Mary Lou Totten, and Martie Tracy. Feedback from students and administrators at Payap University, European Training Programme, Graduate Institute of Applied Linguistics, and Arts in Mission 2011 was also invaluable.

This manual is an imperfect object that will continue to grow and morph, spawning new objects with different shapes in different places. I take responsibility for its current contour and content, including errors and omissions. But now it's yours. You may take it, play with it, add to it, discard parts of it. Now *you* have the responsibility and pleasure to use the manual as an aid to creating astounding bits of artistry on earth that you'll recognize in heaven.

PREFACE

PREPARE

STEP 1

STEP 2

STEP 3

STEP 4

STEP 5

STEP 6

STEP 7

CLOSING

ALL THE ARTS FROM ALL THE WORLD FOR ALL OF GOD'S PURPOSES

REALITY: People communicate in almost seven thousand languages around the world, not just by spoken words, but also through artistically rendered song, drama, dance, visual arts, story, and other special forms.

REALITY: All communities have nonexistent or imperfect relationships with God, and struggle with social upheaval, violence, disease, anger, sexual immorality, anxiety, and fear.

REALITY: God gave every community unique gifts of artistic communication to tell the Truth, and bring healing and hope and joy in response to these problems. Many of these gifts, however, lie dormant, misused, or dying.

The purpose of this manual is to guide your involvement in working toward a new reality, one in which *all* cultures are using *all* of their gifts to worship, obey, and enjoy God with *all* of their heart, soul, mind, and strength (Mark 12:30). In other words, it will help you work alongside local musicians, dancers, actors, painters, sculptors, storytellers, and other artists to spark the creation of new songs, dances, dramas, paintings, sculptures, and stories that help people usher God's kingdom into their community.

We have chosen to organize our activities in the arts in terms of how they can move us toward the kingdom of God. What is this

PREFACE

PREPARE

STEP 1

STEP 2

STEP 3

STEP 4

STEP 5

STEP 6

STEP 7

CLOSING

kingdom? Jesus taught his followers to pray for the kingdom of God to come to earth (Matt 6:10). He described it as centered on himself and his message (Mark 1:15), growing mysteriously but to great size (Mark 4), marked by values contrary to human social systems (Mark 10; 12; Luke 6), and connected in practice to healing and spiritual warfare (Luke 9; 11). The kingdom of God on earth mysteriously but concretely reflects the reality of life in heaven, and God wants us to help it expand.

A basic characteristic of the kingdom of God is that it exists only partially on earth now. Every community has aspects that are more like the kingdom, and those that are less. Now and not yet. No human culture fully expresses God's kingdom, but because God created us in his image, there are glimpses of the kingdom everywhere.

What would a community look like that was deeply shaped by the values and spiritual power of God's kingdom? It would contain an expanding body of Christ-followers who worship God in spirit and in truth. Its members would be growing spiritually, socially, and physically healthier. Older members would be passing on God-reflecting aspects of their cultures to younger members. Everyone in the community would have access to accurate Scripture in the language they understand best so that young and old could remember and apply it to their lives. And the whole community would be marked by justice, honesty, health, joy, and care and love for people in their margins.

Locally available artistic forms of communication are powerful resources for anyone working toward these and other signs of the kingdom. Such communication is embedded in culture, and so touches many important aspects of a society. It marks messages as important, separate from everyday activities; it touches not only cognitive, but also experiential and emotional ways of knowing; it aids memory of a message; it increases the impact of a message through multiple media that often include the whole body; it concentrates the information contained in a message; it instills solidarity in its performers and experiencers; it provides socially acceptable frameworks for expressing difficult or new ideas; it inspires and moves people to action; it can act as a strong sign of identity; and it opens spaces for people to imagine and dream. Perhaps most importantly, local artistic communication exists and is owned locally; there's no need to translate foreign materials, and local artists are empowered to contribute to the expansion of the kingdom of God.

Our approach is to help you work with a community in deciding what aspects of the kingdom of God people want to see flourish, and then explore that community's resources for artistic genres that might help in the accomplishment of those goals. We then describe activities that spark creativity in these genres in ways that meet a community's goals in sustainable ways, and we show how you can

PREFACE

PREPARE

STEP 1

STEP 2

STEP 3

STEP 4

STEP 5

STEP 6

STEP 7

CLOSING

join in. In other words, we join in *others'* creativity, helping them use their existing arts for new purposes that will continue into the future.

ALL?

The title of this chapter uses the word "all" three times. What do we mean? "All the arts" doesn't suggest that God wants to include every art form in its current state in his kingdom. Rather, we want to approach every art graciously, not judging its worth or usefulness for the kingdom until God judges it. All communities and their arts are marred by sin, but God can redeem all things. The process of integrating arts includes a winnowing, a remaking.

For example, not all of a community's arts are equally appropriate for furthering God's goals at a given time. A particular dance might be so strongly associated with immoral or idolatrous activities that its use might pull new believers in Christ back to their old lives. We believe that God will renew everything for himself–see Matthew 19:28–but that it takes insights of local believers and the Holy Spirit to decide what actions are wise at any given point. Don't force kingdom change.

"From all the world" refers to the thousands and thousands of ways people communicate artistically. Because each of us is a finite being with limited experience, we don't naturally recognize arts new to us, especially when they're part of a foreign culture. So one goal of this manual is to both widen and sharpen our vision to see the myriad potential resources. We want to have a little bit more of a God's-eye view of the arts.

"For all of God's purposes" helps us remember that God does not limit his use of the arts to our categories. In Scripture we see examples of artistic communication involved in corporate adoration, teaching, warfare, celebration, ritual, correcting, individual growth, healing, confession, remembering, and many other purposes. We've crafted this manual to nudge each of us to think beyond any particular liturgical role of the arts we're used to.

WHAT ARE ARTS?

In this manual, we treat the arts as special kinds of communication. Like all communication systems, the arts are connected to particular times, places, and social contexts. They have their own symbols, grammars, and internal structures. This means that just as you have to learn how to ask directions in a language foreign to you, you must also learn how to move your arms and neck and eyebrows to tell a story in Thai dance. There is no one artistic language that communicates completely across lines of time, place, and culture. So to understand any art form, you have to interact with its practitioners and study it. Getting to know local artists and their arts is our first job.

PREFACE

PREPARE

STEP 1

STEP 2

STEP 3

STEP 4

STEP 5

STEP 6

STEP 7

CLOSING

But artistic forms of communication differ from other kinds of communication in several important ways. First, artistic communication places greater emphasis on manipulating form than do everyday interactions. Poetic speech, for example, may rely on patterns of sound and thought like rhyme, assonance, and metaphor that a simple exchange of information will not. Circling a drum while repeating a sequence of foot movements relies on form more heavily than simply walking from one place to another. Adopting the facial expressions of a mythical character draws on form to communicate more than allowing a person's face to remain at rest.

Second, the arts reveal their uniqueness as bounded spheres of interaction. Artistic events have beginnings and endings (no matter how fluid), between which people interact in unusually patterned ways. Ethnomusicologist Ruth Stone describes artistic events as "set off and made distinct from the natural world of everyday life by the participants."[1]

In this manual we help you use these and other characteristics to discover and describe the kinds of artistic communication in any community you enter, including your own. We keep our discovery parameters broad so that we don't inadvertently miss an important kind of communication that doesn't fit our existing categories. So our view of an artistic act might refer to a concert of Spanish *flamenco*, rehearsals for a Broadway musical, a painting hanging on a café wall, a father speaking a proverb to his daughter, or rhythmic wailing at a gravesite. There are tens of thousands of kinds of artistic communication that people use around the world, an amazing and too often undervalued resource.

HOW DO ARTS AND CULTURE INTERACT?

The arts may both reflect and influence the cultures in which they exist. Artistic communication reflects the shape of other aspects of culture because it's interwoven with the rest of life. Members of Kaluli society in Papua New Guinea, for example, have a metaphor, "lift-up-over-sounding," that shows up in several aspects of their lives. This idea underlies music-making in which two singers will alternate in taking the lead role, producing interweaving layers of sound. A similar phenomenon occurs in Kaluli conversation when people "interrupt" each other—they are cocreating, lifting-up-over together. So musical form here reflects a more widespread Kaluli communication pattern.

Artistic communication, however, can also effect change in cultures because of its unique abilities to motivate people to action, inspire feelings of solidarity, and provide socially acceptable space to disagree. As an example, women in the African Apostolic Church

---

1   Ruth Stone, "Communication and Interaction Processes in Music Events among the Kpelle of Liberia" (PhD diss., Indiana University, 1979), 37.

PREFACE

PREPARE

STEP 1

STEP 2

STEP 3

STEP 4

STEP 5

STEP 6

STEP 7

CLOSING

in southern Africa are able to symbolically take hold of time in a worship service in order to communicate their grievances against men. While they are not allowed to preach to a congregation, women may interrupt a sermon with a song, containing lyrics such as these: "Men, stop beating your wives. Only then will you go to heaven." Women-led songs provide symbolic protection for their critical content.[2] In this case, artistic communication has the power to change other parts of culture. Arts may also strengthen existing power structures. National anthems are clear examples of this.

WHAT IS CREATIVITY?

Since the purpose of this manual is to help you spark artistic creativity that feeds into God's expansion of his kingdom, it's important to understand how creativity works. We describe it this way: artistic creativity occurs when one or more people draw on their personal skills, the social patterns of their culture, and symbolic systems to produce an event or work of heightened communication that has not previously existed in its exact form. The newness of this event varies according to its constituent parts and their degrees of novelty. Each culture values newness in unique ways.

So to understand how people create in a culture, you have to find out who the creators are and what skills, knowledge, and techniques they need to be able to produce something new. In addition, for created works to enter into a society's life, you must then learn who are the people who strongly influence a community's acceptance of an innovation (gatekeepers), and what taboos or customs the new works might run up against: who influences whether a group values, learns, and passes on a new creation?

Underlying our approach to creativity is an important understanding of tradition. Tradition is not a fixed body of ideas and practices, but something that is constantly being passed from one person to another, one generation to the next. And every act of transmission introduces small or large changes. The French philosopher Paul Ricoeur describes tradition as "the living transmission of an innovation always capable of being reactivated by a return to the most creative moments of poetic activity. . .[A] tradition is constituted by the interplay of innovation and sedimentation."[3] This manual helps you come alongside local creators in their communities, sparking moments of artistic activity that have the capacity to become enduring traditions. Traditions endure when people are continually motivated to transmit them, with the social structures and resources to support their moments of creativity. Or

---

2   Bennetta Jules-Rosette, "Ecstatic Singing: Music and Social Integration in an African Church," in *More than Drumming: Essays on African and Afro-Latin American Music and Musicians*, ed. Irene V. Jackson (Westport, CT: Greenwood, 1985), 119–44.

3   Paul Ricoeur, *Time and Narrative*, vol. 1 (Chicago: University of Chicago Press, 1984), 68.

PREFACE

PREPARE

STEP 1

STEP 2

STEP 3

STEP 4

STEP 5

STEP 6

STEP 7

CLOSING

as food historian John Edge has said, "Tradition is innovation that succeeds."[4]

All of us who have contributed to this manual can point to exceptionally gifted artists who have inspired and motivated us. Sometimes these individuals see the world differently, and feel compelled to play with and change traditions fundamentally. These are the paradigm shifters. We want to encourage them to create for God and his kingdom, which should only increase their genius because it connects them explicitly to the Ultimate Creator. But our focus in this manual is creativity as a communal activity that everyone contributes to. Consider this credo:

In the beginning, God created

- heaven and earth
- day and night
- water and soil
- plants and animals
- man and woman

God created *ex nihilo* (out of nothing)
What wasn't, now was
And it was good

God made us in his image
One way we reflect this image is in our drive and ability to create

We make

- cities and dams
- houses and shops
- clothes and furniture
- stories and songs and dances and masks

We create *ex creatio* (out of what God made)

- every time we write a paper or an email
- when we greet or comfort someone
- when we cook a meal or play a game or dance a swing
- when we paint a portrait or sketch a cartoon
- every time we do something in a way that never quite existed before, for a purpose or context that doesn't duplicate a previous purpose or context exactly

We are acting like God. But love compels us to take one more step, to

---

4   John T. Edge, Twitter post, February 12, 2010, 6:49 a.m., http://twitter.com/johntedge/status/9009036481.

- nurture a small group
- commission someone to write a song or a poem or craft a chair
- help someone translate the Bible into their language
- tutor a refugee
- raise a child

Every time we inspire or prepare *someone else* to create, we are performing one of the highest, most satisfying and enduring acts of love

We are not God, but creativity flows through us
And in that, we are like him

WHOM DO WE ENCOURAGE?

Just as most people in the world speak more than one language, they also perform and experience music, dance, stories, and other arts from multiple traditions and geographical locations. Each community—and each individual within a community—has a unique, changing blend of local, regional, national, and international artistic activity. So how do you know where to join in? Historically, missionaries have answered this question in three ways:

Bring It–Teach It, Build New Bridges, and Find It–Encourage It. As you'll see, these are more like three points on a multifaceted continuum, and they parallel common approaches to mission in general.

THREE APPROACHES TO ARTS IN MISSION

People working cross-culturally in the Bring It–Teach It framework teach their own arts to people in another community. This has been a common practice throughout the history of the church and is still going on. It's why I could sing "Ekangeneli Na Yesu" with a church in rural Democratic Republic of Congo a week after arriving. Previous missionaries produced the song by putting lyrics in the Lingala language to the tune of "Auld Lang Syne."

The Bring It–Teach It approach may ultimately result in a common artistic language that unifies people around the world. It also sometimes contributes to satisfying and pleasurable fusions, and an inspiring sense of mystery surrounding the worship of God. However, Bring It–Teach It also has frequent and dangerous downsides. It often results in miscommunication of emotions and messages, communities that see God as foreign to them, local artists who feel excluded or demoralized, a sense among local communities that Christianity is irrelevant, and a weakening of kingdom diversity.

Someone reaching out in the Build New Bridges approach will learn enough about another community's arts to influence how they use their own arts in ministry. Art therapists, for example, have used

PREFACE

PREPARE

STEP 1

STEP 2

STEP 3

STEP 4

STEP 5

STEP 6

STEP 7

CLOSING

PREFACE

PREPARE

STEP 1

STEP 2

STEP 3

STEP 4

STEP 5

STEP 6

STEP 7

CLOSING

local materials or songs to guide children through a healing process from suffering. This approach could also include collaborations between artists of different cultures for common purposes, where what is produced has characteristics of more than one tradition.

The Build New Bridges model often requires a relatively short time before making initial progress, and it can work in communities who are going through trauma and so don't have energy or resources to do their own arts completely. It may also promote healthy interdependent relationships where everyone equally shares their arts. Problems can arise, though, when there is a significant power differential between the missionary and the artists in the community. The higher global, social capital of an outsider can dampen the resolve and courage of local artists. This approach may also produce unsustainable results; new collaborative artistic production that is not deeply rooted in local traditions and social systems will likely fade away.

In Find It–Encourage It, the missionary learns to know local artists and their arts in ways that spur these artists to create in the forms they know best. You can think of this missionary as a catalyst for someone else's creativity, helping give birth to new creations that flow organically from the community. The approach usually requires longer-term relationships with people and an irrepressible commitment to learn.

Though none of these three categories is untainted by creation's groaning, we wrote *Creating Local Arts Together,* for people working primarily in the third approach. We did this for two reasons. First, we see Jesus as our primary model. As king of the kingdom, he left his heavenly culture to become a human zygote, learning to walk, talk, sing, relieve, and dress himself in a minoritized society for nearly thirty years before entering his full ministry (Phil 2). Like Jesus, we should be with, learn from, and then give to. Second, we believe this approach is being neglected, with often tragic consequences.

YOUR PARTICULAR CALLING

We suggest three criteria to help you in your decisions about how to invest your unique but limited gifts, time, and energies.

First, ask God to show you where he's working. Remember that his might not be the loudest, most obvious voice.

Second, enter a process of discovery with the community. Together you'll be wiser in knowing how and where to work. But remember that your background combined with the approaches in this manual provide you knowledge and experience that they can benefit from. If you have submitted yourself to a locally led decision-making process, don't be afraid to humbly speak the truth as you see it.

Third, give extra attention to local artists who represent older, geographically or ethnically rooted traditions. We encourage this focus on local artists because their skills and knowledge are of unique

PREFACE

PREPARE

STEP 1

STEP 2

STEP 3

STEP 4

STEP 5

STEP 6

STEP 7

CLOSING

value but often endangered; communities need a combination of deeply rooted traditions and innovation to thrive. Here is our working definition of a local art: an artistic form of communication that a community can create, perform, teach, and understand from within, including its forms, meanings, language, and social context.

Societies connect through media and face-to-face interactions. They come in contact with each other through individual choice in the context of social, financial, church, and other local and global forces. People are multilingual, multicultural, multiartistic. A community marked by the kingdom of God reflects on the value and purposes of each form of artistic communication and works toward a combination that glorifies God.

WHO DOES WHAT?

We wrote the manual for you, an *arts advocate*. You want to help a community—perhaps your own—integrate artistic action more fully into their lives so their temporal and eternal futures will be better. Your primary job is to help *others* make new things in genres they already know. If you are an artist, you may need to find outlets to express your own gifts; that's a great thing. But again: your primary job is to help *others* make new artistic things. That is what this manual will help you do.

However, the whole process of artistic cocreation requires people with many kinds of competencies, knowledge, and skills, including these:

- artistic sensibilities and abilities
- ethnographic and form research
- relationships with all parts of local, regional, and national communities
- planning and organizing
- communicating well in modes appropriate to different contexts
- technical aspects of recording and production

No one person or type of person can do everything required to create local arts together. That's why we put "together" and "we" and other plural terms in as many sentences in this manual as possible. We guide you through what needs to be done but don't say who should do it.

We have three kinds of arts advocates in mind. The first group consists of those who have some secondary or university education using the arts in cross-cultural Christian work and want a guide to beginning and planning their work in a new context. The second kind of person has significant experience in this kind of work, but wants to make their impact deeper and more long-lasting. We assume that people in these first two categories expect a relatively

PREFACE

PREPARE

STEP 1

STEP 2

STEP 3

STEP 4

STEP 5

STEP 6

STEP 7

CLOSING

long-term relationship with the communities they work with, and so will eventually use most of the manual. Finally, people who can devote even a short amount of time or energy to strengthening artists in a community can skim the manual and find something helpful to do. We've given a few ideas for this in "If You Don't Have Much Time," at the end of this chapter. Though we've written most of the manual with someone crossing significant cultural boundaries in mind, it is also useful for people hoping to make a difference in their own communities.

Whatever category you're in, our goal is to help you integrate artistic communication into other activities in a community's life. We thus assume that you have access to people and organizations with the basic skills, resources, and knowledge to work toward God's goals in a situation. We don't, for example, include guidelines for deciding whether you should help start a literacy program, or instructions on how to make a primer. Rather, we show how you can use the lyrics of a local song style as an aid to teaching reading, how local dances can play important roles in motivating people to learn to read, and offer tools to understand local visual patterns that could be incorporated into primer drawings. As another example, we don't here develop a theological framework or methodology for starting new churches. Instead, we lead you through a process of getting to know local artists and incorporating their insights and skills into existing church-planting efforts.

On a personal level, if you are new to a community, you probably don't have the skills to actually fashion or compose a new work in one of its artistic genres. Your contributions to the creative process, then, will normally be in helping people in the community discover motivations to create, helping design events and contexts in which skilled people create, helping communities critique what they produce, and figuring out how to help people integrate new forms of creativity into enduring aspects of their lives. You may learn an artistic tradition well enough to make new works in it, and that can have a profound effect on motivating people within a community to create.[5] But we want to help you enter into relationships with people in a community in ways that result in them creating new examples of existing genres that feed into the deepening of God's kingdom.

CREATE LOCAL ARTS TOGETHER

Figure 1 represents the method that this manual will lead you and a community through: a continuous process of researching and creating together, resulting in more signs of the kingdom. We call this process *Create Local Arts Together* (sometimes shortened to the awkward acronym *CLAT*) or *Cocreation*. The knot in the middle represents an event containing artistic communication and is central to the whole process. This ensures that the community's efforts are

5   Read about Tom Avery's work with the Canela people of Brazil in the *Handbook*, Jack Popjes, "Now We Can Speak to God—in Song," chpt. 73.

grounded in a local reality, based on knowing artists and their arts in context. The artistic event serves as the focus for seven steps:

1. <u>Meet</u> a Community and Its Arts
2. <u>Specify</u> Kingdom Goals
3. <u>Select</u> Effects, Content, Genre, and Events
4. <u>Analyze</u> an Event Containing the Chosen Genre
5. <u>Spark</u> Creativity
6. <u>Improve</u> New Works
7. <u>Integrate</u> and Celebrate for Continuity

Finally, the word "Research" sits by itself under the representation of the artistic event, emphasizing that learning should be your primary posture. Fundamentally, this manual is about helping *other* people make new artistic things.

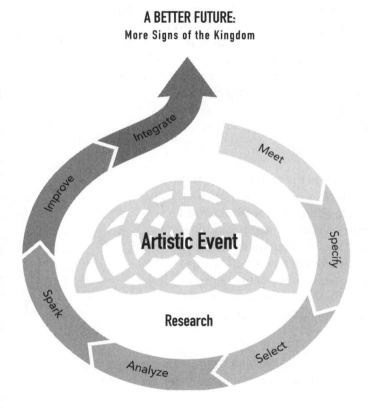

Figure 1: Create Local Arts Together

We now want to whet your appetite for the Create Local Arts Together process by briefly introducing each step with a short illustrative story. In the early 1990s, Brian Schrag and his family lived in northwestern Democratic Republic of Congo (then, Zaire) to help a community translate the Bible into their language, Mono. After describing each component of the cocreation process, Brian will

PREFACE PREPARE STEP 1 STEP 2 STEP 3 STEP 4 STEP 5 STEP 6 STEP 7 CLOSING

PREFACE

PREPARE

STEP 1

STEP 2

STEP 3

STEP 4

STEP 5

STEP 6

STEP 7

CLOSING

tell how he saw that component take place (or not) in the Mono community.

STEP 1: MEET A COMMUNITY AND ITS ARTS

The **meet** component entails getting to know basic information about a community, first making relationships with people, and listing the kinds of arts that run through the community. We draw on research methods from fields like anthropology, ethnography of communication, and performance studies to help you get to know the community. But most of those fancy research methods ultimately boil down to building relationships with other human beings.

Meeting a Mono Community and Its Arts. When we first moved to the village of Bili in Congo, I noticed that church members sang songs in a trade language, not Mono. Some of these songs were translations of European and American hymns, and some were composed in a national pop style. Outside of the church, people played and sang very different kinds of music, in the Mono language. Before we could encourage creativity, we needed to know what to encourage. So I asked the leaders of a local church if we could meet under the *paillote* (straw-roofed gazebo) near our house to talk about their art forms and the Bible. We made a list of about a dozen social contexts when Mono people traditionally make music and dance. These contexts include social dances, rites of passage, personal expression, and giving counsel on the *kundi* (a local harp)–a performance genre called *gbaguru*.

STEP 2: SPECIFY KINGDOM GOALS

Which goals for a more heavenlike life does the community you're working with want to work toward at this time? In the manual, we've placed these signs of the kingdom into several broad categories: Identity and Sustainability, Shalom, Justice, Scripture, Church Life, and Personal Spiritual Life. But this manual is just a beginning—there are thousands, even tens of thousands of signs of the kingdom of God. So act in freedom: specify new signs of the kingdom and new activities that feed into the signs, and tell and write stories of how artistic communication has spread and deepened the kingdom of God.

Specifying with a Mono Community. Still under the *paillote*, the pastor and elders discussed the many purposes of music evident in the Bible, and the fact that God created every person in his image. They said that they didn't use Mono instruments in their church because the first evangelists fifty years earlier had counseled them to burn all physical objects associated with their traditional life. Based on Scripture, the leaders decided that God did want them to reclaim their music for his purposes, including corporate worship. They wanted to relate to God in new, deeper ways. Or at least they were curious about the possibilities.

STEP 3: SELECT EFFECTS, CONTENT, GENRE, AND EVENTS

Once the community has chosen a goal, you can together decide which effects, art forms, content, and events would likely feed into that goal.

> *Selecting with a Mono Community.* The leaders wanted Christians to understand Scripture better and value their traditions, so they thought the familiarity of a church meeting would make it the best place for them to first experience something new. They also decided that the best genre to start with was gbaguru songs, since much of the Bible is about communicating wisdom.

STEP 4: ANALYZE AN EVENT CONTAINING THE CHOSEN GENRE

Creating something in an existing artistic genre for new purposes requires a great deal of knowledge, skill, and wisdom. You'll notice that the bulk of this manual is dedicated to **Step 4**, because it's so easy to assume we understand something, though our understanding is based on superficial knowledge. We help you get to the details of art forms and their meanings so you and the community can identify the elements that will penetrate a community for the kingdom.

> *Analyzing an Event with a Mono Community.* Spurred by my own interests, I had already started to learn about the *kundi*, used to perform *gbaguru* songs. I asked who the best *kundi* player was, and everyone pointed me to Punayima Kanyama. In this case, I analyzed Punayima performing in the *gbaguru* genre in several events: I video recorded him, and transcribed melodies, lyrics, and fingerings. Punayima also taught me to play a couple of songs, which deepened my insights into the forms and themes of the genre. Among many other insights, I learned that *gbaguru* lyrics usually contain Mono proverbs, performances are usually by male individuals, vocal melodies usually follow the tonal patterns of the words in the lyrics, and composers usually require isolation to make new songs.

STEP 5: SPARK CREATIVITY

One sparks creativity by performing an act that results in a new bit of artistry coming into existence. This can be as simple as suggesting that someone carve a new mask or compose a new song for a celebration, or it may require more complex and time-consuming activities, like workshops, commissioning, apprenticeship, festivals, or developing a new version of an existing ritual or ceremony. In whatever activity is chosen, make sure to include all of the people who have an interest in or control over how new works will be integrated into the community.

> *Sparking with a Mono Community.* I asked who could compose new Scripture-based *gbaguru* songs for corporate worship. The history of the kingdom of God among the Mono led to this response: "Nobody in the church knows how to play the *kundi*." So after some discussion, they decided that they would choose some people from the church to learn from a *kundi* master as apprentices. We met weekly, and Punayima taught us how to construct a *kundi*, tune it, and play some simple songs.

PREFACE

PREPARE

STEP 1

STEP 2

STEP 3

STEP 4

STEP 5

STEP 6

STEP 7

CLOSING

PREFACE

PREPARE

STEP 1

STEP 2

STEP 3

STEP 4

STEP 5

STEP 6

STEP 7

CLOSING

STEP 6: IMPROVE NEW WORKS

Evaluation is essential to the cocreative process because we want communities to integrate creativity into their lives that truly results in them meeting their spiritual, social, and physical goals. Evaluation according to agreed-upon criteria helps them make their imperfect artistic communication more effective.

Improving with a Mono Community. Unfortunately we didn't evaluate the early songs that Punayima and others created. They could have been even better. However, we included processes to improve Scripture-based songs that Mono people have composed since then. Bible translators checked for scriptural accuracy and clarity, and Mono musical experts checked that the songs were excellent examples of the genres they represented.

STEP 7: INTEGRATE AND CELEBRATE FOR CONTINUITY

Our desire is that communities will increasingly integrate kingdom creativity into their daily, weekly, monthly, and yearly lives. To do this, they need to teach newly created art works to others and plan for people to keep creating. This means that, at the simplest level, sparking activities like workshops or commissioning should include times to teach new works to other people there. They should also include time to plan for teaching the new works and skills to wider audiences in the future. It may be good to first teach or show them to a small group and get feedback to evaluative questions before presenting the works to a larger group.

Integrating and Celebrating with a Mono Community. Somewhere during our apprenticeship, the others decided to form a *kundi* group, called *Chorale Ayo* (the Love Choir). Punayima composed a song about God creating man and woman from the earth. When we played and sang the song in a church service, the normally boisterous congregation was still and silent. I feared that we had somehow made a mistake, making people think of old gods. So after the service I asked a friend why everyone was so quiet. His reply: "What could we do? The song cut our hearts."

The *Chorale Ayo* continued to sing in congregational meetings, and some of the apprentices began to compose their own songs. After a long hiatus because of war and personal calamities, similar *kundi* groups started springing up in other villages. One part of the Mono community—the Protestant church—was beginning to celebrate good parts of their traditions more. But I was looking for ways to include more people. So when we were planning a big *fête* marking the completion of a new house we had built in the village, I had an idea. I commissioned three songs to be performed at the event—two in traditional Mono genres, and one in a church choral style. That night hundreds of people from all walks of life experienced Jesus' parable of the wise and foolish builders (Matt 7:24–27) in forms they had known since childhood.

HOW TO USE THIS MANUAL

A FLEXIBLE GUIDE

We've organized the *Create Local Arts Together* process as numbered steps because each flows logically into the next. However, though you and the community might plan these activities in this order, they often won't happen that way. In fact, each step might reveal a need for doing more of one of the others, because each is related to all. For example, to **improve** a newly crafted story, the community may need to go back and do more research on the poetic features of good local stories, using guides in the **analyze** step. Ideally, you and the community are trying ideas, learning from what happens, doing more research, trying again, and so on and so on. Act and reflect. Reflect and act. This pattern results in healthy, growing creativity. Think of the steps as a reliable, solid framework you can refer to, but not one etched in stone.

Another caveat to this ordered presentation is that some steps include elements of other steps. Most importantly, we'll describe some activities in **Step 5** that spark the creation of new works that are bundles of several steps. A workshop to produce woven cloth with scriptural marriage advice, for example, may include **analyzing**, **sparking**, **improving**, and **integrating**. As another example, the activity "Help Organize a Festival Celebrating Community Art Forms" includes a larger group in examining and choosing which of their art forms to celebrate—regardless of what genre(s) you choose in **Step 3**. Our emphasis is not on rigidly defining and requiring separate steps, but helping a community make sure that they've included each component somewhere in the big picture of their lives. Please see the accompanying Ethnodoxology Handbook and Manual website for more resources (www.ethnodoxologyhandbook.com).

FEATURES OF THE MANUAL

Scattered throughout the manual, you'll notice activities that have "First Glance" in the title. Because artistic communication is maddeningly complex, it sometimes feels impossible to know how to start. The "First Glance" tools are designed to give you a relatively quick grasp of the most important elements of whatever the task is. We then show you how to go deeper.

You'll also see "Glimpses" every so often, marked by a magnifying glass icon. These are short stories that illustrate a topic we're addressing nearby. Many of them have longer versions in the *Handbook*. Note that only some Glimpses are attributed to someone. The others are stories that seem to have become common property of the Christian ethnoarts community.

PREFACE

PREPARE

STEP 1

STEP 2

STEP 3

STEP 4

STEP 5

STEP 6

STEP 7

CLOSING

PREFACE

PREPARE

STEP 1

STEP 2

STEP 3

STEP 4

STEP 5

STEP 6

STEP 7

CLOSING

EXTERNAL CONNECTIONS

To get the most out of the manual, you'll need to be aware of two related resources:

1. The Community Arts Profile (CAP) is a document you will use to store data you gather from researching and cocreating in a community's arts. More in "Sample Community Arts Profile (CAP) Outline" at the end of the manual, and in Step 1.
2. We are developing a Cocreation Website (www. ethnodoxologyhandbook.com/manual) to post resources that don't fit in this manual. It is also a place where you can interact with others involved in kingdom creativity.

YOU DON'T HAVE TO DO ANY OF THIS

People have been integrating arts into their communities in astounding ways since the beginning of human existence. . .without the help of this manual. Individuals and communities sometimes create arts with no explicit purpose in mind except "I really want/ need to do this!" And sometimes those bits of artistry spread and enliven the kingdom of God in completely unpredictable and positive ways.

Or you may be an exceptional communicator-artist who naturally knows how to listen, learn, and lead. You may work more good for the kingdom by just going and meeting people and learning how to dance or orate on your own. Really.

Most of us and our communities, though, will benefit from the reminders bound up in the structure of this book.

SOME ADVICE AND ENCOURAGEMENT

DISCUSS THE CREATE LOCAL ARTS TOGETHER PROCESS WITH LEADERS

In particular, you should discuss the CLAT process with leaders representing your connections to the community. If you are part of an external organization partnering with the community, all leaders involved need to understand the goals and process described in this manual. Perhaps you can arrange a special meeting to describe this, illustrated with Glimpses or your own experiences.

RESEARCH ALL THE TIME

Learning to know someone else deeply is a fundamental act of love and necessary for success in everything else you do. So whenever you're not sure what to do, go ask a question, practice a dance, observe an event—anything that helps you learn. Research=learning=love. Sometimes your research will take you into realms of belief and practice that contradict your Christian faith. In these cases, whenever possible, adopt an attitude of "temporary

PREFACE

PREPARE

STEP 1

STEP 2

STEP 3

STEP 4

STEP 5

STEP 6

STEP 7

CLOSING

suspension of disbelief." Do not act counter to what God wants you to do, but try to identify with your friends, at least for a moment. This can be a thorny issue, so pray fervently.

IT'S (ALMOST) ALL ABOUT RELATIONSHIPS

Our first priority is whole human beings, not just their art forms. So build relationships, get permission to do things, earn the right to pry, and be respectful of local limitations on what you can do (e.g., don't expect to study female initiation rites if you're a man). Most of the time, it will be your authentic, reciprocal relationships with people that will allow you to enter their lives. Other times you will benefit from others' long-term relationships with the community to connect you. In any case, always remember that we care deeply about the artistic life of people, but they are people first.

WHAT IF THEY DON'T WANT IT?

Even if you do everything in this manual perfectly, humbly, and respectfully (which you won't), you will almost certainly run into resistance. This resistance could come from several sources: a community's low opinion of artists, theological or ideological arguments against certain kinds of arts being used in certain contexts, previous negative experiences with trying to do new things with arts, inertia from long-standing traditions, and underappreciation of the importance and transformative potential of artistic communication. Our whole approach of creating together within a community should lessen much of this, but it won't remove all problems. The following bits of counsel may help you navigate your way with more success and peace.

First, protect, pray for, love, and encourage the artists you work with. Whenever they create something for a public space, they become vulnerable to negative cultural forces. Second, as much as possible, work through existing authority structures. This may not always work, because arts sometimes speak uncomfortable truth to power. However, there are many benefits to sustainability if leaders in a community are willing to listen. Third, you may want to start small with a pilot project. Working to help create a few examples of local artistic genres for kingdom purposes, then presenting them to community leaders, can be a crucial step in them opening the door to further creativity. Fourth, be both winsome and persistent in your relationships. Fifth, don't be afraid to try and fail. Nurture your own humility, knowing that God's plan for you and a community will never be exactly what you think. Sixth and finally, talk with God a lot. He'll tell you what you need to know, because it's his kingdom. Remember: "If any of you lacks wisdom, you should ask God, who gives generously to all without finding fault, and it will be given to you" (Jas 1:5).

WHENEVER POSSIBLE, HELP LEADERS PLAN FOR THE ARTS

One of the most common reasons that communities and organizations don't integrate the arts into their work is that they don't plan for it.

PREFACE

PREPARE

STEP 1

STEP 2

STEP 3

STEP 4

STEP 5

STEP 6

STEP 7

CLOSING

You can help solve this problem by learning the processes through which leaders in churches, nongovernmental organizations (NGOs), and other groups interacting with a community make decisions. Then graciously ask to join those processes in appropriate ways, at key moments. Prepare yourself well, being ready to offer concrete suggestions for how people can draw on the great resources of their community's arts to reach their goals.

Because planning can be so important for long-term integration of kingdom creativity in a community, we've included an overview of one common method in **Step 7**. In fact, our seven Create Local Arts Together steps constitute a planning method that you can relate directly to these other methods. If you're working with an organization that has adopted a particular planning system, adapt the language we've developed in the manual to that of their system in your conversations; we've given an example of how this might work in **Step 7**.

One caveat: regardless of how much you and a community plan, God often works in ways we can't anticipate. So you should plan, but always stay aware of individuals or groups who might be responding to something unexpected that God is doing. Enjoy being surprised.

YOU CAN'T DO IT ALL, BUT YOU CAN DO ENOUGH

Every community and its artistic forms of communication represent an unfathomable degree of complexity and variation. Even the most accomplished master of an art form can learn more and increase his or her skills. To make matters more difficult, the physical and social contexts of these communities are in a constant state of change, sometimes dramatically. In short, there's no way you could fully perform all of the activities we describe in this manual in a definitive way for just one art form, even if you had nothing else ever to do.

But you can do enough.

Insights from academic fields like ethnomusicology, performance studies, anthropology, linguistics, missiology, and neuroscience show that we can understand the important patterns of human artistic communication. In addition, God's view of his final kingdom encompasses every language and nation (Rev 7); we *can* know each other. But because of the complexity, our interactions with communities are more like explorations and adventures than scientific processes. Use this manual to sharpen and broaden your understanding of artistic communication in the kingdom of God, but don't try to do everything. Follow the streams of exploration and creating together that seem most relevant and fruitful.

IF YOU DON'T HAVE MUCH TIME

There may be points in your interactions with a community when you don't have the time or resources to commit to the thorough process we describe in this manual. Or maybe you're just not sure how to begin. If so, this brief section contains suggestions for arts

Prepare Yourself   XXXIII

PREFACE

PREPARE

STEP 1

STEP 2

STEP 3

STEP 4

STEP 5

STEP 6

STEP 7

CLOSING

activities that you can start without much preparation. These will get you going and will feed into more complete actions you may do when you have more time. No artistic exploration or encouragement is ever wasted.

To get started, it helps to look for natural connections you may have with local artists. One connection could be that you are intrigued by a particular art form—you just like it. Or you may have experience or skills related to one of the art forms, such as dance or weaving. Or you may have a personal affinity with a practitioner of an art form. In any case, remember that ultimately you want to get to know and encourage people involved in local arts. Look for ways to make relationships. And if you can only do one thing, ask an artist to teach you something.

Simple arts engagement activities

- Perform part of the "Take a First Glance at a Community's Arts" activity in **Step 1**.
- Attend artistic events and describe them briefly in a notebook.
- Make lists of types of song, dance, drama, visual storytelling, or proverbs.
- Collect instruments.
- Transcribe song texts.
- Do language and culture learning with artists. Spend relaxed social time with them.
- Make systematic audio or video recordings of an art form according to song categories, composer, events in a village, or proverbs.
- Learn to play an instrument, sing, dance, act, weave, or tell a story in a local genre.
- Some things to talk about with local friends and colleagues
  - How did the kinds of arts in the community come about? Who created the things people use or perform?
  - What are people's general attitudes toward people involved in different local art forms? Positive? Negative?
  - Are there parts of a performance that have special symbolic significance? For example, colors, shapes, instruments, or clothes?
  - How does the way people do local art forms now differ from how they did them in the past? Are young people learning how to do them? How does someone get good at them?
  - Are there certain art forms that only men or only women can do?
  - How do people feel when they're involved in different local art forms? Do they ever enter into ecstatic states?
  - How are local art forms connected to religious beliefs?

PREFACE

PREPARE

STEP 1

STEP 2

STEP 3

STEP 4

STEP 5

STEP 6

STEP 7

CLOSING

- What artistic expressions in the culture are not currently being used in the worship of God? Why? How might God want to redeem one for a purpose in his kingdom?

ULTIMATE MOTIVATIONS: A NOTE ON HEAVEN AND HELL

We have invoked signs of the kingdom of God as a central motivation for using this manual: we want God's people everywhere to act in artistic ways that result in more evidence of heaven on earth. But we have so far barely mentioned the first sign of the kingdom of God in communities: each human being's existence. God created people in his image, so every child, woman, and man is a fact that points to God's home, heaven. How should this fundamental sign influence our work?

The answer to this question depends in part on another belief flowing through the manual—that eternity exists in two distinct forms: heaven and hell. Each has substance associated completely, terribly, and only with two distinct realities: heaven with the trinitarian God—Father, Jesus, Spirit—and all that is good; hell with Satan and all that is evil. On earth, however, these realities mingle in excruciatingly complex confusion. Adolph Hitler magnificently developed his oratorical gifts in ways that moved and excited people in invigorating, pleasurable ways; his creative skills dimly reflected those of a creative God. But Hitler used his gifts in ways that resulted in violence, horror, hopelessness, despair, and agony; these effects dimly reflected those desired by a cruel Satan. We believe that heaven and hell are infinitely more extreme and real than we can imagine, both on earth and after.

These truths leave us with a few lessons. First, we must approach every person and his or her gifts as infinitely valuable. We know of one man who travels a lot and sometimes finds that new stimuli from clothes, hairstyles, skin tones, sounds, or smells elicit negative, stereotyping, or lustful responses in his mind. When this happens, he repeats to himself, "Image of God! Image of God!" Each person carries God's mark, so our first attitudes toward them should always be generous, humble, and expecting goodness and beauty. Second, we should study heaven and hell biblically, meditatively, and imaginatively. The more we know these realities viscerally, intellectually, and emotionally, the more discerning we can be. Third, we can't allow ourselves to be lured into thinking that the agonies and ecstasies we encounter on earth are all there is. If we do, we might settle for alleviating hunger without ever caring whether someone connects that satisfaction with the Creator of food.

Finally, we should encourage the spread of all types of signs of the kingdom, for they are all good in themselves. But we can never forget that people need to know the source of all good: God, Creator: Father– Jesus–Spirit. We can ask God to nurture our understandings of both heaven and hell, so that both can motivate us powerfully.

MEET A COMMUNITY AND ITS ARTS

All artistic action exists in the context of more than one person. After God created the universe *ex nihilo* (out of nothing), every being has created *ex creatio* (from something already made and learned). However extreme a person's originality or individualism, his or her artistic creativity at some point references and depends on others. In **Step 1** we guide you through a process of initial discovery and description of a community and its arts. We'll help you

- think about what a community is
- start a Community Arts Profile
- take a first glance at a community
- take a first glance at a community's arts
- start exploring a community's social and conceptual life
- prepare to use research methods to learn more

THINK ABOUT WHAT A COMMUNITY IS

It is likely that you have already identified a community to engage with. Your connection could exist because you were born into the community or have long experience with it. It could be that you are part of a mission or humanitarian or church organization that has directed you to this group in order to fulfill its goals. Whether you have a clear idea in your mind about a particular community or not, it will help in your work to reflect on what a community is. We define a community as a group of people that shares a story, identity, and ongoing patterns of interaction, and that is constantly in flux. As we describe each characteristic, think how it relates to a community.

PREFACE
PREPARE
STEP 1
STEP 2
STEP 3
STEP 4
STEP 5
STEP 6
STEP 7
CLOSING

COMMUNITIES SHARE A STORY

No group of people exists in more than one point in time, but each sees itself as part of a larger story, a history. On any given day, people may refer to events, characters, ideas, and dramatic elements that have occurred over multiple generations, or that took place much more recently. This shared story provides continuity, connections between the past, and an imagined future, providing impetus to keep gathering. For Christian communities, the story that provides ultimate cohesion is this: God created the universe; the first people made a Big Mistake; God sent messengers to show how to overcome the Big Mistake, but it wasn't enough; God sent himself to provide the final solution to the Big Mistake; God is working with his people to grow his kingdom; this kingdom will come to fruition in the new heaven and new earth, at the end of time.

COMMUNITIES SHARE AN IDENTITY

People know they are connected by recognizing and valuing common points of reference in each other. Identity markers tie people in a community together and distinguish them from others. Their shared story may provide a primary marker of this common identity. Other signs of a common identity could include a particular spoken language or accent, food, manner of dress, skills, religion, ideology, geographical location, enemies or allies, taboos, or shared needs or struggles. Artistic forms of communication often provide key points of identity.

COMMUNITIES SHARE ONGOING PATTERNS OF INTERACTION

People in a community communicate with each other in patterned ways, times, and places. Contexts for communication may include these: within a family's living quarters; at meetings designed for rituals, sports, politics, or courtship; during periods of work, business, or education; festivals, celebrations, or entertainment. The communication could be face-to-face, body to body, or mediated through radio, telephones, Internet, or other electronic audiovisual means. Success may be dependent on being geographically close, or proximity may be irrelevant. Whatever the contexts or media, communities depend on common systems of meaning to facilitate comprehension and impact. These systems include spoken and signed languages, visual and video symbolism, movement and tactile sign patterns, and many others.

COMMUNITIES ARE NOT WHAT YOU THINK

Though we've been talking about communities almost as static, coherent objects, they're not. They are composed of individuals who each make their own decisions, enter and leave the community, and respond to external and internal factors differently. Every community has internal variation and changes over time. So beware of saying things like, "Community X sings like this." It may be true for a majority of the group today, but some people may be advocating for a different kind of singing. In five years, things may be very different. The bottom line is that every community displays both continuity and change, internal coherence and diversity. We hold our ideas about them confidently but lightly.

COMMUNITIES IN THIS MANUAL

The initial spark for this manual came from a desire to engage better with communities that have strong ethnolinguistic identities and modes of communication; they represent some of the richest, most underutilized and endangered artistic traditions in the kingdom of God. This remains an important focus. But the world is urbanizing and globalizing, leading to more and more communities made up of people from more than one culture, glued together by diverse interests. So we will also provide guidance for working with artists in multicultural groups. Note that most of the manual applies equally well to monocultural or multicultural communities.

START A COMMUNITY ARTS PROFILE

Where do you keep what you know? We all store thoughts, facts, feelings, skills, experiences, stories, and smells in our brains and bodies as memories. When we need to drive a car, greet a friend, or dance at a wedding, we call on what we've learned to know what to do. This kind of storage is indispensable to life and artistic action. But memories in the mind and body fade and clutter. Written and recorded data provide a crucial, though imperfect, remedy to this natural loss, especially as you're learning about arts new to you. We've developed a tool to help you keep track of what you're learning, called a Community Arts Profile (CAP).

A Community Arts Profile is a place for you to gather everything you and the community learn about its arts. Each community should have its own CAP. It may be in the form of word processing documents, a database, website, or notebook. We have created the outline of such a Profile in .rtf format that you can use. In reality, almost everything you and the community do while creating together will lead to new insights into how a type of artistic activity functions, its meanings, and its place in society; you will do well to capture as much of this as possible in the CAP. This information will prove invaluable when planning cocreative activities, sparking creativity, evaluating artistic output, and integrating the arts into the community. Our hope is that you will add to and draw from the CAP as long as you interact with the community it describes. Open "Community Arts Profile READ ME.rtf" to get started (see www. ethnodoxologyhandbook.com/manual and Closing 2).

PREFACE

PREPARE

STEP 1

STEP 2

STEP 3

STEP 4

STEP 5

STEP 6

STEP 7

CLOSING

PREFACE

PREPARE

STEP 1

STEP 2

STEP 3

STEP 4

STEP 5

STEP 6

STEP 7

CLOSING

TAKE A FIRST GLANCE AT A COMMUNITY

The Community Arts Profile includes a place to include the first bits of information you gather about a community, including its geographical location(s), language(s), important identity markers, and modes of communication.

From this you will decide the scope of your activities. Your scope could be very narrow, restricted to one clan in a village or one multilingual neighborhood in a city, for example. Or it could be very broad, such as everyone who speaks a particular language in a region. "Scope" also refers to how detailed your descriptions will be: you may describe artistic communication from a close-up view (zoomed in), from far away (zoomed out), or somewhere in between.

QUESTIONS TO ASK

- Where is the community and how many of them are there? This includes basic information like village or town, province, and nation. It's likely that community members live in more than one geographical location. It could be that they think of themselves as historically connected to a geographical center, with diaspora in other places.
- What ties the community together? Answers could include factors like language, geography, ethnic identity, and social structure.
- How do they communicate with each other and how often? This question points to languages and modes of communication like these: face-to-face, telephone, and electronic social media. It may be that they have frequent face-to-face communication with those nearby but also make regular trips to visit members who live farther away.
- How do they share their artistic creations? This question points to both face-to-face and electronic sharing, cassettes, compact discs, DVDs, cell phones, Internet sites, written notation, or other means.
- How did they get there? Identify important historical events and patterns that have brought the community to its geographical location and affected its identity.

PLACES TO ASK

Whenever possible, ask these questions of friends, leaders, and other contacts from the community. You can also ask them to point you to other people and resources where you can learn more. In addition, remember that the nearer you live to a community, the more opportunities you will have to learn more.

You can also learn a great deal by reading or watching how members of the community have presented themselves in books, articles, videos, recordings, and other media. Then see how others have described the community through academic research, encyclopedias, or more popular presentations.

TAKE A FIRST GLANCE AT A COMMUNITY'S ARTS

A core feature of our approach is that we help communities create from artistic resources that they already possess. So one of the very first things we have to do is list these artistic genres. We'll show how to make a quick survey, then provide two approaches for making it more complete: "Outside-in" and "Inside-out." If you are working with a Christian community, then you will also want to follow the guides in "Discover a Christian Community's Arts" (**Step 4, Part D**).

MAKE A QUICK LIST OF ARTISTIC GENRES

A productive way to come up with a list of these kinds of communication is to gather a few people together and ask them questions like this:

- When do people in this community sing? play instruments? dance? tell stories? act? carve? paint? use their bodies in unusual ways? play games? build special structures? Remember that each culture divides up and talks about its forms of artistic communication in unique ways, so learn their vocabulary.
- Do people in this community do anything special surrounding the birth of a child? someone's death? someone's passage from childhood to adulthood? For each affirmative answer, ask them to describe what special things happen and make note of the arts involved.

As you list each event, jot down a few basic characteristics of its artistic forms of communication—genres:

- a local name or brief description
- kinds of people involved (men, women, youth, children, specialists, a particular socioeconomic group, etc.)
- when it's usually done (particular days, seasons, months, times of day, etc.)
- purposes of the genre
- anything else that comes up immediately

Don't worry about getting all the details while you're making a survey; we'll guide you through much more detailed investigation in **Step 4**.

PREFACE

PREPARE

STEP 1

STEP 2

STEP 3

STEP 4

STEP 5

STEP 6

STEP 7

CLOSING

EXTEND THE LIST FROM THE OUTSIDE IN: DISCOVER ARTISTIC COMMUNICATION ACTS BY RESEARCHING LIKELY SOCIAL CONTEXTS FOR THEIR PERFORMANCE

In the "Outside-in" approach, you begin with an anthropologist's knowledge that cultures often mark important events and transitions with artistically rendered communication. Use the following outline[6] to help identify rituals and special events that exist in a community. Then explore what arts might be associated with each.

Life-cycle events

- birth (birth announcement, lullaby)
- childhood (funny or nonsense games, teasing, taunting)
- puberty (girl's songs, boy's songs, initiation)
- courting (love, courting, proposal of marriage)
- marriage (wedding, men's events, women's events)
- death (funeral, burial, mourning)

Historical events

- commemorative (disasters, honors, first outsiders, changes in leadership or government, first road, first vehicles, wars, etc.)
- legend (creation, mythology)
- local news

Activities

- work (cutting timber, hunting, fishing, road making, etc.)
- fighting (preparation for battle, battle, victory, defeat, etc.)
- dancing (male, female, both sexes, social, ceremonial, solo, etc.)
- recreation
- worship

Ceremonies

- magic (planting, harvesting, fertility, power, prophecy, etc.)
- social (greeting, farewell, wedding, funeral, completion of a special community project, etc.)

Nature

- animals (pets and wild animals, including birds, fish, and reptiles)
- places and things (mountains, rivers, forests, trees, plants, the heavens—including clouds, sun, moon, stars, and sky)
- time cycles (daily, weekly, monthly, annual)

---

6   Modified from Vida Chenoweth, *Melodic Perception and Analysis* (Ukarumpa, Papua New Guinea: Summer Institute of Linguistics, 1972), 24–25.

This is a basic list of artistic genres of the Mono ethnolinguistic group, Democratic Republic of Congo:

- *agbolo*: children's play songs
- *agidi*: dance for god of water
- *ako'ba*: dance of women healers
- *ambala*: malice dance
- *banda*: male judges' dance
- *gaza aga*: men's circumcision dance
- *gaza mbala*: men's circumcision elephant dance
- *gaza yashe*: women's circumcision dance
- *gbaguru*: proverbs sung to exhort people
- *gbanjele*: social dance
- *gbaya*: celebratory social dance
- *gbenge*: mourning song when village leader dies
- *kowo*: dance for victory or war
- *kpatsha*: dance from Banda people in Central African Republic
- *ku'u agbolo*: lullabyes
- *kuzu*: death celebration dance
- *nganga*: hunters' protection song
- *ngaranja*: male judges' dance
- *yangba*: celebratory social dance

EXTEND THE LIST FROM THE INSIDE OUT: RECOGNIZE ARTISTIC COMMUNICATION ACTS BY THEIR SPECIAL FEATURES

In the "Inside-out" approach, you begin with knowledge you have about art forms themselves, often from your own insights as an artist. You'll recognize many of a community's arts because they have characteristics of singing, dancing, acting, carving, or other arts you're already familiar with. Sometimes, though, the surface structures of the arts we encounter are so different from those in our own experience that we may not recognize them as being artistic at all. In this section we've listed special features of artistic expression that may help you think beyond your experience and identify more of a community's arts. As you go about your daily life, train yourself to notice these characteristics and ask yourself the questions we've provided. When you recognize something as artistic, ask preliminary questions, write down what you learn, and plan to investigate it further.

Arts may have a distinctive performance context

Many times the occasion for artistic communication is different from everyday interaction. It occurs between recognizable boundaries

PREFACE

PREPARE

STEP 1

STEP 2

STEP 3

STEP 4

STEP 5

STEP 6

STEP 7

CLOSING

PREFACE

PREPARE

STEP 1

STEP 2

STEP 3

STEP 4

STEP 5

STEP 6

STEP 7

CLOSING

that set it off from "normal" events, and it usually will have distinctive features such as role changes among the participants.[7] An artistic event might occur at a special time of day (often at night), in a special place, use special language, involve the participation of a large group of people, or participants might wear special clothing and behave in special ways.

Many events are what Milton Singer has called "cultural performances":[8] scheduled, temporally bounded, spatially bounded, programmed, coordinated, heightened (i.e. more pronounced, extreme) public occasions. You can usually find cultural performances relatively easily because they require planning, gathering and allocation of resources, and the involvement of multiple people.

> *Where is everybody going?*
> *Why are people wearing those hats today?*
> *What marks the beginning of this event? The end?*

Arts may expand or contract the density of information

In comparison to everyday communication, artistic expressions often convey a great deal in just a few words. This is often true of poetry and proverbs. Other genres show the opposite effect, such as in Wagner operas, where the dialog and plot unfold almost in slow motion because of the chronological space needed to perform the musical elements. Songs frequently show a great deal of redundancy of texts.

> *How can those people get so much from that little poem?*

Arts may assume more or special knowledge

Jokes are often very difficult to understand for outsiders because insider attitudes and knowledge are assumed by the tellers. It may be important that the assumed knowledge is not made explicit: it spoils a joke if you have to explain it. The implications of references to other artistic works can only be understood if the audience has knowledge of previous works, often of the same genre. Sometimes terminology or alternative meanings of words are specific to a particular artistic genre.

> *What in the world does that mean?*
> *I understand all the words of the joke, but I don't understand what's so funny!*

Arts exhibit special formal structure

Artistic expressions are often limited by constraints of form which do not pertain to everyday communication.

---

7   Muriel Saville-Troike, *The Ethnography of Communication: An Introduction* (Malden, MA: Blackwell, 2002).
8   Richard Bauman, ed., *Folklore, Cultural Performances, and Popular Entertainments* (Oxford: Oxford University Press, 1992), 46.

Why did that person rhyme his last comment? (Clue: maybe it's a proverb.)

Why is this building built differently than others?

Arts may elicit unusual responses

Artistic expressions often produce a strong emotional or physical response from people who experience them.

Why is everybody so excited/upset?

Arts may require unusual expertise

Artistic expressions often seem to take specialized training to perform; not everyone can do them.

How did she sing two notes at once?

START EXPLORING A COMMUNITY'S SOCIAL AND CONCEPTUAL LIFE

Artistic action interacts with its community like threads and themes in an evolving tapestry. To understand an artist and her arts, you have to understand her cultural context. To understand a cultural context, you have to understand its arts and artists. This manual helps you understand arts and artists, but to guide you through a broad exploration of a community is beyond our scope. The field of anthropology has developed a trustworthy set of categories and methods for doing that. If you don't have a background in anthropology, we encourage you to take a course in cultural anthropology or refer to works like McKinney's *Globetrotting in Sandals*,[9] Hargrave's *Doing Anthropology*,[10] or Ferraro and Andreatta's *Cultural Anthropology*.[11] Other important resources are Yale University's *Outline of Cultural Materials* (http://www.yale.edu/hraf) and the *SIL FieldWorks Data Notebook* (http://www.sil.org).

For our purposes, we list here several important anthropological concepts and a few related questions to stimulate your thoughts.

LANGUAGE IN ITS SOCIOCULTURAL CONTEXT

- In what contexts do people use different languages or types of language?
- How do people use silence in their communication?
- What value do people place on different types of speech?

---

9   Carol McKinney, *Globetrotting in Sandals: Field Guide to Cultural Research* (Dallas: SIL International, 2000).

10   Susanne Hargrave, *Doing Anthropology* (Kangaroo Ground, Australia: South Pacific Summer Institute of Linguistics, 1993).

11   Gary Ferraro and Susan Andreatta, *Cultural Anthropology: An Applied Perspective*, 9th ed. (Belmont, CA: Wadsworth, 2011).

PREFACE

PREPARE

STEP 1

STEP 2

STEP 3

STEP 4

STEP 5

STEP 6

STEP 7

CLOSING

PREFACE

PREPARE

STEP 1

STEP 2

STEP 3

STEP 4

STEP 5

STEP 6

STEP 7

CLOSING

MATERIAL CULTURE AND ECONOMICS

- How do people use and value objects?
- How do people produce, distribute, and use goods and services?
- How is labor distributed among genders, classes, and ages?

KINSHIP

- How do people describe their relationships to other people in their community? What are the named categories for blood relatives?
- How do people describe their relationships to their ancestors?
- What social obligations are associated with each kind of relationship?

MARRIAGE AND FAMILY

- How do people define the social union between men and women that results in children? How many men and women are involved, and what behaviors define the relationships between each? Who can marry whom in the community? Where do married partners live?
- What constitutes a household?
- How do households relate to extended family?

SOCIAL ORGANIZATION

- What roles do gender, age, kinship, locality, and shared interests play in organizing social groups?
- How are social groups ranked by status?
- How do people enter or exit groups?

POWER RELATIONSHIPS

- How does a community organize itself politically and relate to government structures?
- How much power does each smaller group hold?
- How do individuals and groups exert, gain, or lose power?

RELIGION

- What sorts of supernatural beings do people talk about or relate to? Do these include ancestral, nature, human, or supreme spirits?
- What rituals does the community perform regularly, and for what reasons?
- How do people use and control supernatural power?

WORLDVIEW AND VALUES

- How do people categorize reality, and what attributes does it have?
- How can people know what is true about reality?
- What do people say they think is important? How does people's allocation of time and resources show what they think is important?

PREPARE TO USE RESEARCH METHODS TO LEARN MORE

Many of the activities we guide you through in the manual require basic research skills. Though we can't teach a course in this, we introduce here the most important methods: Participant Observation, Interview, Note-taking, Audio and Video Recording, Photography, and Library Research. Here's one essential piece of advice, no matter which of these methods you use, especially if it involves equipment: learn to use it before it matters. Practice using a camera, video camera, audio recording device, even writing in a notebook before you need it to capture data. You will thank us if you do.

PARTICIPANT OBSERVATION: LEARN BY WATCHING WHILE DOING

Painting, playing an instrument, dancing, taking part in a drama, learning to tell stories properly: these are all activities that might be part of participant observation for an arts researcher. In a participant observation model of fieldwork, the researcher lives in a community for an extended period to learn something about how that community functions. For the arts researcher, participant observation often includes becoming a student of a master artist in the community or joining a group devoted to an art form. Learning to perform and create gives the researcher an entry into understanding the artistic system, the artists themselves, and the place of the arts in the community. This deep involvement also communicates respect and love. Though it has been a part of research for many years, participant observation became widely popular in the late nineteenth and early twentieth centuries, concurrent with the development of the field of anthropology. American anthropologist Franz Boas and his students employed participant observation techniques in their fieldwork. Ethnomusicologist Mantle Hood stressed the importance of acquiring "bi-musicality"—learning about a musical tradition by becoming a part of it.[12] Many ethnomusicologists now consider bi-musicality and participant observation as common-sense approaches to fieldwork.

Participant observation in fieldwork is rarely neat and tidy, however. Becoming a part of a community means adjusting to

---

12   Mantle Hood, "The Challenge of Bi-Musicality," *Ethnomusicology* 4 (1960): 55–59.

PREFACE

PREPARE

STEP 1

STEP 2

STEP 3

STEP 4

STEP 5

STEP 6

STEP 7

CLOSING

PREFACE

PREPARE

STEP 1

STEP 2

STEP 3

STEP 4

STEP 5

STEP 6

STEP 7

CLOSING

the stresses and expectations of daily living. The researcher must be flexible and willing to abide by the schedule offered by local teachers and guides. "Going with the flow" is a crucial, yet frequently frustrating, part of fieldwork. Dance scholar Felicia Hughes-Freeland describes participant observation as "determined by a process of planning and intention, which is disrupted by accidents and enhanced by serendipity."[13] Participant observation often yields the most satisfying results when the researcher is able to spend long periods of time in the field location.

As relationships deepen and develop, community members will share more information. Trust is crucial in the participant observation relationship. The researcher must be committed to being a wise steward of the information he or she is given, abiding by all proper ethical expectations.

LEARNING AN ART FOREIGN TO YOU: LEARN BY DOING

One of the most fruitful and enjoyable kinds of participation in our work is learning a new art form. Putting yourself in a nonexpert role like this helps you build relationships with people, yields insights into multiple aspects of a community, and increases your understanding of the characteristics of the art you're studying.

I was trying in vain to understand how all of the percussion instruments worked together in a Cameroonian dance group. At one of their rehearsals, I played the simplest instrument—the shaker—and moved around the circle with the rest of the dancers. Somehow in the middle of that dance I noticed how one of the men was playing the wooden slit drum, and everything became clear. "Ahhhh! So my foot moves to the right when the shaker goes down and the slit drum hits a repeated pattern." Performance can lead to many insights. – *Brian Schrag*

Becoming an expert in all of the skills, symbolism, and social patterns of most art forms is likely beyond your capacity; artistic communication is complex, as attested by all of the research activities we describe in **Step 4**. Each of us, however, can gain something. This may include learning the appropriate ways to show appreciation during a performance, how to play an instrument, how to sing a song or do a dance, or how to carve a mask. Your research activities in **Step 4** will give you more ideas of what to learn.

When you decide you want to learn some aspect of an art form, you can enter an existing social context, devise your own system of learning, or a combination. If you want to learn like people in the

13   Felicia Hughes-Freeland, "Dance on Film: Strategy and Serendipity," in *Dance in the Field: Theory, Methods and Issues in Dance Ethnography*, ed. Theresa J. Buckland (New York: St. Martin's Press, 1999), 120.

community learn, first find out how that happens (see "Transmission and Change" in **Step 4, Part C**). Then you can decide whether it fits your life. Local educational systems can range from informal watching to high-expectation apprenticeships. If you decide to figure out your own learning system, here are some things to keep in mind:

- Find out who in the community is best at the part of the art form you'd like to learn. It may be that one person knows all of the songs associated with a social dance, for example, but is not a respected dancer. Ask a friend or two for advice on how to approach your potential teacher, and whether and how it would be appropriate to compensate them.
- Reflect on your own learning style and plan your activities accordingly. One or more of these types might apply to you:[14]

  - **Relational learner**: Wants to relate to people, have variety, and help others develop.
  - **Analytical learner**: Enjoys working independently and integrating data into theoretical models and solving problems.
  - **Structured learner**: Prefers a systematic and organized approach to learning, a chance to apply concepts in a practical way and have hands-on activities and practical solutions.
  - **Energetic learner**: Likes lots of activity and chances to do things with people; lots of variety, adventure, and risk; personal involvement in activities; and hands-on activities.

- Watch, imitate, and practice what you want to learn. You may want to audio or video record a performance so you can review it as many times as you want privately. You can also use the recordings for memorization or analysis, transcribing texts, melodies, and movements.

INTERVIEW: LEARN BY ASKING

One of the most important aspects of your fieldwork is the relationships you build with other people in your host community. You may be adopted into a family, and neighbors may provide for your daily needs. Obviously, it is difficult to learn much about any of the arts without talking to people and asking questions about what you see around you. But talking can be done intentionally, purposefully, not just casually. When you formally arrange to talk with someone about their expressive arts, you are engaging in **ethnographic interviewing**.

---

14   Clay Johnston and Carol J. Orwig, "Your Learning Style and Language Learning," in *LinguaLinks 1999* (Dallas: SIL International, 1999).

PREFACE
PREPARE
STEP 1
STEP 2
STEP 3
STEP 4
STEP 5
STEP 6
STEP 7
CLOSING

PREFACE

PREPARE

STEP 1

STEP 2

STEP 3

STEP 4

STEP 5

STEP 6

STEP 7

CLOSING

Primary benefits

- **Information gathering:** Biographical information; descriptions of performance events; emotional, ideological, critical, and other responses to performance events.
- **Clarification:** Confirm or correct information you have previously gathered or conclusions based on other fieldwork.
- **Comparison:** Learn the different perspectives various people might have about the same performance events. What do the differences tell you?

Elements of ethnographic interviews

- **Explanation of the procedure:** Tell the interviewee about the purpose of the interview, the recording equipment you'll be using, the kinds of questions you'll ask, and how you hope to use the information learned during the interview. Before or after the interview, have the interviewee record a statement or sign a form giving permission to use the interview and the information for your research project. You can modify the "Sample Permission Form" below to do this.
- **Questions:** Before the interview, create a set of questions that might help guide the interview toward the areas you want to learn about. You may not use all the questions, or that particular order, but it can help to think about where the interview might go. Often the best questions are those that allow the interviewee to talk at length, rather than answering with short statements. Avoid asking questions that elicit yes/no responses. Other excellent questions allow insiders to guide your interviews of *other* insiders: Who else should I ask about this? What questions should I ask him or her?
- **Restatements:** At some points during the interview, you may want to restate what the interviewee has said. This helps to clarify that you understand what has been said, and also gives the interviewee the opportunity to say more about what he or she has already said or to correct you.
- **Audiovisual media:** It may be helpful to have recordings ready to play for the interviewee in order to stimulate thoughtful comments about or reactions to performances. Then, when you present your interview as part of your field research, consider whether including recorded documentation could be helpful in understanding the context of the interview.

Ethnographic interviews with groups of people are sometimes preferable to those with individuals. Your questions can spark discussion among the participants that unearths information and issues you had never thought of. We have successfully used group interviews to discover genres of artistic communication in a community, identify and agree on community goals, and explore the meanings of an event. Be aware, though, of social dynamics in group settings—sometimes group members will defer to a respected or authoritative leader, leaving you with just the leader's opinion.

NOTE-TAKING: LEARN BY WRITING

Writing down what you observe and learn forces you to make your impressions clearer, and provides a durable record you can refer to later. Two types of notes are especially helpful, and lead to a fruitful approach to analysis:[15]

Jottings: Initial condensed account

- Done on the spot, immediately after or during the event.
- Write short descriptions and keywords and phrases to help you remember the details for later write-up.
- Do not let jotting become offensive or distract you from observing. Initial impressions are very valuable.

Notes: Expanded account

- This is a more descriptive account, when you have more time to write and are away from the event.
- Can be handwritten, typed, or dictated.
- The writer is aware of her own perspective, biases, and interpretations.

When writing initial fieldnotes, keep in mind two principles:

The verbatim principle: Record everything in the exact words used by the person you're talking with.

- Write: "You have to swallow the beat to play that shaker."
- Not: "Your rhythm was not consistent."

The concrete principle: Use concrete language.

- Write: "She looked out the window of the truck and started to take sharp, rapid breaths. After about a minute, she leaned her head back, made a high-pitched, loud,

---

15   From James Spradley, *Participant Observation* (New York: Holt, Rinehart & Winston, 1980), 63–72; and Helen Myers, "Fieldwork," in *Ethnomusicology: An Introduction*, ed. Helen Myers (New York: Norton, 1992), 38–41.

PREFACE
PREPARE
STEP 1
STEP 2
STEP 3
STEP 4
STEP 5
STEP 6
STEP 7
CLOSING

PREFACE

PREPARE

STEP 1

STEP 2

STEP 3

STEP 4

STEP 5

STEP 6

STEP 7

CLOSING

prolonged sound without recognizable words that dropped rapidly in pitch. Tears began to flow, and she soon repeated the vocalization."

- Not: "She began wailing."

Codings and analysis: Processing fieldnotes

1. Read your fieldnotes. Look for threads that identify larger themes. A cultural theme is any principle that recurs in several domains and defines relationships among sets of meanings.[16] Yale's *Outline of Cultural Materials* provides a huge number of possible themes.
2. When you think you've found a theme, choose a short word or abbreviation to identify it. Whenever you find the same theme, write the code in the margins, on a separate piece of paper, or perhaps in a separate book.
3. Do this after you have observed, interviewed, and written quite a lot.
4. Look for patterns, like themes that often occur together (e.g., food and warfare).
5. You can also code or write about subjects in your fieldnotes when you start to venture hypotheses.

AUDIO AND VIDEO RECORDING: LEARN BY REDUCING LIFE TO MEDIA

"A picture is worth a thousand words." For the fieldworker this is especially true. Verbal description will never show people what the music sounds like or what the dances look like. An important part of every fieldworker's skills is audio and video recording. Refer to *A Manual for Documentation*[17] for more guidance in this area.

History of recording

Documentation of audio and visual data is nearly essential in any field project, and the history of ethnomusicology fieldwork is intimately connected with such documentation. Some of the most iconic photographs of early ethnomusicological fieldwork include ethnomusicologists, such as Frances Densmore, using audio recording equipment. Audio recording and playback began with Thomas Edison's phonograph cylinder in 1877—coinciding with the beginnings of modern anthropology. Audio recording technology progressed from wax cylinders to magnetic tape, and now to digital recording.

The possibility of recording video and audio together developed more recently, in the second half of the twentieth century. Many fieldworkers feel that audio-only documentation is not complete enough; a high value is placed on being able to see the artistic

---

16   See Spradley, Participant Observation, 141.
17   Society for Ethnomusicology, *A Manual for Documentation: Fieldwork and Preservation for Ethnomusicologists*, 2nd ed. (Bloomington, IN: Society for Ethnomusicology, 2001).

event (or even an interview), rather than just hearing it. This is especially true of performances in which movement or dance is a significant element. However, it is also worthwhile to be able to see instrumental performing techniques, facial expressions while singing, and body language.

Choosing recording equipment

The pace of change in recording technology makes it impossible to suggest particular products in a printed manual like this. However, here are some guidelines that should be valid for years to come.

When purchasing audio recording equipment, ask other experienced fieldworkers or look online to find current information about audio recorders. A good recorder should have the following: manual control of recording levels, external microphone input (even if the recorder has internal microphones), high-quality WAV file recording settings, headphone jack, and common media.

For video recording, you want to use a videocamera with good resolution, a tripod mount, high-quality audio, external microphone input, and headphone jack.[18]

Purposes for a recording event

Your purpose in reducing live, human activities to static media will determine how you go about it. We present here four common purposes and their implications for how you record: ethnographic analysis, form analysis, preservation, and production for distribution.

If you want to get a record of an event that allows you to later research the meanings of any or all its elements through ethnographic analysis, then you should capture everything that happens. This means that you will do as much continuous recording of an event as possible, including nonartistic sounds like chickens and babies.

If, on the other hand, you have a particular analytical interest—you'd like to figure out the melody of a particular song, or understand how weight shifts in a dance movement, for example—then you will isolate these elements from a normal performance. Benefits of recording sound and visuals in the field is the ability to go back later and look more closely at what happened. Playback on a computer allows slowing down the speed of a musical performance and freeze-framing video recordings. This can lead to more accurate description. Recordings also make comparative study easier. Different recordings of the same song, for example, can show where stylistic variation is acceptable.

The value of audiovisual recording is not limited to your own needs, but also for preservation. With many of the world's indigenous traditions in decline, this documentation may soon be all that exists to show the variety of creative expression. Many—if not all—of your recordings should be properly archived in local, national, and international collections, with performers' permissions for nonprofit

---

18   For more on this, see accompanying website, www.ethnodoxologyhandbook.com/manual.

PREFACE

PREPARE

STEP 1

STEP 2

STEP 3

STEP 4

STEP 5

STEP 6

STEP 7

CLOSING

PREFACE

PREPARE

STEP 1

STEP 2

STEP 3

STEP 4

STEP 5

STEP 6

STEP 7

CLOSING

and research uses. Future generations and interested researchers will then have access to them. Many archives have high standards for items they accept: audio files should be recorded at 24 bit/48khz, and video files should be recorded at the highest quality possible (there's no agreed-upon standard as of this writing). Get the best equipment you can afford so you can maintain a high quality of recordings for preservation.

Finally, the community you're working with may want to create products from recordings of their arts for sale or distribution. This purpose usually requires using recording standards of existing media in the region. To meet these standards, you may choose to record audio in a studio and use multiple camera shots for video. Rely on local skills and technology for this as much as possible.

Other purposes of recordings include helping you learn to perform something or documenting a process, like making an instrument or weaving fabric. You can modify how you design recording events according to each need.

Documenting recordings

A recording without accompanying contextual information has extremely limited usefulness, because you will eventually forget what's on it. It's essential, then, to create several kinds of metadata— data about the recording—as you go along:

- Speak onto the medium: If you are working with audio, record "This is *your name*, recording *so-and-so person*, at *such-and-such place*, on *such-and-such day*."
- Write as much as you can on the outside of the tape, disc, etc.
- Write in your field notebook: code for the recorded item, date, place, name of the event, participants, instruments used, community(ies) involved, audience description (size, make-up), context, purpose of event, possible ethical considerations for future use of the recording of the event.

Your notes should have a clear coding system of correspondence with the physical media. Your system may simply consist of the year and recording number. "2013-3" would refer to the third recording (perhaps a CD) you made in 2013.

Planning a recording opportunity

- Discuss the event with whoever's in charge—figure out permissions, payment, etc.
- Step through the whole event in your mind, writing down what you hope to do.
- Choose, prepare, and test your equipment.
- Bring backup equipment and batteries.

- Prepare for equipment failure, batteries dying, electricity going out, hurricanes, etc.
- Arrange mechanisms for recording metadata—notebook and pen/pencil always work.
- Prepare permission forms or audio recording of authorization (see "Sample Permission Form" below).

PHOTOGRAPHY: LEARN BY REDUCING LIFE TO STILL IMAGES

Still photographs freeze an object or scene into a two-dimensional image at a precise moment in time. As in each of these research methods, subjects must give you permission to take photographs of them.

Purposes for photography

Pictures can enrich the research process in many ways, including these:

- Document the existence of kinds of objects, like masks, regalia, props, instruments, paintings, house adornments, ritual aids, and representations of supernatural beings. These could be representations of entire objects in use or in an analytical context.
- Reveal details of objects, especially using multiple shots of the same object from different angles. These can lead to insights into construction, coloring, textures, and other features.
- Document artists, their families, and other community members in performance and at repose. Photos provide an excellent channel for reciprocity: you take pictures, then give copies back to the subjects.
- Encourage community members to take pictures to tell their stories and document the things about a performance that are important to them.
- Ask someone to document your presence and activities in the community by photographing you in action.
- Express your own creative impressions of events.

A few tips for photography

Becoming a photographer with professional skills usually takes training, expensive equipment, and technical and aesthetic gifts. If this describes you, then go take some pictures. For the rest of us, here are a few bits of advice about taking pictures. Remember, though, that you may need to change this advice depending on the purposes of the photographs.

- Your basic kit: a camera (or two), a tripod or monopod, extra batteries, extra lenses if you have them, camera use instructions. Have one or two backup ways to take photos.

PREFACE

PREPARE

STEP 1

STEP 2

STEP 3

STEP 4

STEP 5

STEP 6

STEP 7

CLOSING

PREFACE

PREPARE

STEP 1

STEP 2

STEP 3

STEP 4

STEP 5

STEP 6

STEP 7

CLOSING

You may have a fancy camera, but if it stops working (and it will), cheap and lower quality is better than nothing.

- Make sure that the primary element you want to capture is visible and in a prominent place. Many people think that important elements should be off center, and they use the rule of thirds (see glossary). If you can control the focus on your camera, make anything in front of or behind the object be slightly out of focus.
- Make sure that the light reveals what you think is important. Especially make sure that there is no light shining toward you from behind your subject. Force your flash to flash if there is light behind.
- Frame your picture by putting a bit of a wall, tree, or other object at the edge of what the camera captures.
- Keep your horizon lines (e.g., ocean, land) straight.
- Archive your pictures in different places and on different media to be sure that you will not lose them.

PUBLISHED SOURCES: LEARN BY GETTING OTHERS' PERSPECTIVES

Somebody has probably already written or filmed or recorded something about the community you are working with or a similar group. If so, you may benefit greatly from their experiences and insights.

We use the term "publish" here to refer to anything someone puts into an enduring medium to communicate to an audience beyond one or two people. These could include books, theses, dissertations, articles, films, newsletters, and audio and video recordings. The people who produce these resources could be part of scholarly communities or cultural groups, or they could be individuals like travelers, journalists, or missionaries. You'll find resources in libraries, archives, bookstores, people's personal bookshelves, and on the Internet. University libraries, archives, and bookstores in the location of the community often prove a rich source of relevant documents found nowhere else in the world. As with anything you hear or learn, make sure you evaluate these resources in terms of the purposes and credentials of the people who produce them.

LOVE AND LAW

We want all of our interactions with people to be guided and marked by love. This means that when we're researching a community, we are humble, want the best for them, and don't promote ourselves or our agendas at their expense. So explain your actions and their purposes to your friends, and respond to any concerns they may have. In many situations, it will be appropriate—sometimes also legally necessary—to let them sign an authorization form like the example below. Sometimes such forms can increase distrust if your relationship with the performers is not well established. In this case, discuss your needs (e.g., to an archive or publisher) with friends knowledgeable of local customs and come up with a respectful solution. Finally, whatever you take, find a way to generously give something back for it. An excellent way to start is to give copies of photographs, videos, and audio recordings to the subjects of your research. The best thing you can do to perform loving research is to be trustworthy, dependable, generous, respectful, humble, and concerned to build relationships that will last into heaven.

CELEBRATE A COMMUNITY'S ARTS FROM THE START

The overall arc of this manual is to stir up creativity in local forms that meet community goals. But we start with the premise that all people reflect God's image: who they are and what they do now are also inherently valuable. So as you document a community's existing arts, celebrate them. The activities "Publish Recordings and Research in Various Forms and Contexts" and "Help Develop Multimedia Collections of Local Arts" (**Step 5**) are great ways to start.

Our last word to you in this discussion of meeting the community is simply this: keep learning. Nurture your curiosity so you can continue showing this powerful sign of love.

PREFACE

PREPARE

STEP 1

STEP 2

STEP 3

STEP 4

STEP 5

STEP 6

STEP 7

CLOSING

SAMPLE PERMISSION FORM (simplify and adapt to local needs)

RELEASE FORM

PROJECT OR EVENT: _____

DATE(S): _____

Name of Individual Researcher or Organization Representative: _____

Name(s) of Participant(s): _____

_____

_____

Mailing Address of Participant(s): _____

Phone Contact of Participant(s): _____

Email Contact of Participant(s): _____

For the Participant(s): (please circle)

My/our performance may be video recorded.	YES	NO
My/our performance may be audio recorded.	YES	NO
I/we may be photographed for the project.	YES	NO

I wish to be acknowledged in any related publication as (check one):
☐ Name as written above.
☐ This name: (please print) _____.
☐ I wish to remain anonymous.

I/we the undersigned authorize the [*organization or person name*] to publish these materials on CDs, cassettes, videos, or other media, for noncommercial, nonprofit research purposes, and for communicating the value and beauty of [*these artistic events*] to others. We understand that no royalties will be paid to anyone and that no one will personally profit from these recordings without express consent of people involved.

_____   _____
Participant Signature   **Organization Representative Signature**

_____   _____
Date   **Date**

Additional participants may sign below, if desired:

_____   _____

SPECIFY KINGDOM GOALS

In Cambodia during the 1970s, under Pol Pot and the Khmer Rouge, some of the first people who were taken, tortured, and murdered were the creative people who carried the story and the heartbeat of the land. Even instruments were destroyed during this time, and ultimately an estimated total of 1.7 million deaths resulted from Khmer Rouge policies. Cambodian Christian Arts Ministry School (CCAMS) was started by Noren (a survivor of the Pol Pot regime), and an American lady, Gioia. Former street kids, gang members, orphans, and children being used in slavery and prostitution are rescued into a loving home where they are loved, fed, sheltered, and educated. Alongside its regular schooling, the CCAMS family has an emphasis on the arts (music, dance, drama, visual art, and literature). By teaching the children at CCAMS the arts, they not only give the children incredible skills and a means to express their emotions, they are also restoring something that was stolen from the nation and putting God at the center of it.

The Ling family could see no other way to survive than to sell their children into modern slavery. But Noren met them at this crucial time and took the children into CCAMS, where they have flourished. One girl became their lead dancer and, together with her sister, earned enough money performing to help their parents build a house in their home village and farm the land successfully. The mother makes many of the beautiful costumes for the children of CCAMS while another sister teaches them to dance. All of the Ling family are now Christians, and as others hear of their story they are marvelling at the story of God in their transformed lives. — *Martin and Rebekah Neil*

PREFACE

PREPARE

STEP 1

STEP 2

STEP 3

STEP 4

STEP 5

STEP 6

STEP 7

CLOSING

Many of us experience little visceral anticipation of heaven because we've never wholeheartedly tried to grasp its astounding richness and complexity. Every good thing we experience on earth points to something infinitely more satisfying in heaven. These earthly signs of the kingdom are mere glimpses, whiffs, hints, brushes, whispers of that reality. Our goal in **Step 2** is to stir your imagination in ways that release aromas of the kingdom of God, awakening your hunger for heaven. You'll then be more able to inspire that same hunger in the community you're working with. We emphasize the "now and not yet" nature of these signs of the kingdom, recognizing that none will flourish completely until God institutes his perfect realm. There will be significant obstacles along the way, but we can join what God is doing and help make a difference.

To this end, we present six broad, biblically based categories of goals that could indicate that the kingdom of God is thriving in a community: Identity and Sustainability, Shalom, Justice, Scripture, Church Life, and Personal Spiritual Life. In each we briefly describe some specific objectives that a community could adopt, explain how local arts might help meet them, and give a few real-life Glimpses of these goals fulfilled. **Step 5** details activities that communities can perform to help achieve these objectives. Throughout the discussion we illustrate many of the goals with stories of how real communities have drawn on their arts to more fully reflect heaven. The final section of **Step 2** guides you through a process a community can follow to identify the kingdom goals they want to work toward.

IDENTITY AND SUSTAINABILITY

VALUING IDENTITY
WHERE THE KINGDOM OF GOD THRIVES, COMMUNITIES VALUE THEIR CULTURE.

"God created people in his own image" (Gen 1:27 NLT). Not only does every man and woman reflect God's image, but the cultures they form will continue into eternity: "a great multitude that no one could count, from every nation, tribe, people and language" (Rev 7:9) will stand before God's throne. Until Jesus' ultimate reign in the future, of course, cultures show evidence of both God's image and the brokenness and sin that exist. But it is a right, healthy, and holy thing for people to value the good aspects of their societies. In many places, however, minority groups think more highly of other people and so denigrate the usefulness, beauty, or intrinsic value of their own culture. Sometimes other groups—often more powerful—have overtly or inadvertently taught this. Missionaries and colonizers are infamous for this, despite Paul's planting the seed of affirming the equal value of each culture (Gal 3:28). The groups we belong to are all susceptible to either self-exaltation or self-rejection; neither reflects truth in the kingdom of God.

We have seen that the more a community appropriately values its own culture, the more the kingdom of God is likely to thrive. Further, a community's artistic genres constitute some of the most identifiable and valuable parts of their culture. If they see no good in their own arts, they will not use them to worship God or communicate truth to each other. We want to explore ways that a community can affirm its artistic resources and create new works that foster strong, godly cultural identity.

In one South Asian language group with no believers, translators worked on Bible translation for fifteen years. When we arrived, the translators told us that the only time they heard traditional music from these people was when the people were drunk. Those who had become believers said the same thing. Because of this practice, the church borrowed melodies from a neighboring language group for use in their own worship. Some Christian songs were sung in the neighboring language and some songs were translated into their own language.

As we met together with several Christian artists from this community, we explored what God's word says about worship and our call to communicate to others and to the Lord with truth and meaning. Within three days, these artists began revealing knowledge of traditional tunes, dance, and drama styles that were truly their own. One man revealed that he was a poet, and one musician was actually a music guru in his own traditional music system before he became a Christian. These artists soon felt free to compose new song texts with new tunes in their traditional music system.

The Christian artists from this culture said that the reason they suppressed the information about their heart expressions was that they felt that they needed to worship as neighboring language groups worshiped, using other groups' music, song texts, and tunes. They felt that their own artistic genres were not good enough for the Lord. They had not realized how valuable their own arts and culture are. As they embraced this new idea, we challenged them to think about the needs of the believers and nonbelievers in their communities as well as for what purposes they could sing new songs. New songs were birthed and impacted not only their Christian worship, but their entire community. The first CD ever created in their own language and music was distributed throughout their language community.
— *Mary Beth Saurman*

TEACHING CHILDREN
WHERE THE KINGDOM OF GOD THRIVES, COMMUNITIES TEACH THEIR TRADITIONS TO THEIR CHILDREN.

One telling sign of the identity health of a community is how much they pass on good parts of their culture to their children and grandchildren. Identifying patterns of what and how each generation

PREFACE

PREPARE

STEP 1

STEP 2

STEP 3

STEP 4

STEP 5

STEP 6

STEP 7

CLOSING

PREFACE

PREPARE

STEP 1

STEP 2

STEP 3

STEP 4

STEP 5

STEP 6

STEP 7

CLOSING

is passing on artistic knowledge to the next will reveal a community's health in this area.

One South Asian language group, as happens with many cultures desiring a move towards national education, faced a rupture in their transmission process. This meant there was no passing on of their traditional culture and values. Children no longer worked the fields during the day or sat with elders in the evenings, where transmission of cultural knowledge usually took place. With this shift, a generation grew into young adults who did not have interest in their own traditional songs and dances. Soon the songs and dances would be lost.

Through a participatory workshop, the generations came together and discussed what traditions they valued and what was slipping away from them. Together the older and younger adults interacted and planned how they would actively pass on their valuable cultural wisdom and art forms.

One approach included older expert musicians and artists teaching in the public classes about their art forms and cultural knowledge. Books and other reading materials about the creation process and cultural values were also created. The transmission process that was severed was reconnected through a new creative method within the national education system that initially caused the rupture. — *Mary Beth and Todd Saurman*

USING MEDIA

WHERE THE KINGDOM OF GOD THRIVES, COMMUNITIES CONTRIBUTE TO LOCAL, REGIONAL, AND GLOBAL RECORDING INDUSTRIES.

People around the world are constantly figuring out new ways to communicate with each other. A community with an appropriately strong sense of its value will not only receive and learn artistic communication from others, but will also contribute recordings of their own arts through local, regional, and global media.

Among the Akyode of Ghana, there were very few commercially available recordings in their own language. In order to promote local language and culture, five cassettes were recorded from 1994 to 1996. Different sets of recording equipment were used at different times, ranging from a minimal set to a large set (the tape purchasers never remarked on any perceived differences in recording quality). The first tape was recorded with songs already composed (a mix of traditional and choir genres). The second and third tapes used only songs in traditional genres that were commissioned for the recordings. The song texts were biblical narrative portions (Creation and Christmas), and were targeted especially at older, nonliterate, non-Christian community members. By request, the fourth and fifth tapes used choir songs preferred by members of certain churches. Different target audiences preferred different tapes, but the general response to all cassettes was favorable.

Step 2: Specify Kingdom Goals

27

PREFACE

PREPARE

STEP 1

STEP 2

STEP 3

STEP 4

STEP 5

STEP 6

STEP 7

CLOSING

Research was done beforehand to (a) consider which musical genres were preferred by particular target groups; (b) identify composers who worked in those genres; (c) determine if enough tape players were in use within the society to make a cassette program feasible; and (d) prioritize which biblical messages needed to be communicated first.

Most of the planning of the first two cassettes was done by the expatriates of the language team; in later cassettes, more of the planning was done by Akyode people as a sense of ownership developed, and they gained experience in planning and completing a recording.

The initial funds were provided by the expatriates of the language team. The cassettes were sold at a price comparable to other prerecorded tapes in the area. The money from cassette sales was used to purchase more blank tapes for the next recording, and thereby stayed in circulation to a large extent. However, each new cassette was recorded before the previous one sold out completely, which meant that (fairly small) amounts of capital were contributed by the expatriates for each tape duplication run. *– Paul Neeley and Bill Groot*

Dagomba women from a literacy class in Ghana were asked to compose some songs based on the Creation for a video project. Almost all participants were Muslims but content material was acceptable to all faiths, including those practicing traditional religion. Traditional dances were included with the songs on the final video along with more explicitly Christian content. The video was shot by a visiting cameraman, with the creation story being dramatized by local people using gestures, dress etc. . . . that they chose (Adam named each animal three times in accordance with local practice, for example). Editing was done by an expatriate with local input, but despite several copies of the video being made available to the local community through the literacy project office, there was little interest. Possible factors include lack of access to equipment (at this time, there was little provision of electricity in the mostly rural area, and few people had TVs and video players), and poor promotion. However, despite its failure on the media and distribution fronts, this project did serve useful purposes in the community where it was enacted for building interfaith connections and enhancing the status of traditional music, dance, and dramatic styles, especially for Christians in the community. *– Paul Neeley* [19]

SHALOM

HEALING

WHERE THE KINGDOM OF GOD THRIVES, COMMUNITIES RESPOND TO SOCIAL, EMOTIONAL, AND PHYSICAL CHALLENGES IN HEALTHY WAYS.

Jesus entered human society so that his followers would be able to live life to the fullest (John 10:10) and have peace (John 14:27). The Hebrew word *shalom* captures much of what he promised: a state

---

19   Ibid., 22.

PREFACE

PREPARE

STEP 1

STEP 2

STEP 3

STEP 4

STEP 5

STEP 6

STEP 7

CLOSING

of peace, completeness, social harmony, justice, and health. Bryant Myers suggests that while "shalom and abundant life are ideals that we will not see this side of the second coming, the vision of a shalom that leads to life in its fullness is a powerful image that must inform and shape our understanding of any better human future."[20]

The forces arrayed against shalom are formidable: war, natural disasters, sexual exploitation, disease, slavery, hunger, and thirst. A community marked by the kingdom of God responds to these groanings of creation with healing and restoration. Artistic activity plays crucial roles in increasing shalom because it can point suffering people to hope, instill solidarity within a community, and aid emotional and physical healing.

For many suffering people, the sixty-eight Psalms that are laments—and in fact the whole book of Lamentations—are a good model of how we can be angry with God and lament what has happened to us. During trauma healing workshops, participants are encouraged to write their own laments to God, including the six parts found in many of the Psalms (address to God, past faithfulness, complaint, plea for help, answer from God, vow to trust). They are also encouraged to set their lament to music in local ethnic traditional forms used at funerals and other sad occasions. – *Margaret Hill*

One birth-mother's heart rate began soaring beyond control during delivery. The nurses refused my assistance to let her listen to her favorite music, even though I had explained how helpful it would be. Finally, in desperation, they consented. I turned on the *heavy metal music* (the birth-mother's favorite) and immediately her heart rate and the baby's (still in her womb) began dropping and quickly returned to a normal state.
– *Mary Beth Saurman, Music Therapist* [21]

In Sudan, RECONCILE facilitators in trauma healing settings use experiential processes to make the material "come alive" and to give space for the participants to share their insights. One of the activities used, after sharing material and biblical passages on the concept of forgiveness, was to have the multiethnic participants write down situations in which they needed to grant or seek forgiveness on a piece of paper, which they then nailed to a wooden cross. Often the situations they were concerned about had involved other ethnicities present at the workshop. They then made a procession together, singing as they marched, and brought the cross to an area where prayers of forgiveness were offered, and it was burned amidst jubilant singing and dancing representing each of the groups who had wounded each other. – *Debbie Braaksma*

20   Bryant L. Myers, *Walking with the Poor: Principles and Practices of Transformational Development* (Maryknoll, NY: Orbis, 1999), 51.
21   Mary Saurman, "The Effect of Music on Blood Pressure and Heart Rate," *EM News* 4, no. 3 (1995): 2.

Step 2: Specify Kingdom Goals

29

PREFACE

PREPARE

STEP 1

STEP 2

STEP 3

STEP 4

STEP 5

STEP 6

STEP 7

CLOSING

In Benin, I met a community nurse who had realized that singing about health can inspire people to change their behavior. Yerima, the nurse, told me that he started to sing about health issues out of frustration. He had noticed that the women who came to his village's two-room health center for prenatal care paid little attention to his lectures on topics such as nutrition and childhood vaccinations. Yet when he composed and performed songs with the same information, he found that his audience became much more interested, and they sang with him in the common call-and-response form of the region.

Given the threat of a cholera epidemic at the time of my visit, I asked whether he could write a new song to communicate fundamental ideas about water hygiene. Yerima disappeared into the back room while the clinic director gave a lecture on cholera, which received scant attention. Five minutes later, Yerima returned and began to shout that cholera causes diarrhea. The crowd responded with sounds of disgust. Yerima then began to sing, repeating a response line for them: kolera baradarorwa (cholera will kill you). Gradually, he began to sing lines of information between the response lines, advising the women to boil their water and urging them to wash their hands and those of their children before eating. In less than ten minutes, a new song had been learned and a new message communicated: simple, fast, effective, memorable. — *Matthew Davis*[22]

We communicate our messages primarily through music, dance, and drama. Counseling on our site is also done through music and drama. When we organize a play or music, we don't just compose any song or meaningless drama. First we recognize the experiences and needs around us. If we pass along those experiences in drama we find that we help people enormously. We can show a drama demonstrating how younger girls acquire HIV because they want to get rich, to become "smart" at an early age. We can show what happens when women go to witchdoctors instead of testing centers. We can pass along some songs in places where AIDS has hit aggressively. Music is our most powerful tool . . . for affecting change in Uganda![23]

RECONCILIATION

WHERE THE KINGDOM OF GOD THRIVES, COMMUNITIES RECONCILE WITH EACH OTHER AND WITH OUTSIDE COMMUNITIES.

Human beings don't get along. We fight, denigrate, mock, disdain, undermine, exploit, deceive, and exclude each other. We justify our sickly outrages through appeals to self, ethnicity, class, religion, ideology, and pleasure. But God emptied himself to flood us with

22   Matthew Davis, "Health through Song: Outreach Workers in Benin and Guatemala Use Lyrics to Promote Health," *Harvard Medical Alumni Bulletin* 73 (1999): 36–41.
23   Meeting Point spokesman, in Gregory Barz, *Singing for Life: HIV/AIDS and Music in Uganda* (New York: Routledge, 2006), 168.

PREFACE

PREPARE

STEP 1

STEP 2

STEP 3

STEP 4

STEP 5

STEP 6

STEP 7

CLOSING

a unifying love, a God-human reconciliation that models human-human fellowship. Brittle turns to soft. Furrowed brow turns to open smile. "Everyone will know that you are my disciples, if you love one another" (John 13:35). In the kingdom of God, there are no lasting human distinctions that put some of us above others (Gal 3:28; Col 3:11; Jas 2:5).

Artistic communication can help us open our arms to each other and feel unity that draws on something deeper than our histories. Singing and dancing together require us to mold our individuality into coordinated sound and movement. The joy, pleasure, and solidarity that arts evoke pull us out of patterns of distrust and lift our eyes from our hurt to transcendent truths. Artistic forms of communication can lead to powerful moments of repentance, forgiveness, solidarity, love, and lasting reconciliation.

REST AND PLAY[24]

WHERE THE KINGDOM OF GOD THRIVES, COMMUNITIES BALANCE PRODUCTIVITY WITH REST AND PLAY.

Foundational to Jewish and Christian faith is the fact that God wants everyone to follow his example of integrating a pattern of rest into work. God created in six days and rested the seventh (Gen 2:2). Isaiah connects restoration and keeping Sabbath to delight (58:12–14). God decreed Sabbath for human benefit (Mark 2:27), heaven will include rest (Heb 4:1–11), and Jesus offered to give rest to weary people (Matt 11:28). God even wants land to enjoy rest (Lev 26:34). So part of shalom is a satisfying mix of fruitful work, rest, celebration, and play. Artistic forms of communication provide exceptional opportunities for playful restoration: they can contribute to reduced stress, heightened hope, and improved emotional and physical health. The world's communities engage in an astounding variety of sporting activities that both display artistry in themselves and are integrated into larger events full of arts.

---

24   For further study, consult Mark Buchanan, *The Rest of God: Restoring Your Soul by Restoring Sabbath* (Nashville: Thomas Nelson, 2007); Abraham Joshua Heschel, *The Sabbath* (New York: Farrar, Straus, & Giroux, 2005); Wojciech Liponski, *World Sports Encyclopedia* (St. Paul, MN: MBI, 2003).

PREFACE

PREPARE

STEP 1

STEP 2

STEP 3

STEP 4

STEP 5

STEP 6

STEP 7

CLOSING

 Aceh, Indonesia, recently stopped thirty years of war. In these areas everyone is traumatically affected by the war, and their ability to heal from the trauma is essential to the whole society. To help individuals learn the skills they will need to recover from trauma, Nadine Hoover of Friends Peace Teams to Indonesia has developed an advanced level "Alternatives to Violence" workshop that includes role playing and games (http://avpinternational.org). The workshop focuses on the following:

- Safety and self-care
- Companionship and accompaniment
- Facing traumatic incidents
- Stress, trauma, and reactions to trauma
- Remembering without reliving
- Loss, grief, and mourning
- Rebuilding social relationships

JUSTICE

SOCIAL JUSTICE

WHERE THE KINGDOM OF GOD THRIVES, COMMUNITIES LOVE AND STRENGTHEN THE POOR AND OTHERS IN THEIR MARGINS.

God has communicated clearly and repeatedly throughout Scripture that he cares for people without power. He highlights orphans, widows, and foreigners (Deut 10:18; Jas 1:27), people without enough money (Deut 15:7,8; Ps 9:18; Luke 4:18; 6:20), the politically and socially oppressed (Neh 9:15; Luke 1:46–55), prisoners (Ps 146:7), and hungry and homeless people (Isa 58:6–11; Matt 25:34–40). Jesus made a special point of telling the poor that they could have the kingdom of God (Luke 6:20–26). And God shows how the lack of justice for marginalized people often—though not always—results from the callousness and sin of people in power (Ps 12:5; 35:10; 72:12–14; Prov 22:22,23; Isa 10:1–3).

In response to these realities, God told people *with* resources to be generous (Deut 15:7,8; Prov 11:24,25; Rom 12:13; 2 Cor 9:6–13; Jas 2:15–17) and kind to the marginalized (Prov 14:31), to defend them (Prov 31:8,9) and break the systems that keep them down (Isa 58:6–11). Communities can work toward kingdom justice by drawing on their arts' abilities to instill hope, speak unwelcome truth to those in power, and encourage solidarity.

PREFACE

PREPARE

STEP 1

STEP 2

STEP 3

STEP 4

STEP 5

STEP 6

STEP 7

CLOSING

In the early 1900s, some white men gave blankets to some Mi'kmaq people (eastern Canada). It seemed like a wonderful gift, but it turned out that these blankets had previously belonged to families who had died from smallpox. The blankets carried the smallpox virus and as a result of the "gifts," the resulting epidemic reduced the Mi'kmaq population from over thirty thousand to just over three thousand people. Several of my Mi'kmaq friends have told me this story; they see this incident as a deliberate act against the Mi'kmaq people—and it still hurts them to think of it.

So, when some of the ladies from church groups who pray for me asked me what they could do to bless the Mi'kmaq people, I thought and prayed about it and this idea came to mind: "What if people made 'blankets of blessing'—that carry not a hidden killer virus, but prayers and good wishes?"

I shared my vision, and now many women's groups have embraced this project and are making an overwhelming number of beautiful blankets. What a wonderful way to pour love on my friends here! I see these gifts as making a step towards acknowledging what happened to the Mi'kmaq people.

When I told some of my Mi'kmaq friends about the blankets being made, they were thrilled, especially when they found out that the women have prayed over these blankets for God to bless the Mi'kmaq. *– Dianne Friesen*

Games and sport can energize a community, help develop identity, and transmit cultural values in ways that might not otherwise occur. A prime example of such a game is *castells* (human towers). *Castells* are found in the Catalonia region of Spain and have been in existence since the eighteenth century, generally occurring during festival times. These human structures are visually impressive, sometimes with ten levels of people standing on each other's shoulders with a supporting base of hundreds of assistants. Variations of these towers not only add to the complexity of the tower and success of the *castell* team but also to the visual beauty. As a nonprofessional sport, participants wear specific clothing to indicate their regional identity, and unique songs are played while the *castells* are being built. UNESCO has recognized the value of the *castell* and placed it on their list of the Intangible Cultural Heritage of Humanity. *– Cory Cummins*

Step 2: Specify Kingdom Goals

33

PREFACE

PREPARE

STEP 1

STEP 2

STEP 3

STEP 4

STEP 5

STEP 6

STEP 7

CLOSING

"Dancing changed my life. For the first time I felt that I was doing something I liked," recalls Shampa Roy. The eighteen-year-old from Kolkata lived in children's homes from the age of five after her parents died. "I was always angry, I didn't know why. I beat up other inmates at the slightest provocation; people used to avoid me. I didn't respect my teachers or my elders," she admits. And then she discovered dance. Roy realized she could express her inner turmoil through dancing. It was, she says, a discovery of joy. Roy is now an assistant dance instructor, sharing her discovery with other women.

She was trained by Kolkata Sanved (which means "sensitivity" in Bengali), a local NGO that uses dance to help people cope with mental trauma. A main area of Sanved focus is working with trafficked girls and women, with Kolkata a significant source and destination for trafficked women.

Sanved was set up in 2002 by Sohini Chakraborty, a sociology graduate from Kolkata. Chakraborty first started to use dance as a form of therapy when she volunteered with another NGO, Sanlaap, which works with former prostitutes. Using her background in classical Indian dance, Chakraborty initially taught the girls a combination of classical and contemporary dance movements. However, they didn't respond to the classes. So instead she began to create a series of body movements based on everyday actions, such as making chai or sweeping the floor, and this clicked with the girls. She would ask a girl to imagine that she was a tree. How would she project it? Gradually the girls started to open up and learned to express their emotions through their movements. It was only later that Chakraborty realized that this form of movement is a recognized therapy, known as Dance Movement Therapy (DMT), which was devised in America in the 1940s.

As Chakraborty explains, the women she works with often feel a deep inferiority and have extremely low self-esteem. "DMT encourages them to think, 'I am creating my own body through my own expression.'" By taking control of their bodies, they are able to rebuild their confidence and begin to cope with mental trauma.

Kolkata Sanved has since expanded its work to other groups. Today Chakraborty collaborates with NGOs working with street children, young people living in red-light areas, those living with HIV, and also people with mental health issues. The NGO also helps elderly women living in shelter homes. Workshops are held regularly in rural areas in collaboration with outreach organizations. Sanved also runs projects with domestic workers, including one held on the platform of the main train station where many workers pass through daily.

Indrani Sinha, director of Sanlaap, says, "A lot of pain and hurt haunts these women, but there's a lot of beauty too. We have to look for their wellspring of beauty, try to bring it to the surface, and not treat them as only case studies. DMT helps them to rise above the brutalities they have gone through." *– Ranjita Biswas*[25]

---

25   Ranjita Biswas, "Dancing Away the Pain," *Guardian Weekly*, October 12, 2010, edited by Sue Hall-Heimbecker.

PREFACE

PREPARE

STEP 1

STEP 2

STEP 3

STEP 4

STEP 5

STEP 6

STEP 7

CLOSING

Around the world, deaf community members are regularly treated as low-caste citizens by the hearing majority. The church is often unwittingly one of the greatest culprits. Hearing ministers and missionaries teach not only the Bible, but hearing culture, forcing deaf Christians to conform to hearing learning methodologies which tend to frustrate and bore the deaf. Often deaf church attendees never learn the story of Jesus Christ because they are not told through their languages and their artistic learning norms.

Upon visiting the Woodhaven Baptist Deaf Church in Houston, Texas, I was pleased to find a church where Deaf culture and arts were central to church community. American Deaf culture celebrates the gift of American Sign Language in all its artistic glory, and Deaf community members often gather for storytelling and poetic performance. Adjacent to the church building is a community center in which stands a large room which serves as both cafe and performance space. A raised stage against one wall stands in the line of sight of all present, including the baristas, who are stationed at the opposite wall. The room is full of small round tables, for ease of signed communication, which requires sustained eye contact within a group. There is extra space left between tables, so that conversants can easily shift their chairs for a clear view of the performance space. In this way, Woodhaven Baptist has fully integrated Deaf artistic culture into their community center. – *Maan Di Thomas*

EDUCATION

WHERE THE KINGDOM OF GOD THRIVES, COMMUNITY MEMBERS LEARN WHAT THEY NEED TO SUCCEED IN AND CONTRIBUTE TO THEIR SOCIETIES.

Communities *not* marked by the kingdom signs of health and valuing their identity often have weak educational systems. Rapid social change—when new economic and political realities devalue previous knowledge—can also leave people without the knowledge or training to thrive. Because the arts are such penetrating and memorable systems of communication, communities can integrate them into all educational subjects and teaching contexts.

Cherry Faile smiles when she hears villagers singing songs in the Manpruli language about how to properly nurse children or cook nutritious meals. In a place where accurate statistics are tough to track, the songs affirm that the public health programs she helped develop at the Baptist Medical Centre in rural Ghana are working.

"You'd hear them singing those songs everywhere," says Faile. "You'd be surprised how quickly those messages spread and become part of the thinking in the community." That's just one example of the unique public health programs the hospital uses to educate and minister to the large local community, most of whom still live in simple huts and have little formal education.

35

PREFACE

PREPARE

STEP 1

STEP 2

STEP 3

STEP 4

STEP 5

STEP 6

STEP 7

CLOSING

As Faile began putting up a public health building years ago, she realized, "I really wanted [it] to belong to the people so they would feel comfortable coming here." So she invited village chiefs to send villagers to help with construction. Together, they built the traditional huts used as exam rooms and administrative offices.

The hospital offers other special health education programs building on community values. A rustic pavilion beside the hospital provides a place for mothers to nurse their malnourished children back to health. Every morning the mothers sweep camp together, attend devotionals, and learn how to prepare healthy meals using local foods. Each afternoon, with babies strapped securely to their backs, the women prepare the food in giant cast-iron pots. "They come every day until their children reach a healthy weight," Faile explains. "They may stay six weeks." – *Emily Peters*

LITERACY

WHERE THE KINGDOM OF GOD THRIVES, COMMUNITIES READ AND LISTEN TO THE BIBLE AND OTHER LITERATURE.

Members of a community marked by the kingdom of God will be able to access Scripture and other literature through written and aural means. Since many decisions affecting people's lives in private and government relationships involve written documents, the ability to read and write provides minority communities tools to help protect their interests. Literacy goals relate to both technical (e.g., understanding language structure) and social issues (e.g., wanting to read and write in a language, and feeling capable of acquiring these skills). This makes it likely that artistic forms both with heavy language components (e.g., songs, drama, storytelling, proverbs, and riddles) and those without (e.g., dance, visual arts) will feed into these goals.

Muslims in Dagbani communities of Ghana feared literacy because of a history of school learning leading to Christian conversion. Leaders of a literacy project there asked students questions like these: "Why are you learning to read? Why is it worth the trouble? Make a song about it." Then the songs were collected on cassette and transcribed into a booklet with pictures done by a local artist. The songs were rerecorded for quality in a makeshift studio in the office, and copies of the tape and booklet given to all the class supervisors. They typically used them by writing a song on the blackboard for a class, teaching the song orally or from the tape, and having learners join in, following the text. The songs were a learning tool, but more importantly built community motivation for engaging with the process of learning to read. The students' reasons for wanting to read included being able to write and read letters, becoming "enlightened" so that no one could fool them, being like other people groups locally who had classes, and helping their children with school work. – *Sue Hall-Heimbecker*

PREFACE

PREPARE

STEP 1

STEP 2

STEP 3

STEP 4

STEP 5

STEP 6

STEP 7

CLOSING

A literacy specialist in the Central African Republic felt that an alphabet song was needed to strengthen the reading readiness component of the Sango literacy program. She commissioned a local choir director to set a poem to music. It was to accompany a one-page alphabet chart which teachers distributed to learners and posted in their classrooms. A local artist had illustrated it. The chart had a key word and illustration to go along with each letter. "The Sango Alphabet Song" used alliteration, and Sango literacy teachers taught the song to help students learn the sounds of each letter. Here is part of it:

a. Bâgara tî âta agä,
   Grandfather's cow came,
b. lo buba bongö tî babâ.
   It ruined father's clothes.
d. Deku adö dödö tî lo.
   The mouse did his dance.
e. Ë te lê tî këkë sô.
   We eat fruit from this tree.

Singing the song fostered group enthusiasm and built team spirit. Churches sang it enthusiastically when certificates were presented to graduating students; students in some classes sang it while passing around an offering cup to collect coins for their teacher.

Six local literacy supervisors trained over one hundred volunteer literacy teachers in Sango-speaking churches. They, in turn, taught thousands of Central Africans how to read so they could benefit from health booklets, cultural materials, and Bible portions, as well as use their new skill to learn French. "The Sango Alphabet Song" was one of the strongest motivators to encourage new students to attend Sango literacy classes and learn how to read.

One pastor was among the students who received their reading certificates after learning how to read. He read to his church from the third chapter of the Gospel of John and encouraged everyone in his congregation to be in the next reading class. "Don't be ashamed to admit you don't know how to read," he said. "I learned. So can you!" Another student said, "When I didn't know how to read, I was like a blind person. Today I am happy to say I am like the blind man of Jericho. My eyes are opened, and I can see!" – *Michelle Petersen*

Mary Stringer in Papua New Guinea encouraged teachers to use a different song to go with each week's literacy theme. They made up songs about rats, frogs, women, houses, and other themes. – *Mary Beth Saurman*

ECONOMIC OPPORTUNITY
WHERE THE KINGDOM OF GOD THRIVES, ALL COMMUNITY MEMBERS CAN WORK TO CONTRIBUTE TO THEIR MATERIAL WELL-BEING.

From God's own crafting of the universe (Gen 1) to putting Adam in charge of the garden of Eden (Gen 2:15), and admonitions to be productive (Prov 18:9; Col 3:23; 2 Thess 3:10; 1 Tim 5:18) and to reward labor (1 Tim 5:18), Scripture shows that humans are meant to work. The members of a community marked by the kingdom of God have opportunities to engage in meaningful, materially rewarding endeavors. Artists benefit from their activities when people pay for performances or objects. Artistic communication can also grease the wheels of commerce in advertising, and can motivate and coordinate people who are laboring. A thriving community values and rewards the contributions of its artists to its material health.

The Wagogo people of Tanzania, Africa, are renowned for their musicality. A British couple under their charity Voices from the Nations have recorded audio, pictures, and video entitled "Sing to the Well" to bring their story of hope in adversity to a wider audience. The CD and DVD were recorded in a mud hut and designed to appeal to a Western audience. The recording is a collection of songs taken from everyday life in a beautiful but harsh environment, where famine and drought are often just around the corner. Through an agreement between the local community, musicians, and the producers, sales of this production have provided water sources, a clinic, and other emergency help to the Mnase area implemented by a local development committee. *– Martin and Rebekah Neil*

SCRIPTURE

TRANSLATING SCRIPTURE
WHERE THE KINGDOM OF GOD THRIVES, COMMUNITIES TRANSLATE SCRIPTURE.

A community marked by the kingdom of God will know what he has communicated through Scripture. To do this, they must first have access to a translation of the Bible that is faithful to the original documents, communicates in ways that are clear to the vast majority of its members, renders texts in the most appropriate and penetrating forms of the local language, is interpretable by various Christian traditions, and can be transformed into oral communication forms with ease. Since the Bible is riddled with artistic forms of communication—parables, proverbs, stories, song lyrics, poetry— insights into local artistic genres will help a community translate Scripture in ways that feed into these goals.

PREFACE

PREPARE

STEP 1

STEP 2

STEP 3

STEP 4

STEP 5

STEP 6

STEP 7

CLOSING

I knew that one of the most common features of biblical poetry is semantic and accentual parallelism. Translators often indicate this poetic device through typographical conventions, using indentation and line breaks. In my preparations to help Baka speakers in Cameroon translate the Bible into their language, I discovered that Baka poetic "lines" are not constructed in quite the same way. They do not mark poetic lines through accentual parallelism, but through periodic parallelism; that is, through musically metered lines. This means that Baka poetic lines are primarily bound by repeated groups of musical pulses ("beats"), not by repeated groups of patterned word stresses, as in Hebrew poetry.

Parallel Baka poetic meters may be formed of 4, 8, 12, or 16 pulses per song line, depending upon the song genre in question. The texts of these metered song lines are then grammatically segmented according to generic line lengths. Generic story-song poetic texts, for example, typically include an average of 11 words per line (ranging 7–16 words per line) and an average 21 syllables per line (ranging 20–22 syllables per line). Thus, when preparing the text for the "Song of Moses" (Ex 15) for translation, the Baka translation team knew beforehand that the traditional text load of any single poetic line should contain between 7 and 16 words, and between 20 and 22 syllables. By respecting such grammatical parameters, the translators could be reasonably confident that they were meeting traditional Baka expectations regarding some of the most fundamental rhythmic and syntactic phenonema of Baka poetic texts. – *Dan Fitzgerald*

Ellen and Ross Errington helped the Manobo (Philippines) Old Testament translators improve the naturalness of their translation by asking them to draw the Bible story and tell it to neighbors before writing it down.

The Bible translation team in a dialect of Arabic wanted to translate the book of Proverbs in a way that would impact hearers and readers as strongly as traditional proverbs. They first gathered and analyzed traditional proverbs such as this:

Al-bituchch diginah
hu bichimm afanatah.
(The one who burns his beard will smell the odor.)

Then they considered particular features of each proverb, such as these:

- **Overall meaning**: If you cause problems, you are the one that will bear the consequences.
- **Subject**: The consequences of actions.
- **Verbal type**: Declarative, imperfect.
- **Rhythm**: Two lines, first line six syllables, second line seven syllables. Lines are roughly balanced in length.
- **Rhyme**: Uses the *a* sound at the end of each line.
- **Total number of words**: Five.

- **Metaphor**: To burn a beard = to search for problems; uses a body part (others might use animals, plants, or objects).
- **Interesting grammatical features**: The article *al-* is used as a relative pronoun "he who" or "whoever." This seems to render the proverb more general.
- **Other features** they looked for included homonyms, context, and exaggeration in this proverb.

The team was then able to use what they had learned about traditional proverbs in their translation of biblical proverbs. Here is how they translated Proverbs 10:5: *Al-yilimm akilah fi wakt al-gati' aagil ziyaada wa al-yunuum fi al-darat yiwassif fasaadah* (He who gathers his food at cutting time is very intelligent but he who sleeps during harvest shows his depravity).

This translation uses features that are similar to traditional proverbs: theme—consequences of actions, two lines, roughly balanced in length; rhyme—each line ends in the *a* sound; article *al-* used as a relative pronoun to provide a general subject. *– Sue Hall-Heimbecker*

ORAL SCRIPTURE
WHERE THE KINGDOM OF GOD THRIVES, COMMUNITIES ACCESS SCRIPTURE THROUGH FAMILIAR FORMS.

A community marked by the kingdom of God will have access to Scripture in many forms. Local art forms—especially those that people use to tell stories—can play key roles in integrating Scripture into communities' lives.

A Tibetan language group completed a full set of oral Bible stories. These stories accurately paralleled the stories from Scripture. People, however, were not embracing them or passing them on.

The believers prayed together, asking the Lord to show them the barriers. They studied the biblical stories in more depth. They then contextualized the stories through cultural lenses. The believers also looked at their own local storytelling and expressive art forms. They realized that their traditional way of storytelling is not just through words. Storytelling within their culture occurs through poetry, songs, dances, dramas, and visual arts.

With this new awareness, these believers created more relevant Bible stories. These artistically infused stories now emphasize both the needs and the cultural issues within their Tibetan communities.

The story of the prodigal son, expressed through several songs and a dance, contains a song sung by the father. "This will reach the hearts of our people," said the composer, "because a father's expressed care for his children is so important in our culture. Now, people will listen, understand, and grab this story." *– Mary Beth and Todd Saurman*

PREFACE
PREPARE
STEP 1
STEP 2
STEP 3
STEP 4
STEP 5
STEP 6
STEP 7
CLOSING

In some cultures, the person who works with the words as a poet, and the one who works with the musical notes as a composer, may not be the same.

In Cambodia, a threefold process was used to develop indigenous hymns at United Bible Society translation workshops. The first step was to accurately translate the chosen passages (from Matthew 5 and Philippians 2) into prose; then poets were given the translated texts and "were assigned to turn this prose text into good Cambodian poetry, using their own traditional rhyming patterns and poetic forms." In the third step, musicians were asked to work with the poets to create translations that could be actually sung. – *Howard Hatton and David Clark*[26]

CHURCH LIFE

CORPORATE WORSHIP

WHERE THE KINGDOM OF GOD THRIVES, CHRIST-FOLLOWERS GATHER TO WORSHIP IN WAYS THAT PROMOTE DEEP COMMUNICATION WITH GOD AND EACH OTHER.

In its deepest sense, biblical worship is a life completely sacrificed and given to God (Rom 12:1,2). It is the moment-by-moment choice to live for God's glory and not one's own. But this whole life of worship includes particular times of gathering with other believers for heartfelt adoration of God and communication with him (Ps 95:6; 96:9; Acts 2:42; Heb 10:24,25; Rev 19:10). Local arts provide languages for these moments of worshiping God and listening to him that involve our whole heart, soul, strength, and mind (Ps 100:2; Mark 12:29,30). Jesus taught that it doesn't matter where you worship, as long as it's done in spirit and in truth (John 4:21–24). This opens the door to people from every nation and language using their own forms of communication to honor God.

To express such corporate worship, the Bible urges us to be filled with the Holy Spirit (Eph 5:18–20) and to use languages and forms that are clearly and deeply understood by others (1 Cor 14:6–19). This includes not only spoken words (v. 9) but songs (v. 15) and symbolic forms that are unambiguous in meaning to all culture members (see the analogies in vv. 7,8).

---

26   Howard A. Hatton and David J. Clark, "From the Harp to the Sitar," *Bible Translator* 26, no. 1 (1975): 132–38.

In Senegal, a group of Wolof believers used songs translated from English or French—but they sang with little joy. One day, they discussed the use of indigenous arts in worship. All of a sudden a Wolof man began to praise God in a chanting style typical of the way Wolof express joy. Within seconds the whole room exploded in spontaneous praise. After further probing questions about how the Wolof express joy and reverence, this group of Wolof believers redesigned many aspects of their gatherings. First, they decided to sit on mats on the floor (not on chairs), to chat informally outside but not inside the building, to remove their shoes before entering quietly and kneeling reverently to prepare their hearts. These changes provided greater flexibility and expressed biblical worship in Wolof ways. Secondly, indigenous repetitive chants were devised to praise Jesus. Often the congregation explodes in sound and movement. One believer, trained in Qur'anic chant, set New Testament passages to chant. Even those usually opposed to Christ can sit for hours repeating the Bible stories they have heard presented in such an acceptable way.[27]

STUDYING AND REMEMBERING SCRIPTURE
WHERE THE KINGDOM OF GOD THRIVES, COMMUNITIES UNDERSTAND AND REMEMBER SCRIPTURE.

A community that is coming more and more under the rule of the kingdom of God will study, remember, and understand Scripture. Jesus marked its defining authority on his life and that of others (Matt 22:29; Mark 12:24; Luke 4:21; 24:45), the early church used Scripture to explain and verify their faith (Acts 8:35; 17:2,11), and God uses it to regularly guide followers of Christ (Rom 15:4; 1 Tim 4:13; 2 Tim 3:16). The more ways we learn Scripture—including through local arts—the more likely we are to remember it. Studies have shown that memorizing words through song and/or motions involves more areas of the brain. In addition, when people from more than one culture are present in a Bible study, the leader needs to work with people in a variety of ways reflecting the variety of cultural learning styles, arts, and languages of all of those present.

In Nigeria, Yoruba Christians found that when they studied the Bible in Yoruba song forms as well as in print, they strengthened their memory of the content. Herbert Klem organized Yoruba Bible study groups in which Bible study leaders taught the first six chapters of the book of Hebrews to four groups in four ways. Klem then evaluated the effects of various teaching modalities on comprehension. The four different Bible study groups studied the first six chapters of the book of Hebrews in four different ways:

27   Richard Shawyer, "Indigenous Worship," *Evangelical Missions Quarterly* 38, no. 3 (2002): 326–34.

PREFACE

PREPARE

STEP 1

STEP 2

STEP 3

STEP 4

STEP 5

STEP 6

STEP 7

CLOSING

- Participants in the first group held Bible studies in which they studied the *written text* of Hebrews 1–6 in Yoruba.
- Participants in the second group held Bible studies in which they studied both the *written text* of Hebrews 1–6 and a *cassette* of Hebrews being *read* aloud in Yoruba.
- Participants in the third group held Bible studies using the *written text* and a cassette of Hebrews 1–6 being *sung* in a traditional Yoruba song style.
- Participants in the fourth group held Bible studies using the Yoruba Hebrews *song cassette* alone, without any written text.

Klem trained a group of Bible study leaders so any of them could lead a group using any of the four teaching styles. Then the Bible study leaders rotated among the four groups to minimize the effects of having different teachers. They wanted to see if the way people learned made a difference in how much they remembered, not just find out if one teacher was better than another teacher. At the end of the Bible study, all four groups had a test to see how much they remembered of Hebrews 1–6. The highest scoring group was the third group. They used *both the text and the song* of Hebrews 1–6 in a traditional Yoruba song style. The next highest scoring group was the second group. They used the *text and the cassette of the text being read aloud.* The group using *only the song* came in third, and the group using *only the text* came in last for their test scores.

The two highest scoring groups learned in two ways. The two lowest scoring groups learned in only one way. This shows us that the more ways we learn, the better we remember and understand the message of Scripture. Because the group with only the text came in last, we should increase the variety of forms in which we study Scripture, so we can remember it better.[28]

CHRISTIAN RITES
WHERE THE KINGDOM OF GOD THRIVES, CHRIST-FOLLOWERS MARK CRUCIAL EVENTS WITH CEREMONIES.

Where the kingdom of God is strong, people mark important moments with intense spiritual events. These could include weddings, Communion or the Eucharist, funerals, rites of passage, and agricultural feasts. Artistic forms of communication mark these events as special, provide historical continuity through unique repertoire and forms, and open up holistic channels of communication with God.

Pilgrims regularly travel to a special shrine a day's travel from the capital of Ghana, Accra. They bring offerings to the shrine in hopes that its god will make their farms fertile. An arts advocate started a discussion with the small number of Christians in one of the nearby ethnolinguistic communities about how they could express their need to God for spiritual help in their own farming.

---

28   Herbert V. Klem, *Oral Communication of the Scripture: Insights from African Oral Art* (Pasadena: William Carey Library, 1982).

PREFACE

PREPARE

STEP 1

STEP 2

STEP 3

STEP 4

STEP 5

STEP 6

STEP 7

CLOSING

They looked at over twenty scriptural references to God's involvement in agriculture. From these they developed a series of vows and entreaties to God, acknowledging their ultimate dependency on him. This ritual has become a seasonal part of this Christian community's life. – *Paul Neeley*

Dinka believers (Sudan) are experiencing the help of God and the reality of Scripture in their lives. One central result is that they are becoming more able to forgive and heal within their communities, rather than seeking revenge. They are choosing to carry ebony crosses decorated with fragments of metal found on the ground—the debris of the war that has surrounded them for years. These crosses indicate the bearer to be a follower of Jesus, willing to help others in the refugee camps and village communities where many Dinkas have been scattered by the turmoil of the last two decades. These communities are "beating" the tools of war into ebony crosses, fit to articulate their suffering and their trust in God. – *Karen Campbell*[29]

WITNESS

WHERE THE KINGDOM OF GOD THRIVES, NON-BELIEVERS IN COMMUNITIES LEARN ABOUT GOD.

A community marked by the kingdom of God will learn that he is their Creator and Savior. Local arts provide penetrating means for communicating truth about God because they are often intertwined with both special and daily activities of life: important life events, social interaction, entertainment, teaching, and the like.

I commissioned three people to compose songs they would perform at the dedication of my new house in the Mono village of Bili, Democratic Republic of Congo. Two of the songs were in genres closely tied to Mono traditions, and one in a church choral style. The content of the songs came from Jesus' parable of the wise and foolish builders, thematically connected to the building of the house. We invited scores of people from Bili, served lots of food, and provided a time for the local composers to perform their new songs. Many people heard biblical truths that evening in familiar musical and poetic languages. – *Brian Schrag*

---

29   Karen Campbell, "'God Looks Back on Us': Healing Songs for a Suffering Nation," in Frank Fortunato, *All the World Is Singing: Glorifying God through the Worship Music of the Nations*, with Paul Neeley and Carol Brinneman (Tyrone, GA: Authentic, 2006), 110–115.

PREFACE

PREPARE

STEP 1

STEP 2

STEP 3

STEP 4

STEP 5

STEP 6

STEP 7

CLOSING

Most members of the evangelical church in Brazil look askance at everything associated with the annual festival of *Carnaval*, especially its *samba* music; immoral connotations are extremely strong. Christian leader, writer, composer, and performer Atilano Muradas believes that God can redeem even this. He has formed a *samba* school of Christians that has more than five hundred members. They prepare all year and perform Scripture-based *samba* songs during *Carnaval* in southern Brazil. Their troupe has won awards not only because of the excellence of the costumes and music, but because people are drawn to their holy, healthy, exuberant version of *samba*.

As the Ifé churches grew stronger in Togo, they realized that there might be a more communal and effective way of reaching out than sending a lone preacher to a village with his Bible. They called together sixty active Baptist church members to consider how storytelling, song, drama and dance might combine to create a uniquely Ifé way of sharing the good news of Jesus with other communities. They were encouraged by the example of an older, illiterate grandmother who had seen three churches established as she composed new Ifé songs and taught them to children. As they learned to tell Bible stories by hearing others read to her, the participants grew excited about the potential of culturally-relevant evangelism. After two days of teaching, experimenting, and polishing their presentations, four teams headed out into villages to put into practice their new ideas. All returned excited about how they were received in communities, with a great deal more openness to the gospel message since it came in a relevant and attractive presentation. Many villagers had been drawn by the music and dancing, and had stayed to watch the dramas and hear the testimonies. The group approach to witness left these believers eager to share more of Jesus in Ifé terms back in their home communities. – *Tom Ferguson*[30]

What started as a unique ministry in a small reservation church has grown into walking out the gospel of Jesus among Native peoples from Montana to the Zapotec people of the southern Mexican state of Oaxaca. Using Native dancing, drums, flutes, and other instruments to worship our Creator has touched the hearts of many people, both Native and non-Native alike.

All of this has led our ministry to put on an annual traditional powwow in Flagstaff, Arizona. We work together with traditional Native people to make this happen. Through this bringing together of peoples, we are seeing many people touched and healed. We recognize the hurts of the past while working together to see hope for the future. We have seen Native and non-Native people touched by the Holy Spirit through the songs and dances. One woman came up to me after a service where we had some traditional powwow singers sing drum songs for us. The woman said, "Those songs made me want to worship God, is that OK?" From Montana to Mexico and at our Native Christian gatherings in

30   Tom Ferguson, "Music, Drama, and Storying: Exciting Foundations for Church Plant-ing," in Frank Fortunato, *All the World Is Singing: Glorifying through the Worship Music of the Nations* (Tyrone, GA: Authenic, 2006): 199–204.

Flagstaff we are seeing lives changed. The dancing and traditional songs are helping to break down the barriers that keep many Native people away from the Church. – *Bill Gowey*[31]

PERSONAL SPIRITUAL LIFE

PRAYER AND MEDITATION

WHERE THE KINGDOM OF GOD THRIVES, INDIVIDUALS HAVE VIBRANT PRAYER LIVES.

A community marked by the kingdom of God will have followers of Christ who communicate with God frequently and wholeheartedly. Artistic forms of communication can help this happen because they are enjoyable and connect deeply to people's emotions and wills.

Tami Diagne has had much sorrow in her life. She suffers ill health, her young adult sons are in trouble, and her non-Christian family has treated her badly since her husband abandoned her. Yet she wakes with songs in her heart during the night. And these are not just songs she heard on the radio—they are songs full of passion and yearning for her Savior Jesus, songs pouring out her heart full of sadness to him, and songs full of confidence that he will meet her in her sorrow. These powerful testimony songs are a source of deep reassurance to Tami, and they speak powerfully to Christian and non-Christian Senegalese women as she finds opportunities to share them. These songs begin as a personal prayer to "*the God* of her life" but overflow into a life that witnesses to the power of Christ to overcome suffering. – *Sue Hall-Heimbecker*

SPIRITUAL FORMATION

WHERE THE KINGDOM OF GOD THRIVES, CHRIST-FOLLOWERS EXPERIENCE SPIRITUAL GROWTH.

Where the kingdom of God is strong, Christ-followers grow in their knowledge and experience of God, their obedience to God, and in godly character traits and habits. Artistic forms of communication can energize and provide structure for formal and informal spiritual training, coaching, and mentoring.

31　Bill Gowey, "Walking Out the Gospel among the People," *Mission Frontiers* (September–October 2010), http://www.missionfrontiers.org/issue/article/walking-out-the-gospel-among-the-people.

PREFACE

PREPARE

STEP 1

STEP 2

STEP 3

STEP 4

STEP 5

STEP 6

STEP 7

CLOSING

PREFACE

PREPARE

STEP 1

STEP 2

STEP 3

STEP 4

STEP 5

STEP 6

STEP 7

CLOSING

The Kenra Christ-followers grew in number to about thirty within two years. They established a church and borrowed songs from a neighboring language group, with followers for over ten years already. Kenra believers could sing the songs.

An ethnoarts workshop was later held for Kenra believers. They composed new Christian songs in their mother tongue and music for the first time. When the composers checked the songs for clarity, the believers asked questions related to the song texts. They asked about Creation, following Jesus, ways to serve the Lord, and more.

The Kenra pastor asked them to sing some of the borrowed Christian songs they used in church. After finishing the song he asked them to explain the meaning. The people could not. They said, "We don't understand this song or the other songs we sing in church. But these new songs you've brought us have a clear message. Are we supposed to understand the songs we sing as believers?"

The Christians created new songs in their own traditional style in order to clearly communicate biblical truths and respond to questions about their faith to those in their communities. – *Mary Beth and Todd Saurman*

PERSONAL BIBLE STUDY
WHERE THE KINGDOM OF GOD THRIVES, INDIVIDUALS EXAMINE SCRIPTURE ACCURATELY AND FAITHFULLY.

Acts 17:10–12 gives a great example of the importance of studying Scripture:

The brothers [in Thessalonica] immediately sent Paul and Silas away by night to Berea, and when they arrived they went into the Jewish synagogue. Now these Jews were more noble than those in Thessalonica; they received the word with all eagerness, examining the Scriptures daily to see if these things were so. Many of them therefore believed, with not a few Greek women of high standing as well as men. (ESV)

When community members integrate artistic forms of communication into their personal Bible study, they remember, understand, and are changed more.

In South and Southeast Asia, tigers abound in the jungles. People are fearful as they hike through these jungle areas. A traditional way of handling this fear for many groups is to close one's ears with index fingers and sing songs as loud as possible when walking through these areas and feeling afraid. There is hope that this activity will scare away nearby tigers. Some believers in two different language groups in this region created songs from Scripture passages about not being afraid and about God's protection over his children. These songs helped believers learn these scriptural truths and walk with less fear through the jungle. One believer said, "Now we don't need to close our ears or sing loudly out of fear, we can sing with joy about God's promises to us and walk confidently knowing he is with us through whatever we face." – *Mary Beth and Todd Saurman*

APPLYING SCRIPTURE

WHERE THE KINGDOM OF GOD THRIVES, COMMUNITIES APPLY THE BIBLE TO THEIR LIVES.

A community becoming more and more like the kingdom of God will apply the teachings of Scripture to their daily life experiences. Yet the Bible was written to people in different cultures and at different times. How can we accurately apply it to our lives today, in all our various cultures? Local artistic communication can help people connect scriptural truths to their lives in memorable, motivating ways.

Scripture Relevance Dramas by West African dramatists show stories that apply Scripture to typical life situations.[32] In each of their half-hour weekly radio dramas, they follow the story of a person or a family who develops some difficulty. A friend or neighbor then tells them a Bible story that helps them resolve their difficulty.

The program's scriptwriters think of typical questions their audience will be likely to ask about each Bible story. The characters hearing the Bible story ask the storyteller those questions. Background information they need to make sense of the story is given through dialogue. The difference the story makes for the audience today is shown as appropriate applications of the Bible story are shared by the characters. The Bible story teller sometimes relates the point of the Bible story to the point of a local proverb, to show that the Bible affirms many cultural values.

As the play's conflict is resolved, personal applications dramatize the point of the story for the main character(s), and the radio audience hears possible biblical ways they could deal with their problems, too.

---

32   Michelle Petersen, "Scripture Relevance Dramas," *Ethnodoxology* 4 (no. 4, 2010):22–31.

PREFACE

PREPARE

STEP 1

STEP 2

STEP 3

STEP 4

STEP 5

STEP 6

STEP 7

CLOSING

PREFACE

PREPARE

STEP 1

STEP 2

STEP 3

STEP 4

STEP 5

STEP 6

STEP 7

CLOSING

Christian leaders suggest changes and approve the scripts before they are acted out and recorded by the drama group. Their programs began airing on one radio station and spread to fifty-seven radio stations in three countries.

Like drama, storytelling and other arts can also communicate the relevance of Scripture. Colgate discusses what he calls "relational Bible story telling" as an alternative to simple Bible story telling. He encourages Bible story tellers to first listen to people's stories, then tell their own personal stories, and only then tell Bible stories that relate thematically to their local friends' personal stories.[33] You don't need a radio station to do what the radio drama program did. You too can say to a friend, "Your problem reminds me of something I went through once and how God helped me with this Scripture. May I tell you a story?"
– *Michelle Petersen*

STEPS TO SPECIFYING KINGDOM GOALS

As this whirlwind tour shows, God's kingdom shows up in incredibly diverse ways around the world. In this section, we outline a process that you and a community can follow to choose one or more signs of the kingdom that they can encourage. We want this procedure to be marked by maximum participation of the community. This means that everything we do should demonstrate respect for local knowledge and intelligence; emphasize discussing, listening, and building consensus; help community members become agents of change; and advance sustainable changes. This mindset plays a crucial role in deciding what goals a community wants to work toward. You may be familiar with some formal methods people use to specify community needs and goals in participatory ways, with names like Appreciative Inquiry, Force Field Analysis, Stakeholder Analysis, and Participatory Action Research. We draw on a few of these here, outlining an activity that you can modify to fit different situations.

Be aware also that unless you are working with Christians, the community you're with will not be motivated to work toward goals stated in terms of the kingdom of God. But because all humans are created in God's image, we all yearn for many of these signs: peace, health, joy, significance, and justice; you may simply call them "Signs of a Better Future." So when a community wants these things, we can join wholeheartedly in helping according to our skills and calling. If we are working with a local church, then their goals will also naturally include deepening their relationship to God. The ultimate King of the kingdom of God is Jesus. As we journey alongside individuals and communities who don't know Jesus, our love and words can point them to him.

---

33   Jack Colgate, "Relational Bible Story Telling Part 1," *International Journal of Frontier Missions* 25 (no. 3):135–142. http://www.ijfm.org/PDFs_IJFM/25_3_PDFs/colgate.pdf.

Creating together will include a continual process of specifying and refining community goals. This section provides a place to start.

 Between 1986 and 1991, artist-animators from the University of Dar es Salaam helped organize a series of two-week "Theatre for Development" workshops in Tanzania. They led participants through identifying local art forms, elicited problems in the communities, and helped participants address these problems through communication in local performance genres. Problems often included many particular to women, such as frequent cases of being beaten by men.[34]

1. GATHER VOICES

Your first task is to talk with and listen to people. You may join conversations about goals that people already have in social structures like traditional or government organizations, rotating savings and credit associations, churches, or mosques. Or you may have this conversation as part of an event that's already happening, like a conference or workshop. Work toward including people from as many parts of the community as possible, especially those not usually given a voice.

2. EXPLORE STRENGTHS

All communities have strengths and weaknesses. Identifying strengths and aspirations first gives people courage and may suggest solutions to problems. Based on our experience and the biblical premise that all people reflect God's image, we expect to find good arts in every community. Ask people questions like these:

- What is your community known for doing well?
- What hopes do you have for your children? For yourself? For the community as a whole?

List answers to these questions, then think together how they relate to goals for the kingdom (or a better future). Here's a reminder of the goal categories we used above:

- **Identity and Sustainability**: Valuing Identity, Teaching Children, Using Media
- **Shalom**: Healing, Reconciliation, Rest and Play
- **Justice**: Social Justice, Education, Literacy, Economic Opportunity
- **Scripture**: Translating Scripture, Oral Scripture

34   Penina Mlama, "Reinforcing Existing Indigenous Communication Skills: The Use of Dance in Tanzania." In *Women in Grassroots Communication*, edited by Pilar Riaño (London: Sage, 1994): 51–64.

PREFACE   PREPARE   STEP 1   STEP 2   STEP 3   STEP 4   STEP 5   STEP 6   STEP 7   CLOSING

PREFACE

PREPARE

STEP 1

STEP 2

STEP 3

STEP 4

STEP 5

STEP 6

STEP 7

CLOSING

- **Church Life**: Corporate Worship, Studying and Remembering Scripture, Christian Rites, Witness
- **Personal Spiritual Life**: Prayer and Meditation, Spiritual Formation, Personal Bible Study, Applying Scripture

List the most closely related goal category next to the strengths, or make up a new one. You may come up with something like this:

Strengths and Aspirations	Goals for the Kingdom / a Better Future
Respect between generations	Identity and Sustainability
Celebration	Identity and Sustainability
Hospitality	Shalom
. . .	. . .

3. EXPLORE PROBLEMS

Ask people questions like these:

- What issues are difficult for your community?
- What causes you significant worry?
- What is worse in your community now than five years ago? Ten? Twenty?

List answers to these questions, then think together how solutions would relate to goals for the kingdom (or a better future). List the most closely related goal category next to the problems, or make up a new one. You may come up with something like this:

Problems	Goals for the Kingdom / a Better Future
Disease: HIV/AIDS, malaria	Shalom
War, crime, violence	Shalom
Intergenerational conflict, loss of traditions	Identity and Sustainability
Fear of death	Personal Spiritual Life
Exploitation: slavery, prostitution	Justice
Inability to read or write	Justice
Lack of access to the Bible	Scripture

Lack of spiritual growth	Personal Spiritual Life
Lack of unity in Christian community	Church Life
Some groups left out of worship	Church Life
Inadequate communion with God	Personal Spiritual Life
Poor education	Justice
Hunger	Justice
. . .	. . .

4. CHOOSE A GOAL

Ask the community to decide which problem they would most like to address, or the strength they would most like to build on. If you are not a decision-maker in the community, your role in Step 2 is now complete. The goal must emerge from and be owned by the community, not inserted from outside.

PREFACE

PREPARE

STEP 1

STEP 2

STEP 3

STEP 4

STEP 5

STEP 6

STEP 7

CLOSING

PREFACE

PREPARE

STEP 1

STEP 2

STEP 3

STEP 4

STEP 5

STEP 6

STEP 7

CLOSING

STEP

3

SELECT EFFECTS, CONTENTS, GENRE, AND EVENTS

Priscille Ndjerareou feels that a primary means of promoting solidarity and passing on important knowledge has all but disappeared from her Ngambay (Chad) community; hardly anybody gathers around the fire to sing, talk, and tell stories in the evening *tà pòr ndàāl*. She also wants to encourage young Christians to value traditional *su* storytelling and be courageous in their faith. To this end she developed a plan to revitalize the *tà pòr ndàāl* event by modifying it in three ways. First, she would find and invite people who are excellent *su* storytellers to come. Second, she would tell Scripture stories in another story form, and encourage other Christians to do the same. Third, she would commission new songs in the *pa nō gōr* genre with Christian themes. She believes that these innovations will attract people to gather, result in transmission of crucial life knowledge, raise the younger generation's sense of Ngambay identity, and instill biblical knowledge that will lead to stronger discipleship. She is looking for ways to put this plan into action.

Once a community has identified a goal or goals that they want to work toward, it's time to figure out how their arts can help them get there. Each genre is particularly apt for communicating certain kinds of content and producing certain kinds of effects. So in **Step 3** we explain a process that you and a community can follow to

- choose the desired effects of new artistry
- choose the content of new artistry

PREFACE

PREPARE

STEP 1

STEP 2

STEP 3

STEP 4

STEP 5

STEP 6

STEP 7

CLOSING

- choose a genre that has the capacity to communicate the content and produce the desired effects
- imagine events that could include performance of new works in the genre that would produce the effects in its experiencers

You may want to have this conversation with the same people you gathered for **Step 2**, or include others. Also note that each of these points needs to be addressed, but the discussion need not follow this order. And as in the Ngambay anecdote above, the community may innovate both genres and types of events. Finally, though this almost appears to be a mechanical process that guarantees effects, this is certainly not the case. Human beings are complicated, sinful, diverse, and make their own choices. So hold your expectations lightly.

CHOOSE THE DESIRED EFFECTS OF THE NEW ARTISTRY

Think back to the stories we told in the introductory chapter about a Mono church community in DR Congo. Though they may not have expressed them as completely as this at the time, they had these kingdom goals: deeper communication with God, fuller understanding of Scripture, affirmation of good arts in their culture, and witness to the rest of the community. To reach these goals, people in the community needed to think differently about their arts, sing new kinds of songs in church and out, and experience Scripture in a communication genre closer to their hearts.

So the first task to connecting kingdom goals with local arts is thinking through the effects you want those arts to produce in the community. These are common effects of artistry that can move people toward goals:

- They understand an important message.
- They act differently.
- They change an unhelpful or dangerous behavior.
- They do something new.
- They think differently.
- They feel solidarity with others.
- They experience hope, joy, anger, remorse, elation, peace, satisfaction, relief, empathy, surprise, or other emotions.

So together, ask:

- How do we want people to change in ways that move them toward these goals?
- Then enter the results of the discussion in the Community Arts Profile.

CHOOSE THE CONTENT OF THE NEW ARTISTRY

If the desired effects depend on people learning ideas through arts, then it's crucial to make sure that those ideas are trustworthy. In the Mono case, church leaders wanted others to hear and understand Scripture, so they needed to have excellent translations available. The lesson is this: study the truth content to be taught so that an accurate message is conveyed. If the message is about how malaria may be prevented, make sure you know the facts about how malaria is actually prevented: talk to your health care professional. For Scripture, study the passage before creating a message based upon the passage: talk to Bible scholars and translators. Talk about the content with God, other artists, and leaders. Together discuss these questions:

- What content do we want to communicate?
- How can we make sure that the content is reliable?
- Enter the results of the discussion in the Community Arts Profile.

CHOOSE A GENRE THAT HAS THE CAPACITY TO COMMUNICATE THE CONTENT AND PRODUCE THE DESIRED EFFECTS

Every artistic genre has characteristics that affect the messages it conveys and the effects it has. Because one of the effects that the Mono community wanted was that people would understand Scripture better, they chose the *gbaguru* genre for their initial activities. It was a relatively straightforward genre to start with for this purpose because it can include lots of words, is used to communicate advice that people respect, and doesn't have distracting connotations like sexuality or ancestor worship. Note that sexual connotations could be appropriate for goals having to do with marriage, but not for this situation.
So together:

- Show the list of artistic genres you produced in the activity "Take a First Glance at a Community's Arts" in **Step 1**. This could be on a big piece of paper, a chalkboard or whiteboard, an overhead projector, or a digital projector.
- For each genre, ask:

  - Would a new artistic work in this genre have the effects we've chosen? If not, why not?
  - Would a new artistic work in this genre communicate the content we've chosen well? If not, why not?

PREFACE

PREPARE

STEP 1

STEP 2

STEP 3

STEP 4

STEP 5

STEP 6

STEP 7

CLOSING

PREFACE

PREPARE

STEP 1

STEP 2

STEP 3

STEP 4

STEP 5

STEP 6

STEP 7

CLOSING

- Narrow the list to one or two genres that would be the best for effecting these changes and communicating this content now.
- Perform "Take a First Glance at an Event's Genre" (**Step 4, Part A**) for each of these genres. This new glance might cause you to reconsider genres you've chosen or rejected. **Step 4** will then lead you through more detailed exploration of the genre or genres you finally decide on.
- Put the results of this discussion in the Community Arts Profile.

Remember that all artistic genres have characteristics that can be redeemed for God's purposes, but that not all are appropriate at a given moment in a community's life. Encourage all involved to pray a lot, and listen for the wisdom of the Holy Spirit. Don't force a genre into new uses in a community unless leaders involved see it as wise and you are certain that God wants it to happen now.

IMAGINE EVENTS THAT COULD INCLUDE PERFORMANCE OF NEW WORKS IN THE GENRE THAT WOULD PRODUCE THE EFFECTS IN ITS EXPERIENCERS

When an individual or group acts artistically alone, it can be deeply satisfying, cathartic, or healing for them. This is of great value. The focus of this manual, though, is artistic action in the context of community. This means that a new dyed cloth, play, or poem has limited value for the kingdom if it remains hidden. It has no effects on anybody else unless it is part of an event where communication happens. The Mono apprentices of Punayima felt that and performed in a corporate worship setting as *Chorale Ayo*.

Before we start planning how to create new works in a genre, it's important to start imagining the contexts for their presentation and how they work as communication. We started you thinking about events with artistic content in **Step 1**. Here are a few more examples of an infinite number of such communication contexts:

- Mass, worship service, Bible study, Sunday school, home group, outreach, weddings, funerals, baptisms
- harvest celebrations, courting rituals, birth rites, rites of passage, teaching contexts
- listening to an audio recording, watching a video recording, transmitting live audio or video to other locations, viewing a sculpture in a museum, looking at a skyscraper in a city
- concert, rehearsal, gig, awards ceremony, sporting event

- intimate family discussion, smoking a peace pipe, court, war

Each of these examples has certain components that typify communication events, illustrated in Figure 2.

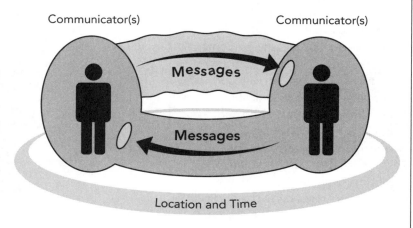

Figure 2: Components of an Artistic Communication Event

This figure illustrates how people interact by directing messages through various artistic genres to other communicators at particular places and times. The place and time could be one evening in a concert hall, or spread out when someone watches a film created previously by someone else in a different location. The people involved in the communication event consist of at least two individuals or groups who may or may not be physically close, and may or may not exist materially; humans often perform for spiritual beings.

We represent artistic genres in the diagram by the tubes enclosing and connecting the communicators. Note that some genres are more regular and predictable than others—these are depicted in the front with smooth lines. Others include more variability or improvisation, which we've shown with the curled edges. Messages are the thoughts or feelings that take form when mediated by a genre. People at the event experience this content when they hear, see, feel, smell, taste whatever other communicators produce with their singing, dancing, painting, cooking, and the like. Finally, you'll see that communication happens in particular directions (indicated by the arrows), but is always eventually reciprocal. People who experience a bit of artistry may respond with verbal, physical, or visual encouragement or discouragement, joining in a performance, notable silence, or many other ways. It's this response that so often feeds back into the performance, resulting in more energy, pleasure, and creativity.

PREFACE

PREPARE

STEP 1

STEP 2

STEP 3

STEP 4

STEP 5

STEP 6

STEP 7

CLOSING

PREFACE

PREPARE

STEP 1

STEP 2

STEP 3

STEP 4

STEP 5

STEP 6

STEP 7

CLOSING

So together:

1. Make a list of kinds of events that new works in the artistic genre could be part of. Let your minds run free with possibilities at this stage. Include both presentations where performers and other participants are in the same place, and those in which people experience the arts through sound, visual, video recording, or broadcast.
2. Remind yourselves of your choices thus far: effects, content (messages), and genre.
3. Choose a few of the event types you came up with and briefly describe them in terms of their communication components: Who are the communicators? When and where might such an event happen? What senses will participants use in experiencing the content? How will the genre affect the messages that people experience? When people experience the artistry, will it have the effects you'd like? How will people respond to the original communicators?
4. Choose one or two events that would be likely goals for cocreative activities. You can always choose other events in the next steps, but this will help you plan.

Make sure you put the results of this discussion in the Community Arts Profile.

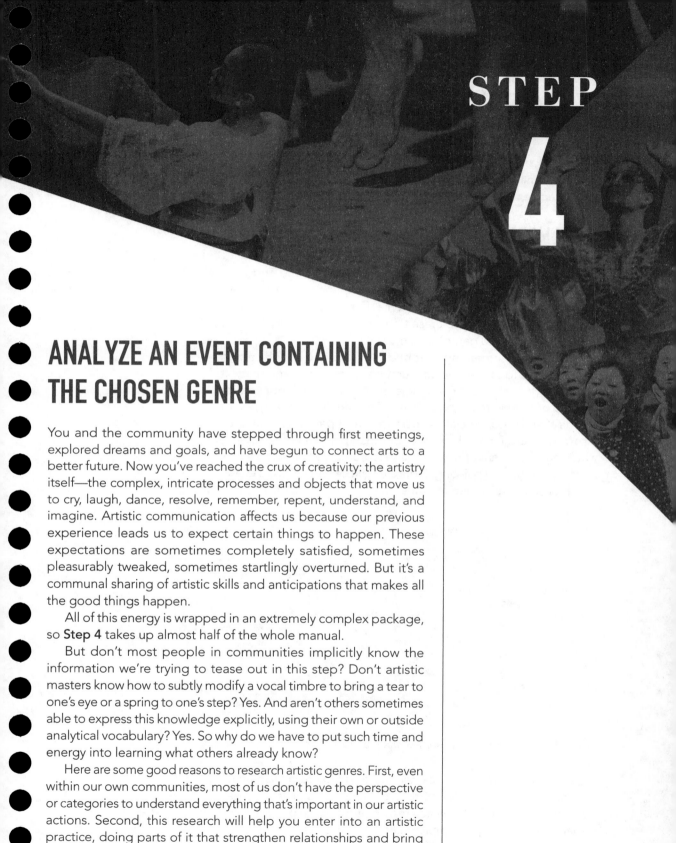

ANALYZE AN EVENT CONTAINING THE CHOSEN GENRE

You and the community have stepped through first meetings, explored dreams and goals, and have begun to connect arts to a better future. Now you've reached the crux of creativity: the artistry itself—the complex, intricate processes and objects that move us to cry, laugh, dance, resolve, remember, repent, understand, and imagine. Artistic communication affects us because our previous experience leads us to expect certain things to happen. These expectations are sometimes completely satisfied, sometimes pleasurably tweaked, sometimes startlingly overturned. But it's a communal sharing of artistic skills and anticipations that makes all the good things happen.

All of this energy is wrapped in an extremely complex package, so **Step 4** takes up almost half of the whole manual.

But don't most people in communities implicitly know the information we're trying to tease out in this step? Don't artistic masters know how to subtly modify a vocal timbre to bring a tear to one's eye or a spring to one's step? Yes. And aren't others sometimes able to express this knowledge explicitly, using their own or outside analytical vocabulary? Yes. So why do we have to put such time and energy into learning what others already know?

Here are some good reasons to research artistic genres. First, even within our own communities, most of us don't have the perspective or categories to understand everything that's important in our artistic actions. Second, this research will help you enter into an artistic practice, doing parts of it that strengthen relationships and bring you and your friends pleasure. Finally, a common language that flows from genre research will help a community design sparking

PREFACE

PREPARE

STEP 1

STEP 2

STEP 3

STEP 4

STEP 5

STEP 6

STEP 7

CLOSING

activities in **Step 5**, improve new works in **Step 6**, and integrate new creativity in **Step 7**.

To help you access these benefits, this introduction will show you how to:

- think more clearly about genres and events
- understand **Step 4**'s structure
- decide what analysis to do (which is not everything)

THINK MORE CLEARLY ABOUT GENRES AND EVENTS

An artistic event is something that happens in space and time that includes artistry. Artistry is anything someone produces from knowledge and skills related to a genre. For the analyses in **Step 4**, it will be helpful to explore these terms further. So, more precisely, we define event and genre as follows:

An **event** is something that occurs in a particular place and time, related to larger sociocultural patterns of a community. It is divisible into shorter time segments. An **artistic event** contains at least one enactment of a genre. Communities have types of events that include social expectations and patterns. Examples of event: festival, church service, birthday party, rite of passage, watching and listening to a music video on an electronic device, studying a museum painting. Figure 3 represents an artistic event, with multiple, intertwined features.

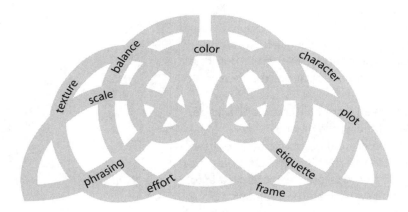

Figure 3: Sample Intertwined Artistic Features in an Event

An **artistic genre** (which we often shorten to **genre** in this manual) is a community's category of artistic communication characterized by a unique set of formal characteristics, performance practices, and social meanings. A **genre enactment** is an instantiation of a genre during an event. Examples of genre: *olonkho* (Siberia), Broadway musical (New York City), *kanoon* (Cameroon), *huayno* (Peru), *haiku* (Japan), praise and worship (Euro-America), *qawwali* (South Asia).

Here are some implications of thinking this way:

Events may contain enactments of more than one genre

A commemoration of the death and life of a Bamiléké (Cameroon) king may last a month—one event with many subevents. During this time, performers from other kingdoms visit to pay their respects, usually including performances of one or more genres, each with unique combinations of music, dance, drama, and visual elements.

Events are longer than enactments of a genre

At a wedding, for example, you may perform a solo that is in a love song genre. Enactment of the love song genre is just one part of a larger event that includes rituals and other elements.

Enactments of genres may be found in more than one kind of event

Certain kinds of acrobatic feats, for example, may appear both in circuses and gymnastics competitions.

Many events entail strong expectations of what kinds of genres they can include

For example, an Orthodox icon might jar worshipers in a Baptist sanctuary. There may be an inflexible association between a certain type of event and a certain genre, or participants in an event may have the freedom to switch out elements from different genres. In **Step 3**, you already explored this a bit. We'll help you think about it more in **Step 5**.

Genres and events are always changing

Old ones die, new ones are born, creative people innovate. Genres like Christian Kiswahili rap have multiple origins wrapped in unique ways; such fusions are common. So don't hold your definitions too tightly. As you describe more events and genres, you will be able to understand their boundaries and flexibilities more and more.

UNDERSTAND STEP 4'S STRUCTURE

Step 4 is devoted to exploring an event that has actually occurred in time and space. We emphasize this so much because we want to make sure that everything you do with a community is based on reality, not a disembodied idea. So all of the research activities we include require direct experience with and/or recordings of an event. We augment these with secondary research, often in the form of interviewing people with more direct experience. The knotted shape in the figure above represents the artistry in such an event.

After helping you choose what event to analyze, we guide you through four kinds of analysis of an event and its artistry:

PREFACE
PREPARE
STEP 1
STEP 2
STEP 3
STEP 4
STEP 5
STEP 6
STEP 7
CLOSING

PREFACE

PREPARE

STEP 1

STEP 2

STEP 3

STEP 4

STEP 5

STEP 6

STEP 7

CLOSING

- Part A: Describe the Event and Its Genre(s) as a Whole
- Part B: Explore the Event's Genre(s) through Artistic Domain Categories
- Part C: Relate the Event's Genre(s) to Its Broader Cultural Context
- Part D: Explore How a Christian Community Relates Artistically to Its Broader Church and Cultural Context (includes specialized research that we will put aside for the moment)

Here we show you a small sample of the kinds of information you would learn from each of these, using Brian and Barb's wedding as an example event. We focus on one genre enactment: performance of a love song.

CHOOSE AN ARTISTIC EVENT TO ANALYZE

You may explore anywhere from one to hundreds of events—each will make your understanding of a genre richer. Here are a few guidelines to get started.

Essential elements

- You need to be able to witness the event or objects firsthand, or have a good video recording of the event. Any event at all is better than people's words about something you can't experience. A bird in the hand is worth two in the bush.
- It needs to contain an example of the genre the community has chosen to work with.
- It must be done by people in the community.

Elements that may make your analysis more immediately fruitful

- A typical example of this type of event will help you understand more quickly the normal elements of such an event.
- An example of the event performed by artists whom the community states are the most skillful will help you understand aesthetic and performance values.

PART A:
DESCRIBE THE EVENT AND ITS GENRE(S) AS A WHOLE

Take a first glance at an event: Brian and Barb's wedding

This short questionnaire leads you to basic information like this: it's the coalescing of a bifamily community; California (USA); May 18, 1985; inside a church; ornate regalia; kin and fictive kin of bride and groom; stylized walking; organ, piano, voice, oratory; scriptural themes; joy and sadness; affirmation of Christian marriage; much time, money, and activity invested.

Look at the event and its genre(s) through lenses on forms and their meanings

This section helps you take a closer look at the forms of the artistry in the event through the lenses of space, materials, participant organization, shape of the event through time, performance features, content, and underlying symbolic systems. Doing a few of these research activities on the wedding would lead to the following kinds of insights: the front of the church sanctuary was reserved for the most sacred activities; the bride and groom exchanged rings that symbolized love and eternity; the groom's brother had the role of bringing the groom's ring; the event's ritual expectations were followed closely; performance of the love song genre included the groom's three siblings as singers, the brother as pianist; the song emphasized romantic love in the context of God's love.

PART B:
EXPLORE THE EVENT'S GENRE(S) THROUGH ARTISTIC DOMAIN CATEGORIES

The guided research in this section is divided into five Euro-American artistic domains. You only need to delve into those that the genre in question contains. The wedding event contained several artistic genres: classical organ music; love song; processional and recessional instrumental music; oratory; blessing; storytelling. For this example, we've decided to learn more about the artistic features of one of these genres, the love song. The primary artistic domains that this genre draws on are music and oral verbal arts.

From examination of the song through a few of the research activities in "Music in an Event," we discover a strophic form of verse / chorus / verse / chorus / gentle, floating outro; the groom's brother played the piano (a struck chordophone) and sang, and his sisters sang; they used narrow vibrato at the end of phrases; the chorus was contrapuntal; the song used a divisive meter of ¾; quarter note equals 94 beats per minute; tonal center was G.

From examination of the song's lyrics through some research activities in "Oral Verbal Arts in an Event," we discover phrase repetition, metaphor, lexical substitution, rhyme, and that overall form parallels song form.

PART C:
RELATE THE EVENT'S GENRE(S) TO ITS BROADER CULTURAL CONTEXT

This section leads you to connect the artistry in the event with other elements in the community. Applying a few of these research tasks to the wedding lead to the following kinds of knowledge: the performers and composers of the love song are siblings in a family with historically notable singers and instrument players, rooted in Mennonite choral traditions; the performers enjoyed a transiently high status in the eyes of many experiencers during the event, but their skills were not esteemed as enduringly valuable by most; the

PREFACE

PREPARE

STEP 1

STEP 2

STEP 3

STEP 4

STEP 5

STEP 6

STEP 7

CLOSING

PREFACE

PREPARE

STEP 1

STEP 2

STEP 3

STEP 4

STEP 5

STEP 6

STEP 7

CLOSING

new love song resulted from collaboration between two siblings; high aesthetic value was placed on new lyrics and melody, with highlighted vocal harmonies; the creativity components—creators, language and other symbolic systems, and gatekeepers—were all within the family; many in the audience experienced a combination of pleasure and melancholy.

Figure 4 shows the categories of insights each of these three kinds of research produced in this example. We've bolded the categories related to the genre example we chose: love song. Note that you only have to investigate the artistic domains (music, dance, drama, oral verbal arts, visual arts) that the genre under investigation contains.

Event: Brian and Barb's Wedding			
Enactment of Genre 1: Love Song		Enactment of Genre 2: Blessing	
Unique set of relations to broader cultural context (Part C)	**Unique form and meaning description through seven-lens view (Part A)**	Unique form and meaning description through seven-lens view (Part A)	Unique set of relations to broader cultural context (Part C)
	Unique set of musical and verbal characteristics (Part B)	Unique set of verbal and visual features (Part B)	

Figure 4: Categories of Insights

Each kind of analysis will help you understand what goes on in the others. So let your mind roam from very detailed information about minute features of an event to broad cultural themes and back again. We never know whether a single note, vocal timbre, feather, facial expression, eyebrow movement, color, or any number of other elements could hold meaning that either frees or stifles creativity for the kingdom.

The more you and the community know the range of art forms available and understand how each one works, the more you can reflect together with God on how to best use them. We provide research activities in this step, but they are only a start. If you're not learning anything interesting from our directions, think about these questions: What other questions could I ask? What other ways could I find out about this phenomenon? What is true about this genre that doesn't fit any of the categories here?

DECIDE WHAT ANALYSIS TO DO
(WHICH IS NOT EVERYTHING)

Not every research activity we include in **Step 4** is relevant to the artistry you're investigating. Even if it were, you don't have enough time to do it all. So here are a few ways you can focus your research.

First, always do anything that starts with "Take a First Glance at . . . " These provide a lot of insight requiring a relatively small amount of energy and time. Second, scan the research activities we describe in these sections with a community friend and pick at least one from the seven lenses and one or two in "Relate the Event's Genre(s) to Its Broader Cultural Context" (**Part C**); we've created indexes of these activities that will help you in this. Choose what seems most pertinent or interesting. Third, notice that many of the sparking activities we describe in **Step 5** note research someone needs to do to complete the activity. While performing these activities, go back to **Step 4** to do the research. Fourth, if you have an advisor or more experienced arts specialist available, work with him or her to design a research plan that includes strategically chosen activities.

PREFACE

PREPARE

STEP 1

STEP 2

STEP 3

STEP 4

STEP 5

STEP 6

STEP 7

CLOSING

PREFACE

PREPARE

STEP 1

STEP 2

STEP 3

STEP 4

STEP 5

STEP 6

STEP 7

CLOSING

ANALYZE
AN EVENT
CONTAINING THE
CHOSEN GENRE

PART A:
DESCRIBE THE EVENT AND ITS GENRE(S) AS A WHOLE

In this section, we lead you through a quick overview of a complete event containing artistic content, and then a more detailed exploration of its components.

TAKE A FIRST GLANCE AT AN EVENT

Use the categories here to capture your preliminary observations, brief interviews, and assessments of an artistic event. You will explore each category in more detail later in **Step 4, Parts A, B,** and **C.**

CONTEXT

Name of community: _____

Location: _____

Date(s): _____

Your name: _____

PREFACE

PREPARE

STEP 1

STEP 2

STEP 3

STEP 4A

STEP 5

STEP 6

STEP 7

CLOSING

The following characteristics relate fundamentally to forms of artistic communication.

SPACE
Was the event inside or outside? Where were people placed in the location? How did use of space change at different times?

MATERIALS
What clothes, costumes, musical instruments, electronic media, amplification, and lighting did you notice? Take photos and draw sketches if possible and desired.

PARTICIPANTS
Who was here? How many people of each gender were there? age group? other demographic variable? social status? What were they doing? How were they interacting? Who organized, advertised, and promoted the event?

SHAPE OF THE EVENT THROUGH TIME
How long did the event last? When did the event occur? What were the major internal sections of the event itself?

PERFORMANCE FEATURES
What was everybody doing? What activities were associated with this event, including pre- and post-event activities?

CONTENT
What kinds of plot, text, morals, themes, and language(s) were used?

UNDERLYING SYMBOLIC SYSTEMS
What meanings may be associated with the elements above?

The following characteristics relate fundamentally to how arts fit into a culture.

APPARENT PURPOSE(S)
What was the occasion for the event? Did people have a name for the event? What were the people trying to achieve or accomplish in this event? How were they trying to achieve it? Were there any secondary goals that were either explicitly stated or tacitly understood? How did the goals affect the event itself?

EMOTIONS

How did the participants feel about the event? How did others feel about the event? What feelings were expressed through the event or in individual parts of the event, like a speech or song?

COMMUNITY VALUES SHOWN

Did you see signs of hierarchical vs. egalitarian social structure, free vs. rigid atmosphere, conformity vs. nonconformity? Were there clues in texts, spatial relationships, or interactions between participants?

COMMUNAL INVESTMENT

How many and what kinds of resources did the community invest in this event? This could include time in preparation, finances, length of performance, number of people involved, and status markers.

TAKE A FIRST GLANCE AT AN EVENT'S GENRE

These simple questions help you focus on the type of artistry used in an event. There may be more than one type of artistic genre in an event, but apply these questions to only one at a time:[35]

- *What* artistry do people produce? E.g., name of genre, kinds of activities like painting or acting or singing or dancing.
- *Who* normally performs or creates it? E.g., women, men, children, caste members. Also, gather names of prominent performers or creators.
- *Where* do people normally perform or create it? E.g., outdoors, indoors, special place.
- *When* do people normally create or perform it? E.g., day, night, ceremony, weekly rehearsal, spontaneously for pleasure.
- *To whom* do people normally perform or present it? E.g., potential suitors, ecstatic audience, God.
- *Why* do people normally perform or present it? E.g., express emotions, make money, motivate to action, affirm identity, play.
- *With what connotations* do people normally perform or present it? E.g., partying, a certain age group, spiritual, sexual.
- *How* are new instances normally created? E.g., solitary individual, dreams, group experimentation.

---

35   See Anthony Seeger, *Why Suyá Sing: A Musical Anthropology of an Amazonian People* (University of Illinois Press, 2004).

PREFACE

PREPARE

STEP 1

STEP 2

STEP 3

STEP 4A

STEP 5

STEP 6

STEP 7

CLOSING

PREFACE

PREPARE

STEP 1

STEP 2

STEP 3

STEP 4A

STEP 5

STEP 6

STEP 7

CLOSING

LOOK AT AN EVENT'S FORMS

In Papua New Guinea the Sing Sing Festival is an important cultural event for many language groups: it is where the songs, dances, stories, and dress convey the culture of that group from one generation to another. In one language community, Christians decided that they could not participate. An outsider began to question the Christians about what prevented them from participating. After a time, the offense to the Holy Spirit was narrowed down to one red feather worn in the headdress. The outsider asked the Christians, "If you remove the red feather, would there be anything else in the Sing Sing that you think would be offensive to God?" The answer came back, "No." So the Christians didn't use a red feather in their headdresses and felt free to participate in their Sing Sing.

As in this story, identifying the unique attributes of the form of an artistic act of communication allows you to enter more accurately into its creation, improvement, integration, and celebration. Any small element of the form may evoke significant symbolic or emotive meaning. Because of the potential importance of details like these in meeting a community's goals, it's crucial that we have a way to notice them. In this section, we do this by helping you look at an event through specially chosen lenses.

In physical terms, a lens is a piece of glass that has been polished or otherwise changed in a way that alters any light coming through it. Depending on its maker's goal, someone who looks through a lens at an object may see that object as closer, farther, or perhaps with one color intensified. A lens, then, is a way of looking at something to make one of its aspects clearer. We are using this same idea metaphorically to guide our research in the arts. In particular, we present a method that will guide your eyes, ears, and bodies to reveal seven categories of detail: Space, Materials, Participant Organization, Shape of the Event through Time, Performance Features, Content, and Underlying Symbolic Systems.

Note that each of these lenses may interact very closely with others, describing the same thing from a different perspective; don't be surprised if you come up with recurring patterns. Also, each lens may not reveal insights equally well in any given event, so if a lens does not seem to help much, move on to another.

Discussion of each of these lenses contains the following parts:

- Basic description of the lens.
- Research questions to guide your exploration of the event through the lens under discussion.
- Research activities that are particularly relevant to answering these research questions. Put the results of these activities into the description of this event in your Community Arts Profile.

- <u>Artistic domain connections</u>, a discussion that highlights commonly important connections between each lens and arts domains. You can follow up on these connections by performing exploratory activities in the next section's discussions of music, dance, drama, oral verbal arts (especially storytelling, poetry, oratory, and proverbs), and visual arts.
- <u>Meaning connections</u>, a brief reminder to relate your findings to meanings, symbolism, and broader cultural themes.

We've designed these lenses to help you understand more about a particular event with artistic content. If it is the first event you have seen of its type, you won't know yet if it is a normal example or if it differs in significant ways from what usually happens. As you use the lenses to describe more events of this same type, you'll see patterns and points of divergence. Remember to focus your inquiries on the genre you chose in **Step 3**.

SPACE

BASIC DESCRIPTION

Space is the location, demarcation, and physical characteristics of the area used, which can affect the form of artistic communication. Space is the canvas upon which the performance event is painted. It affects the movement of participants and their relationships to one another, lengthening or shortening the time it takes for participants to move around it, and other elements of a performance.

Write what you learn about how this event uses space in the Community Arts Profile. Include drawings, photographs, and other representations to help explain what's going on.

RESEARCH QUESTIONS TO HELP YOU KNOW WHAT TO EXPLORE

- Did it occur inside, outside, or both? If inside, give type and size of building.
- What are some characteristics of the place where it happened (shape and size, for example)?
- What parts was the space separated into? Were there physical and/or conceptual markers to separate these parts?
- What activities were associated with each part?
- Who designed, controlled, or owned the space for this particular event?
- How did each participant's location in the space and proximity to other participants affect their contribution to

PREFACE

PREPARE

STEP 1

STEP 2

STEP 3

STEP 4A

STEP 5

STEP 6

STEP 7

CLOSING

PREFACE

PREPARE

STEP 1

STEP 2

STEP 3

STEP 4A

STEP 5

STEP 6

STEP 7

CLOSING

the event? How did it affect other participants' experience of their contribution?
- What meaning(s) do people attach to these elements of space?
- From what you know of the genre of this event, did people use space in normal ways? uncommon ways?

RESEARCH ACTIVITIES TO HELP YOU ANSWER THE QUESTIONS

- Draw a floor diagram, including boundaries and demarcations.
- Take photographs of the place and its surroundings.
- Ask questions of participants and other cultural insiders about what happened. You may want to do this while watching a video of the event.
- Make a list of local names for the elements of space used in the event.

ARTISTIC DOMAIN CONNECTIONS

In an artistic event, features that interact most closely with space are often associated with drama and dance. In addition, creators of art objects manipulate space to create formal structure through features like proportion, rhythm, balance, and the like.

MEANING CONNECTIONS

Explore how what you've discovered by looking at an event through the lens of Space relates to meanings, symbolism, and broader cultural themes. "Relate the Event's Genre(s) to Its Broader Cultural Context" (**Part C**) below will provide direction for this.

MATERIALS

BASIC DESCRIPTION

Materials are all of the tangible things associated with an event, like clothing, regalia, instruments, props, and lighting. Some objects are more important to the execution and experience of the event than others. They may be made by humans (as in a mask) or appropriated to fill a function (as an eagle feather marking regalia as royal). Objects may serve multiple purposes, conveying meaning at many levels. For example, the Atumpan drum (Ghana) serves both as a functional member of the musical ensemble, while indicating royalty by its shape, colors, and construction; it plays both a functional and symbolic role. As another example, *kanoon* dancers in Cameroon move shakers in patterned ways that both add to the dance (experienced through visual channels) and produce sounds integral to the rhythm (experienced through auditory channels).[36] Note also

---

36   Brian Schrag, "How Bamiléké Music-Makers Create Culture in Cameroon" (PhD diss.,

that some objects in the space where an event takes place may be incidental to what's going on.

Write what you learn about how this event uses materials in the Community Arts Profile. Include drawings, photographs, and other representations to help explain what's going on.

RESEARCH QUESTIONS TO HELP YOU KNOW WHAT TO EXPLORE

- What were all the objects involved in the event?
- What is each object like physically?
- What meaning(s) do people attach to these objects?
- Were some objects treated in unusual or special ways?
- From what you know of the genre of this event, did people use objects in normal ways? uncommon ways?

RESEARCH ACTIVITIES TO HELP YOU ANSWER THE QUESTIONS

Make a list of objects associated with the event. Do this by observing and asking yourself and others questions like these:

- What objects were present, including structures (like buildings)?
- What objects did people bring expressly for the event?
- What did people wear?
- What did people hold? kick? otherwise manipulate with their bodies?
- Were there objects on surfaces, like walls, floors, or ceilings?
- Were there technologies that produced atmospheric effects and performance enhancements such as lighting, sound amplification, smoke, incense?
- Were there live objects, like animals or plants, in the event?
- Were there foods or drinks involved in the event?
- Were there man-made or natural objects that were repurposed for this event?

Describe each object by examining it and asking questions like these:

- What are the object's physical characteristics? This may include materials, design, construction, weight, and length. Kinds of source materials include fibers (from plants or animals), minerals, metals, plastics, and wood.
- What are local and other names for the object?
- Take photographs that reveal details of objects (close-ups, from various angles).

University of California, Los Angeles, 2005), 177–230.

PREFACE

PREPARE

STEP 1

STEP 2

STEP 3

STEP 4A

STEP 5

STEP 6

STEP 7

CLOSING

PREFACE

PREPARE

STEP 1

STEP 2

STEP 3

STEP 4A

STEP 5

STEP 6

STEP 7

CLOSING

Describe the functions and interactions of objects in the event through observation, interview, and other activities:

- Draw a floor diagram, showing placement of objects.
- Take photographs of the objects in their locations.
- Describe who interacted with each object, and in what ways.
- Imagine and ask how participants might have modified their actions because of the presence of objects. For example, a short microphone cord limits the range of movement of an actor. You can also ask how the presence of an object might have constrained the participants' use of space.
- List all of the ways an object contributes to the execution of the event.

Learn and document how to make or use an object. Ask questions of participants and other cultural insiders about the uses and construction of objects. You may want to do this while watching a video of the event, looking at pictures of objects, or interacting with the objects themselves.

- To whom does each object belong?
- How old is each object? Was it created especially for this event or kind of event?

ARTISTIC DOMAIN CONNECTIONS

In an artistic event, objects can play significant roles in all of the artistic domains. Drama uses costumes and props to show characterization and provide dramatic settings. The most common objects used to produce musical features are instruments. In dance, costumes and props may highlight motion. A storyteller might use a prop to symbolize an event in her story, and visual artists use all sorts of materials to create objects. Finally, cooks gather and process ingredients and spices to create food. Remember that each object can play roles in multiple artistic domains.

MEANING CONNECTIONS
Explore how what you've discovered by looking at an event through the lens of Materials relates to meanings, symbolism, and broader cultural themes. "Relate the Event's Genre(s) to Its Broader Cultural Context" (**Part C**) below will provide direction for this.

PARTICIPANT ORGANIZATION

BASIC DESCRIPTION

At an artistic event, virtually everyone present (and sometimes people who aren't even there) participates in some way. We focus here on the people involved in the event in terms of the roles they play, the ways they interact with each other through time, and how they use the space around them. Each participant in an event plays a role (given by genre and personal proclivities) that affects the form of the performance. Roles can include creators, performers (e.g., singers, instrument players, actors, dancers, storytellers), audience (e.g., aficionados, mass, cognoscenti, hecklers), helpers (e.g., set builders, stage managers, gaffers, ticket takers, bouncers, ushers), producers, directors, and so on. Also relevant to the formal characteristics of an event are participants' histories, skills, kin, and other relationships to each other, status and role in everyday life, and ethnic, religious, and social identities. For example, a priest may be the only one who can play certain roles in a religious ceremony.

Write what you learn about participants in this event in the Community Arts Profile. Include drawings, photographs, and other representations to help explain what's going on.

RESEARCH QUESTIONS TO HELP YOU KNOW WHAT TO EXPLORE

- How many participants were there (be sure to include ancestors or gods that are not physically present)? What were each of their roles?
- How did the participants use performance features to interact with each other? Were there obvious patterns (etiquette)?
- How did participants interact with different sections of the event space? Were any roles associated with particular places?
- Which participants exerted creative control and to what degrees?
- Are there local names for the participant roles used in the event?
- Who is fulfilling each role?
- Why and how did each participant come to fill his/her role?
- What are salient characteristics of each participant, in terms of their training, ability, reputation, and professional/ caste status?
- What meaning(s) do people attach to each participant role?
- From what you know of its genre, were the number and roles of participants similar to other similar events?
- Did any participants receive payment in goods, services, or money for performing their role?

PREFACE

PREPARE

STEP 1

STEP 2

STEP 3

STEP 4A

STEP 5

STEP 6

STEP 7

CLOSING

PREFACE

PREPARE

STEP 1

STEP 2

STEP 3

STEP 4A

STEP 5

STEP 6

STEP 7

CLOSING

RESEARCH ACTIVITIES TO HELP YOU ANSWER THE QUESTIONS

- Make audio, video, and photographic recordings of the event.
- Ask a friend involved in the event what role(s) you might be able to fill in this type of event. Note what background and competencies you would have to have or acquire to fill different roles. When appropriate and possible, prepare to perform a role for a future event of this type.
- Draw a floor diagram, showing where participants were at different times, or what roles were associated with certain places.
- Make a time line, noting participants' actions and interactions.
- Ask questions of participants and other cultural insiders about what happened. You may want to do this while watching a video of the event.
- Make a list of local names for participant roles. Ask what privileges or obligations are associated with each named role.
- Take photographs that reveal details of participants' clothing, props, pertinent facial expressions, gestures, and the like.

ARTISTIC DOMAIN CONNECTIONS

Many roles in artistic communication are associated with the artistic domain categories we've included in the chapters below. Essentially all artistic events require an audience of some sort, someone to experience the communication. Beyond that, some typical dramatic roles include actor, spect-actor (someone who both watches and enters into a drama), set designer, and director. Musical performance may have singers, instrument players, and composers. In dance, people fill roles of choreographer, soloist, and ensemble. Various oral verbal arts performances may include a teller, listener, sidekick, crafter, and affirmer. Visual arts require at least one creator, manipulator, and experiencer. Food creation roles commonly include recipe maker, chef, food manipulator, and presenter. Research these roles in more depth in the artistic domain chapters, and remember that one person could fill roles in multiple artistic domains.

MEANING CONNECTIONS

Explore how what you've discovered by looking at an event through the lens of Participant Organization relates to meanings, symbolism, and broader cultural themes. "Relate the Event's Genre(s) to Its Broader Cultural Context" (**Part C**) below will provide direction for this.

SHAPE OF THE EVENT THROUGH TIME

BASIC DESCRIPTION

One way to describe the shape of an event is by splitting it into sequential segments in a hierarchical fashion. You can identify the time at which one segment ends and the next begins by noting significant changes in elements of the event as viewed through each of the other lenses. These changes are called markers. For example, markers could include pauses, sudden contrasts in features or participants, beginning and ending of participants' activities, beginning and ending of songs, and the like. The shortest segment we are interested in for this lens is the *motif*: the smallest meaningful collection of performance features.

Write what you learn about the shape of this event in the Community Arts Profile. Include lists, time lines, and other representations to help explain what's going on.

RESEARCH QUESTIONS TO HELP YOU KNOW WHAT TO EXPLORE

- What were the segments of the event?
- How did you know when one segment ended and another began? What marked these transitions?
- Were there parallel segments happening at the same time? How were they related?
- What were the important parts of each segment (onset, nucleus, coda)?
- What meaning(s) do people attach to these segments at each level?
- From what you know of its genre, was this event longer or shorter than normal? Did it have the same number and size of segments as normal?

RESEARCH ACTIVITIES TO HELP YOU ANSWER THE QUESTIONS

- Make audio and video recordings of the event.
- Create a Hierarchical Segmentation Time Line. You may use one or more of the following approaches:

    - From a top-down perspective (in other words, macro to micro):

        - While watching or listening to the recording, make a time line of the event, highlighting its major segments by listing the transition markers with the time they occur.

PREFACE PREPARE STEP 1 STEP 2 STEP 3 STEP 4A STEP 5 STEP 6 STEP 7 CLOSING

- While watching each major segment, make a time line of its subsegments, listing the transition markers with the time they occur.
- Continue dividing subsegments at finer timescales, down to the level of your research interest. This may be at the level of the motif.

- From a bottom-up perspective:

  - While watching or listening to the recording, make a time line of the event, identifying the smallest meaningful chunks (sequences of performance features), their beginning and ending times, and how they're assembled to create larger segments.
  - See how these small segments are in turn assembled into larger ones.
  - Continue assembling supersegments at longer timescales until you've described the whole event.

- From a basic level-out perspective:

  - While watching or listening to the recording, make a time line of the event, identifying the most salient activities and how they're assembled to create larger segments or divided to create smaller ones.
  - Continue this process.

- Create a Hierarchical Segmentation Time Line from a basic level-out perspective:

STEP ONE

Time	What Happened
13:30	Storytellers began to arrive
. . .	. . .
. . .	. . .
14:27	Everyone left the area

STEP TWO

Segment 1 (5 min.)	Segment 2 (12 min.)	Segment 3 (10 min.)	Segment 4 (3 min.)
. . .	. . .	. . .	. . .

- Make a list of local names for the segments of the event.
- Ask questions of participants and other cultural insiders about what happened. You may want to do this while watching a video of the event.

ARTISTIC DOMAIN CONNECTIONS

Artistic domains each have traditions of splitting their performances into smaller and smaller chunks. Drama may start with a genre like a play, broken into acts, scenes, and eventually to gestures and movements. An example of music's highest hierarchical level could be a concert or song, split into movement, phrases, and notes. Dances may consist of pieces, motifs, and gestures. An oral verbal art like a poem may contain stanzas and lines and beats. Visual and culinary arts do not change through time like others, though how people view objects and eat food can be split into subparts. You can explore more relationships between the Shape of the Event through Time and these art domains in the chapters that follow.

MEANING CONNECTIONS

Explore how what you've discovered by looking at an event through the lens of Shape relates to meanings, symbolism, and broader cultural themes. "Relate the Event's Genre(s) to Its Broader Cultural Context" (Part C) below will provide direction for this.

PERFORMANCE FEATURES

BASIC DESCRIPTION

Performance features are observable, patterned characteristics of a performance that emerge from an event's unique combination of physical and social context and participants' actions. They are the skills, processes, and conventions that the performers in an event must master to make the event successful. In more detail, a **feature** is a characteristic of a performance that

PREFACE

PREPARE

STEP 1

STEP 2

STEP 3

STEP 4A

STEP 5

STEP 6

STEP 7

CLOSING

PREFACE

PREPARE

STEP 1

STEP 2

STEP 3

STEP 4A

STEP 5

STEP 6

STEP 7

CLOSING

- is produced by participants (e.g., singers, dancers, storytellers, hecklers, playwrights),
- who choose embodied actions (e.g., sing, move, gather together, play instrument, wear a certain color)
- that derive from formal systems (e.g., movement, vocal production, conceptual development, color symbolism, social interaction)
- and temporal patterns (e.g., metricity, flow, timing).

The performer(s) chooses his or her actions by taking into account the

- intended messages, content, and subject matter;
- other participants (seen and unseen) and their responses;
- location;
- genre expectations: acceptable variation, source materials (e.g., written forms, orature);
- and the performer's abilities and preferences.

Each feature

- is experienced by participants (e.g., performers, observers, audience)
- through communication channels (e.g., auditory, visual, tactile, spatial, olfactory).

In short, performance features are things people do that can be transcribed. Transcription is reducing elements of a communication act to writing and graphics. Performance features are our attempt to name the elements most useful for understanding the structure of an event; it's impossible to focus on everything, so this vocabulary and process help us to begin finding out what's important. Transcription can draw on existing notation systems such as Time Unit Box System (TUBS, for rhythm), staff (melody, harmony, and rhythm), Laban (movement), and writing down verbal content. It can also consist of prose descriptions of performance features using specialized vocabulary.

Note that transcribing verbal features of an event requires access to knowledge of a language not immediately necessary with transcriptions of other kinds of features. This document does not teach transcription; you must learn specialized notation systems elsewhere, perhaps in the classroom with an expert. Depending on your interests, search for schools or programs accessible to you that teach notation for music, language, dance, visual arts, or drama.

Write what you learn about performance features in this event in the Community Arts Profile. Include prose descriptions and notation to help explain what's going on.

RESEARCH QUESTIONS TO HELP YOU KNOW WHAT TO EXPLORE

- What do people do to send messages through communication channels?
- How are performance features or clusters of features patterned?
- What meaning(s) do people attach to each performance feature or cluster of features?
- From what you know of its genre, did participants produce performance features in ways similar to other events in this genre?
- What are the stock motifs, or clichés that emerge? These are memorized bundles of performance features.

RESEARCH ACTIVITIES AND ARTISTIC DOMAIN CATEGORIES

Make audio, video, and photographic recordings of the event.

- There are several ways to train yourself to attend to features of people's performance:
  i. focus on the communication channels through which you perceive the features (sight, sound, smell, touch, taste);
  ii. focus on the common producers of features (voices, bodies, objects, and minds); and
  iii. focus on similarities and contrasts between clusters of performance features (dynamics and rhythm).
- To access each of these three windows onto performance features, watch and listen to a video of the event multiple times, answering the questions below.

Feature perception (through communication channels)[37]

Write a free-flowing account of your answers to the questions below, noting patterns as well as unique occurrences. Make educated guesses on what seems important, based on what you've learned by looking through the other lenses. This is just a start.

- What sounds did you hear?
- What movements, colors, lights, and shapes did you see?
- What aromas did you smell?
- What sensations did you feel?
- What flavors did you taste?

---

37   For further study on communication channels, see Ruth Finnegan, *Communicating: The Multiple Modes of Human Interconnection* (London: Routledge, 2002).

PREFACE

PREPARE

STEP 1

STEP 2

STEP 3

STEP 4A

STEP 5

STEP 6

STEP 7

CLOSING

PREFACE

PREPARE

STEP 1

STEP 2

STEP 3

STEP 4A

STEP 5

STEP 6

STEP 7

CLOSING

Feature production

- What did participants do with their voices? Common vocal actions include singing, acting, orating, narrating, or producing sound effects.
- What did participants do with their bodies? Common bodily actions include acting, instrument playing, and dancing.
- What did participants do with their words? Common word-related activities include poetry, singing, acting, orating, and narrating.
- What did participants do with objects? Common actions with objects include instrument playing, acting, spectacle, dancing, oratory, narrating, and presenting a communicative object.

Similarities and contrasts between clusters of performance features

- How did people express intensity, weight, flow?
- How did people organize time?

Advice on knowing what features to attend to, out of an infinite number of possibilities

- Look for repeated actions.
- Look for actions that seem to provoke a strong reaction in participants.
- Note heavy contrast between bundles of features and the next set of bundled features.
- Use your own imperfect intuition to notice what might be important.
- Note where participants are focusing their attention.
- Remember what participants and other knowledgeable folks have told you is important. Look there.

Other research activities

- Listen to an audio recording of the event, noting patterns of things you hear.
- Stare hard and long at a photograph of the event, noting patterns of colors, shade, size and shape, balance, and lines.
- Note when certain feature combinations occur. These co-occurrences may provide clues to underlying symbolic systems that participants all refer to explicitly or implicitly during the event. To get at some common kinds of combinations, ask these questions:

- How did people advance the plot through dancing or singing? See the "Drama in an Event" section (**Step 4, Part B2**).
- How did people relate their movements to melody or rhythm or create movement motifs? See the "Dance in an Event" section (**Step 4, Part B3**).

- Make a list of local names for performance features or clusters of features. You can describe these using the analytical vocabulary in this chapter.
- Ask questions of participants and other cultural insiders about what happened. In particular, ask about meanings and emotions evoked by certain actions or points in the event. You may want to do this while watching a video of the event.
- When appropriate and possible, learn to perform part of this kind of event. Write down what people tell you to do when teaching you, how they correct you, and insights you gain and questions that arise by attempting to produce features with your own body.

Other kinds of socially meaningful actions and their performance features

- Participants may produce features not associated with a particular artistic domain in order to express opinions and emotions. These opinions and emotions could be to affirm or reject, encourage or discourage, express pleasure or displeasure, attract or repel, assist or impede, unify or divide, goad or hinder aspects of the performance. Examples of such features include hand clapping, stomping, cheering, ululating, heckling, "the wave," throwing rotten fruit or candy, holding up lighters / cell phones.
- Participants may express basic emotions by crying, laughing, screaming, or wailing. These expressions often take on artistic form.
- People may produce other bits of communication with their bodies that contribute to an event that you may not have categories for. These could include actions like snapping fingers, belching, whistling, or producing vocal overtones. Keep all of your senses open to bodily communication.

ARTISTIC DOMAIN CONNECTIONS

We've grouped the way performance features relate to artistic domains in these categories: vocal, body movement, object manipulation, visual, rhythm, narrating, and poetic.

PREFACE

PREPARE

STEP 1

STEP 2

STEP 3

STEP 4A

STEP 5

STEP 6

STEP 7

CLOSING

PREFACE

PREPARE

STEP 1

STEP 2

STEP 3

STEP 4A

STEP 5

STEP 6

STEP 7

CLOSING

Participants manipulate **vocal features** in drama to help them act, in music to help them sing, in dance to coordinate breath with movement patterns, and in oral verbal arts to create effects by changing the pitch or timbre of their voices.

Participants **move their bodies** in ways that contribute to acting, characterization, and space organization in dramatic aspects of performance; instrument playing in music; movement dynamics, phrasing, and body and space organization in dance; and gesturing in oral verbal arts.

People manipulate **objects** to help them act and produce spectacle, both related to drama; to help them play instruments and modify their voice in music; to support or facilitate movement in dance; to emphasize oratorical elements in oral verbal arts; and in making or presenting a communicative object in visual arts.

Visual features play important roles in dramatic elements like costuming, makeup, puppets, and spectacle; dance that includes costuming and makeup; and visual arts that include design and composition.

Rhythm features contribute to musical characteristics like poly-, proportional, or free rhythm. How does external rhythm (e.g., music experienced through auditory channels) affect movement in dance? What about meter used in oral verbal arts?

Narrating features play significant roles in presenting or recounting events in drama and oral verbal arts.

Finally, participants may use **poetic devices** for acting in drama, song lyrics in music, and throughout oral verbal arts. You can research these and more relationships between Performance Features and artistic domains in the sections that follow.

Each of these artistic domain categories varies according to its proportional focus on referential meaning vs. form qualities. Performance traditions that rely more on referential meaning (e.g., storytelling, song singing, drama) will normally have more features that require a greater understanding of a language to recognize and understand.

Notes about performance features

- Any specific artistic event will likely draw on multiple features, each of which may exist within different groupings in other performance traditions.
- Performers may add unexpected features, purposefully or accidentally, and with varying degrees of skill and social license.

MEANING CONNECTIONS

Explore how what you've discovered by looking at an event through the lens of performance features relates to meanings, symbolism, and broader cultural themes. "Relate the Event's

Genre(s) to Its Broader Cultural Context" (**Part C**) below will provide direction for this.

CONTENT

BASIC DESCRIPTION

Content is the subject matter or topic of an artistic event. It is most closely tied to symbols like words, and movements in signed languages or dances. There may be multiple layers of meanings, which may be implied or explicit.

Write what you learn about the content of this event in the Community Arts Profile. Include transcriptions of language and other content signs to help explain what's going on.

RESEARCH QUESTIONS TO HELP YOU KNOW WHAT TO EXPLORE

- How did participants communicate the subject matter at different points in the event?
- What was the event about? What else was it about? What was its most important point? Second most important point?
- What assumed background knowledge does an experiencer need to understand the subject matter?

RESEARCH ACTIVITIES TO HELP YOU ANSWER THE QUESTIONS

- Record the event. Ask a friend to write down important words that people uttered, and meanings of any symbolic motions that occurred.
- Ask participants what they intended to communicate during the event.
- Ask participants what emotions or actions they hoped to elicit in other people because of the event.
- Ask participants what topics were angering, humorous, boring, or rousing?

ARTISTIC DOMAIN CONNECTIONS

In an event, features that interact most closely with content are mostly associated with drama, oral verbal arts, and songs in music.

MEANING CONNECTIONS

Explore how what you've discovered by looking at an event through the lens of Content relates to meanings, symbolism, and broader cultural themes. "Relate the Event's Genre(s) to Its Broader Cultural Context" (**Part C**) below will provide direction for this.

PREFACE

PREPARE

STEP 1

STEP 2

STEP 3

STEP 4A

STEP 5

STEP 6

STEP 7

CLOSING

PREFACE
PREPARE
STEP 1
STEP 2
STEP 3
STEP 4A
STEP 5
STEP 6
STEP 7
CLOSING

UNDERLYING SYMBOLIC SYSTEMS

Participants draw on all sorts of rules, expectations, grammatical structures, motivations, and experiences to decide what to do at any given moment of a performance. This is their cognitive and emotive environment, the hidden set of knowledge that participants share which allows composition and interpretation.

Some underlying systems are simple and easily discoverable. For example, the cyclic pattern of an Indonesian *gamelan* piece is quickly discernible by noting the regular interval at which the big gong in the ensemble sounds. Similarly, the metric division of a Strauss waltz into groups of three beats, with an accented first beat, does not require extensive analysis. As another example, stock characters in Thai *likay* drama are easily recognizable after a brief description of their behavior and costume conventions.

However, deriving some systems may take intensive, methodologically rigorous analysis, interview, and participation. For example, grammatical rules governing melodic or rhythmic structure of a song, the permitted movements in a dance, or the use of space in a painting are often not immediately evident. Though much of this complex analysis is beyond the scope of this manual, the sections in **Part B** on music, drama, dance, oral verbal arts, and visual arts provide some tools to explore underlying systems.

One underlying system that's common to each artistic event is the degree of variability its genre allows. You can research this by asking a wide variety of people questions like these:

- Which characteristics do people state must exist in order for an event to be a good example of this genre?
- What is acceptable but not necessary?
- What is not permitted?
- Is any of this contested?

ANALYZE
AN EVENT
CONTAINING THE
CHOSEN GENRE

PART B:
EXPLORE THE EVENT'S GENRE(S) THROUGH ARTISTIC DOMAIN CATEGORIES

Genres of artistic communication consist of a unique set of characteristics: how, when, why, where, with whom they happen, and their formal features. Because of this uniqueness our first goal is to describe each community's genre in its own terms. But it's also true that we humans share a great deal—bodies, cognitive structures, patterns of interaction—with the world. It's therefore not unusual to find similarities in the ways we communicate, even in different cultures. In this section we draw on these commonalities to show how deeper investigation into five common categories of artistic expression provides more detailed knowledge that can inform cocreation processes like sparking creativity (**Step 5**) and improvement (**Step 6**). These five categories are music, drama, dance, oral verbal arts, and visual arts. You could perform similar investigations into other artistic domains with specialized features that we haven't included in this manual, like food arts, games, architecture, and film.

In each artistic domain section we lead you through activities that will help you discover artistic elements of a genre. Note that we've grouped these activities in the same way we grouped your event analysis above in "Look at an Event's Forms": Space, Materials, Participant Organization, Shape of the Event through

PREFACE

PREPARE

STEP 1

STEP 2

STEP 3

STEP 4B

STEP 5

STEP 6

STEP 7

CLOSING

Time, Performance Features, Content, and Underlying Symbolic Systems. This provides continuity with what you've already found out. Note that the research tasks we suggest for each domain consist mostly of participant observation, dialogue with practitioners, written description, and transcription. Write what you discover in the Community Arts Profile.

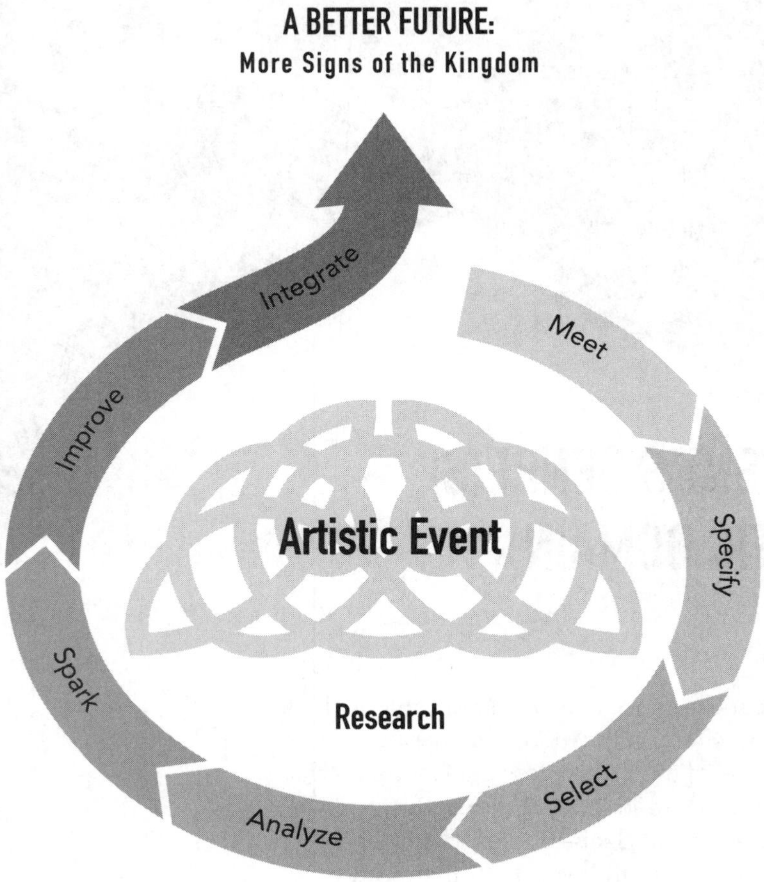

A BETTER FUTURE:
More Signs of the Kingdom

Integrate

Meet

Improve

Specify

Artistic Event

Spark

Research

Select

Analyze

Figure 1: Create Local Arts Together

As you look at the artistic characteristics of this event through the lenses, keep in mind what you've already learned about it in "Look at an Event's Forms." Artistic characteristics are always intertwined with other realities in communities; you won't be able to fully understand the music, drama, dance, oral verbal arts, or visual arts without a more complete picture. In particular, locate the event in its broader physical context relating to the Space lens (nationally, regionally, and locally), and its broader temporal context, connecting to the Shape lens (month, day, hour, season, and occurrence in the overall event).

You should also remember that arts are complicated and you can't be an expert in everything; there are things you won't be able to understand about analyzing artistic production using just these sections. For you to make the most of some of these activities—especially those related to Performance Features and Underlying Symbolic Systems—you will need to study their specialized vocabulary with an expert.

Before we get to the artistic domain analysis guides, we'll give you some recording and collecting advice that may come in handy.

RECORD A BUNCH OF SIMILAR ARTISTIC THINGS

After a brief review of reasons to reduce artistry to recordings, we'll highlight a purpose especially helpful for deeper genre analysis: recording a body of similar artistic work.

SOME PURPOSES FOR DIFFERENT KINDS OF RECORDINGS

We introduced these concepts in **Step 1**, but will now expand them for applications to analysis.

Integral performance contexts

An integral performance is one that is familiar to the performers and has a high number of normal social and artistic components. Here are some reasons to record arts in integral settings:

Video recording
- to discover overall flow of a performance through time, including subdivisions
- to see how sounds are produced and by whom
- to see how movements, dynamics, phrases, and relationships are produced
- to see how artists create visual objects

Audio recording
- to transcribe melodic, rhythmic, movement, plot, and other patterns in simple performance

Analytical performance contexts

An analytical performance context is designed by the researcher in order to isolate features of artistic production. One important purpose for such recordings is to collect components of an artistic genre for analysis and comparison; these might include songs, proverbs, dances, or stories. Here are a few other reasons to design recording events in analytical settings:

Video recording
- to enable subsequent feedback (performers and others can watch and verbally annotate the video recording of a performance with the researcher)
- to describe playing or movement or acting techniques

PREFACE

PREPARE

STEP 1

STEP 2

STEP 3

STEP 4B

STEP 5

STEP 6

STEP 7

CLOSING

PREFACE

PREPARE

STEP 1

STEP 2

STEP 3

STEP 4B

STEP 5

STEP 6

STEP 7

CLOSING

- to document movement in the clearest manner for future viewing
- to transcribe melodies, rhythms, and texts

RECORDING A BUNCH OF SONGS, PROVERBS, OR OTHER BITS OF ARTISTRY

Some of the research and analysis activities we describe in the following sections will benefit from a collection of basic products of an artistic genre. Such collections will help you find patterns, contrasts, themes, and limits to variation in the genre. They will also be key in contributing to archives of the artistry for protection and sharing. Here we present guides to collecting audio recordings of songs and proverbs, but you can apply similar steps to photographs of woven bags, video recordings of dances or plays, and many other bits of artistry.

How to collect songs

Songs are a nearly universally occurring type of artistic object composed of musical and verbal characteristics.

1. Discover an artistic genre that includes songs (see "Inside-out" or "Outside-in" in **Step 1**).
2. Ask people you know: Who are the best performers of this kind of song? Who knows the most songs (often older people)? Please introduce me to this person.
3. Create an analytical recording context: meet the person, describe what you'll do, get permission to record.
4. Slate the recording: at the beginning of the recording, say, "This is *your name*, recording *so-and-so person*, at *such-and-such place*, on *such-and-such day*." Then, before each song, say, "This is song number *one*, etc."
5. After each song, record someone translating the main elements of the lyrics into a language of wider communication.

How to collect proverbs

The vast majority of languages include condensed, specially formed bits of wisdom that we call proverbs. To truly understand a proverb, you need to learn what its words mean and other cultural information it refers to. You also need to know how it is performed in a social context: who can use it and for what purpose(s)? There is an important place for you to perform integral video or audio recordings, recording them in natural use. This is hard and usually time consuming, but possible.

However, there are many analyses that benefit from an analytically recorded collection of proverbs. Here are a few tips to making such a collection:[38]

---

38   See Peter Unseth, "Collecting, Using, and Enjoying Proverbs" (SIL Forum for Language Fieldwork 2008–002, September 2008).

1. Gather people together, turn on a recording device, have everyone speak in the vernacular if possible, and ask people to think of as many proverbs as possible.
2. Suggest situations in which proverbs might be used. These could include what a mother might say to a daughter who is angry with a friend, or a father to a son who is misbehaving. You can also suggest topics that proverbs might address, like laziness, animals, children, or food.
3. Suggest kinds of people that proverbs might mention, like debtors, merchants, old people, midwives, children, hunters, or ancestors.
4. Listen to the recording with someone who knows local proverbs well and can help you translate them in a language of wider communication. When a proverb occurs in the recording, stop the device, and have your friend(s) help you write and translate it.

MUSIC IN AN EVENT

This section will help you describe more completely the patterned, stylized sounds we describe as music in an event. To understand this section best, you should first work through some of the activities in "Look at an Event's Forms" (**Part A**). We use the same seven lenses here, but introduce descriptive categories particularly pertinent to music. You will gather your discoveries about the musical characteristics of this event and others like it in the Community Arts Profile.

Musical things are primarily experienced through auditory channels, though visual channels play important roles in helping the experiencer understand auditory information. Isolating the part of a single drum in a percussion ensemble, for example, may require visual attention to the drummer's playing. Watching a person play an instrument may also be the only way to understand playing technique, as in a rattle rhythm produced by complex, multidirectional movement.

Actions that produce sounds most frequently include singing and other vocal production, and participants' interaction with instruments, their own bodies (e.g., in clapping), or other parts of their environment (e.g., in stomping the ground).

The conceptual systems that participants draw on when performing these actions structure sound through time and frequency relationships (e.g., in rhythm and melody). Musical systems interact most commonly with systems in verbal (e.g., in song texts and

PREFACE

PREPARE

STEP 1

STEP 2

STEP 3

STEP 4B

STEP 5

STEP 6

STEP 7

CLOSING

PREFACE

PREPARE

STEP 1

STEP 2

STEP 3

STEP 4B

STEP 5

STEP 6

STEP 7

CLOSING

speech surrogates) and movement (e.g., in dance and instrument playing) domains.

Research activities most helpful in understanding the musical aspects of performance include audiovisual recording, ethnographic interview, and participant observation.

SPACE

Space is the location, demarcation, and physical characteristics of the area used, which can affect the form of artistic communication.

SUMMARY AND RELATIONSHIP TO OTHER LENSES

Space relates to musical action primarily in how performers place themselves to affect the sounds they produce and hear. Performers may choose to be near each other in order to hear and respond to each other more clearly and quickly. In addition, physical characteristics of the performance space will affect how participants produce and experience musical sounds. Singers, for example, may generate more strident and louder sounds in a larger space. Finally, space is closely related to participant organization in musical production. For example, groups using antiphonal ensemble structure may dedicate two separate areas of a performance space to create a stereophonic effect.

EXPLORE HOW PARTICIPANTS CHANGE THEIR MUSICAL BEHAVIOR IN RESPONSE TO THEIR PHYSICAL SPACE

Videotape an event and arrange a meeting with participants. While watching the video, ask questions like the following:

- Why were you that distance away from other performers at this point? How would your experience of the music have changed if you were farther apart or closer?
- Would you have changed how you sang/played if the space had been smaller? Larger?

EXPLORE HOW PARTICIPANTS DESIGN OR USE SPACE TO AFFECT MUSICAL SOUNDS

Building designers may create physical spaces to enhance acoustic characteristics of musical sound. Roman amphitheaters, for example, were designed to carry sound from the stage through the audience. In addition, Gothic cathedrals were created to accentuate reverberation of organs and choirs. Designers may also demarcate areas for specific types of performers.

If someone designed the space in which they performed, ask him or her: Did you think about how your design would affect the sounds produced by the performers? How so?

SHAPE OF THE EVENT THROUGH TIME

Shape of an event refers primarily to its constituent segments, organized hierarchically.

SUMMARY AND RELATIONSHIP TO OTHER LENSES

In "Look at an Event's Forms" you may have described an event with musical content like a concert, festival, religious service, or ritual. In this manual we focus on two closely related types of musical segments that are often part of such events:

Song: A composition consisting minimally of rhythm, melody, and text.

Piece: A composition consisting minimally of rhythm and melody. Be aware that some cultures do not have a metaterm to distinguish a song with text and a piece of music without text.

We describe the shape of songs and pieces in terms of their form. Form is composed of smaller segments of phrase and motif, which in turn consist of notes and beats. Definitions of these segments from highest to lowest place in a hierarchy follow:

Form: The organization of musical materials. Songs and pieces consist of patterned combinations of textual, rhythmic, and melodic segments. Assigning these segments letter names can reveal the overall structures that their combination produces. We use the following naming conventions:

A, B, C, etc.	phrases
a, b, c, etc.	motifs, or subphrases within a phrase
a^1, B^2, etc.	variation of the original motif or phrase by one change
b^a, C^b, etc.	motif or phrase upon which a new one is based

Phrase: A brief section of music, analogous to a phrase of spoken language, that sounds somewhat complete in itself, while not self-sufficient.[39] Phrases consist of motifs, which may be elaborated or varied.

Motif: A salient combination of notes.

Note: A minimal structural unit of pitch or rhythm produced by a voice or instrument.

Beat: A single time unit, sounded or not.

---

39   Kay Kauffman Shelemay, *Soundscapes: Exploring Music in a Changing World.* (New York: Norton, 2001), 358.

PREFACE

PREPARE

STEP 1

STEP 2

STEP 3

STEP 4B

STEP 5

STEP 6

STEP 7

CLOSING

PREFACE

PREPARE

STEP 1

STEP 2

STEP 3

STEP 4B

STEP 5

STEP 6

STEP 7

CLOSING

DETERMINE THE FORM OF A SONG OR PIECE

You must first identify a song or piece. You can do this by choosing a segment you have already elicited and recorded as part of a collection. Another method is to look at a time line of an event that you created following guidelines in "Look at an Event's Forms," noting the beginning and ending times of a song or piece. Listen to a recording of this segment many times, marking repeated sections and points of change. If you can, transcribe its melody. Direct observation or watching a videotaped rendition of the song or piece may also help.

After becoming familiar with the song or piece, note in the Community Arts Profile whether its form follows any of the following common patterns:

Call and response (responsorial): Singing in which leader and chorus alternate. ABAB. E.g., much African song.

Antiphonal singing or playing: Music in which two groups sing or play alternately. E.g., Renaissance choral music, Mamaindé song teaching (Brazil).

Strophic: "Designation for a song in which all stanzas of the text are sung to the same music, in contrast to a song with new music for each stanza [through-composed]."[40] E.g., hymns are songs with strophic structure. They often also have a refrain.

Through-composed: Melodic structure with no large-scale repetition. ABCDEFG.

Progressive: Each section has completely different material. Differs from through-composed in that it has a fixed number of repetitions and the repetitions are generally shorter than through-composed. AABBCCDD, etc.

Theme and variations: A basic theme is presented and then different variations of it are subsequently presented. A A1 A2 A3 A4 A5, etc.

Litany-type: Consists of only one short phrase that is reiterated throughout.[41]

PARTICIPANT ORGANIZATION

Participant Organization highlights the people involved in an event in terms of the roles they play, the ways they interact with each other through time, and how they use the space around them.

SUMMARY AND RELATIONSHIP TO OTHER LENSES

Common roles of participants in musical production are singers, instrumentalists, and composers. Participant organization interacts with musical structure at two main levels: texture and song form. In terms of melodic or rhythmic texture, roles relate to the horizontal and vertical relationships of participants' contributions. For example, a solo singer will produce monophony, but multiple singers will be

---

40   Willi Apel, *Harvard Dictionary of Music* (Cambridge, MA: Belknap Press of Harvard University Press, 1972), 811.
41   Bruno Nettl, *Music in Primitive Culture* (Cambridge: Harvard University Press, 1956), 69.

responsible for producing polyphony or homophony when a genre requires it.

In terms of song form, participants' roles may be directly related to sequential segments required by a genre. For example, hocketing requires each participant to produce a small number of notes in the formation of a larger melodic line, as in a bell choir, *anklung* ensemble (Indonesia), or a Mamaindé Toré puberty ceremony (Brazil). As another example, participants in some African choirs create call-and-response form by dividing into the roles of leader and chorus.

IDENTIFY THE ROLES OF MUSICAL PRODUCTION

Watch a video recording of an event with people who participated, either as performers or observers. Point out someone who is singing, playing an instrument, or otherwise making sound, and ask them questions like these:

- Who is that person? What is he or she doing? How did he or she qualify to do this? What path in his or her life did they follow to get there?
- Does what he or she is doing have a name? What would allow someone else to be able to do this?
- What does this role add to the event? What would be missing without it?
- Repeat this, asking about others who are making other sounds.

Note that individual performance genres associate participant roles with characteristic musical output. These genre-defined roles may be based on musical structure, difficulty of parts, and social status associated with the roles. For a given performance, individual participants may occupy these genre-defined roles based on their own abilities and social status. In a trombone quartet, for example, there may be four named roles: first, second, third, and bass trombone. The first trombone part may be the most difficult to perform, and the player with the greatest ability may fill this role. However, in a particular performance event, someone may play the bass part because he's the only one who has a bass trombone.

MATERIALS

Materials are all of the tangible things associated with an event.

SUMMARY AND RELATIONSHIP TO OTHER LENSES

The most important materials related to music are instruments. The presence of musical instruments and the way they are designed affect the creation of music performance features. Also, elements of their design may reveal some of the genre's underlying symbolic systems. For instance, instrument tuning may reveal musical scales or harmonic systems. Or an instrument may be "sight tuned"; for example, the finger holes on a flute are drilled where the fingers naturally fall on a flute rather than according to the pitch the hole makes.

PREFACE

PREPARE

STEP 1

STEP 2

STEP 3

STEP 4B

STEP 5

STEP 6

STEP 7

CLOSING

PREFACE

PREPARE

STEP 1

STEP 2

STEP 3

STEP 4B

STEP 5

STEP 6

STEP 7

CLOSING

LIST MUSICAL INSTRUMENTS

Using each genre in the Community Arts Profile as a starting point, ask friends and experts to tell you all of the sound-producing objects. Write down the name of the instrument in the local language and any other languages used in the area.

DESCRIBE EACH MUSICAL INSTRUMENT IN SEVERAL WAYS

You can base your descriptions of an instrument primarily on interviews with knowledgeable people, personal observation and handling, and insights you gain from learning to play it. You can also take photos of the instrument in use and from different angles to expose physical features. Here are a few approaches to get you started:

1. **Construction and materials:** Interview someone who has made an instrument to find out what materials they use (include local names) and the construction process. You can also document someone making the instrument with video or still photography.
2. **Sound production:** The Sachs-Hornbostel organology system groups instruments by the part that is activated in vibration to make a sound. **Aerophones** (such as flutes, trombones) use a resonating vibrating column of air to sound. **Chordophones** (such as harps, guitars) sound from vibrating strings. **Membranophones** (such as drums) have a membrane stretched over a frame and are often struck to make a sound. **Idiophones** (such as cymbals, xylophones) vibrate the entire material of the instrument. Decide what category the instrument you are working with fits in.
3. **Playing techniques:** Participants blow, suck, hit, scrape, pluck, bow, shake, and do other actions with objects in order to produce sounds that relate to melody, rhythm, texture, and text. Describe these interactions according to body parts, action types, instrument parts, constraints the instruments place on potential actions, resulting sounds, and their relationships to other aspects of performance. These techniques often come with local vocabulary. Note that people will modify their techniques to change the qualities of sounds that their instruments produce, such as timbre (see "Performance Feature Categories" below).
4. **Musical function:** Another way to classify instruments could be according to musical function in the texture: melodic or rhythmic, solo or ensemble. Note that it does not necessarily follow that aerophones and chordophones are for melodic/harmonic use and membranophones and idiophones are for rhythmic use. To explore musical functions of an instrument, begin performing the activities in "Performance Feature Categories" below. Then note which instruments produce each feature category.
5. **Visual design:** Instrument design also often includes shaping or adornment using visual art features. Describe and analyze these following the research activities in "Visual Arts in an Event" later in **Step 4, Part B5**.
6. **Tuning:** Using a fixed pitch producer like a pitch pipe, melodica, or electronic tuner, write down the note names that correspond most closely to the pitches

produced by the instrument. Note if a pitch is slightly higher or lower than that on the fixed pitch producer. There are software programs and devices that can identify the exact frequency of a pitch. Also be aware that the relationship between pitches is more important than the pitches' individual frequencies; different players may tune their instruments differently, and the community may tolerate a fairly wide variance in an instrument's tuning.

7. **Cultural integration:** Ask for names of different parts of the instrument. Sometimes a part will have a human attribute (e.g., male and female strings on a harp) and reveal cultural values (e.g., the male and female strings should follow a prescribed structure to sound pleasant). You can also ask whether there are conventions for who should play an instrument (e.g., male, female, child), how it is constructed, all the genres it is used in, and whether there are connections to broader cultural themes.

PERFORMANCE FEATURE CATEGORIES

Performance features are observable characteristics of a performance that emerge from an event's unique combination of physical and social context and participants' actions.

SUMMARY AND RELATIONSHIP TO OTHER LENSES
Performance features associated with music relate primarily to how participants organize sounds through time, frequency, and volume.

DESCRIBE INSTRUMENTAL AND VOCAL TIMBRES
Performers manipulate their voices or instruments to produce various timbres.

Timbre: The quality ("color") of a tone produced by a voice or instrument. This is determined by the relative loudness of the harmonics, the presence of accompanying noise, and the noises occurring at the attack of the note. Initial descriptions of timbre might include rough, smooth, raspy, breathy, nasal, or creaky.

To begin to understand how singers produce the sounds they do, first watch and listen to how they do it. Then ask them how they produce the sounds, how they learned to do it, and how they describe good sounds. Finally, you might ask someone to teach you to do it. Write the results of your explorations in the Community Arts Profile, using the terms below when appropriate. Note that vocal timbres are most often determined by gender (e.g., male/female, soprano, alto, tenor, baritone, bass) and the ways singers modify their voices. Listed below are some techniques you may come across:

Vibrato: A minute fluctuation in volume and/or pitch in a sustained note.

PREFACE

PREPARE

STEP 1

STEP 2

STEP 3

STEP 4B

STEP 5

STEP 6

STEP 7

CLOSING

PREFACE

PREPARE

STEP 1

STEP 2

STEP 3

STEP 4B

STEP 5

STEP 6

STEP 7

CLOSING

Yodeling: Singing style where the performer alternates frequently between the natural chest voice and falsetto tones.

Sprechstimme: A vocal style in which the melody is spoken at approximate pitches rather than sung on exact pitches.

Overtone singing: A vocal technique in which a single vocalist produces two, three, or four distinct notes simultaneously. This is accomplished by separating and manipulating the voice's natural harmonic overtones, which we typically hear as "color" or timbre, but not as individual tones.

DETERMINE THE NUMBER OF NOTES PER SPEECH SYLLABLE IN A SONG

Write down the text of a song. Transcribe the melody associated with the text if you can. If not, listen to a recording of the melody and mark on the text when more than one note is associated with a single syllable. Note in the Community Artyts Profile whether any of the following types describe its relationship of note to syllable:

Syllabic: Usually one note per syllable (e.g., most nineteenth-century hymns).

Neumatic: Usually two to three notes per syllable (e.g., "Amazing Grace" sung "folk" style).

Melismatic: Frequent use of one syllable sung on two or more notes (e.g., refrain of "Angels We Have Heard on High").

DETERMINE AND DESCRIBE THE TEXTURE(S) OF A PIECE OR SONG

Texture describes the horizontal and vertical relationships of musical materials, comparable to the weave of a fabric.[42] To find out the texture of a song or piece, listen to a recording of it several times, focusing your attention each time on different pitched sounds. Then note in the Community Arts Profile whether any of the following types describe its texture:

Heterophony: Musical texture in which the same melody is played by all voices and instruments but with variations and omissions depending on the particular nature of each (e.g., Javanese *gamelan*).

Polyphony: Musical texture composed of two or more voices sounding on different notes (not octaves).

Parallel organum: Polyphony composed of a melody and a second part that parallels it (e.g., Maxacalí, Medieval Organum).

Drone: Polyphony composed of a melody supported by one or two unchanging pitches (e.g., Scottish bagpipe, much South Asian music).

Homophony: Polyphony composed of a melody supported by chords (e.g., most hymns and popular songs of European derivation).

Independent polyphony: The melodic voices move in different directions. (The term "independent polyphony" is not necessarily recognized as standard, but

---

42   Willi Apel, *Harvard Dictionary of Music* (Cambridge, MA: Belknap Press of Harvard University Press, 1972), 842.

it is useful to illustrate a point. Some scholars restrict the term "polyphony" to mean "independent polyphony.") For example, any of Bach's harmonizations of "O Sacred Head."

Imitative polyphony: The melody of one voice is based on another; it imitates it (e.g., Baroque fugues).

Canon (or round): All or almost all the material of the first voice is repeated by one or more following voices (e.g., "Row, Row, Row Your Boat").

DETERMINE AND DESCRIBE THE RHYTHM(S) OF A PIECE OR SONG

Rhythm describes the whole feeling of movement in music, or the pattern of long and short notes occurring in a song. To find out the rhythm of a song or piece, listen to a recording of it several times. As you're listening, try to clap a regular beat that coincides with patterns you hear. If you can do this, the rhythm is likely to be polyrhythm or proportional. Otherwise, it may be based on speech or have free rhythm. Note in the Community Arts Profile whether any of the following types describe its rhythm:

Proportional rhythm: Smaller rhythmic units are simple proportions of larger units.

Polyrhythm: The simultaneous use of strikingly contrasted rhythms in different parts of the musical fabric.

Speech rhythm: Rhythmic system of a musical composition wherein the rhythm is determined by the rhythm of the spoken text without reference to proportionality or other factors.

Free rhythm: Notes of irregular lengths with no discernible pattern.

DETERMINE AND DESCRIBE THE TEMPO(S) OF A PIECE OR SONG

Tempo is the speed at which beats occur. It may play an important role in describing meter, and may convey meaning itself. It is usually indicated in beats per minute, marked as MM (short for Maelzel's metronome). Note also that performance genres specify ranges of allowable tempos for a piece or segment thereof, or their increase or decrease.

While listening to a recording of a piece or song, count the number of beats that occur during a period of fifteen seconds. Multiply that number by four and you have the tempo. Note if the tempo changes at different points in the piece.

PREFACE

PREPARE

STEP 1

STEP 2

STEP 3

STEP 4B

STEP 5

STEP 6

STEP 7

CLOSING

DETERMINE AND DESCRIBE THE DYNAMIC(S) OF A PIECE OR SONG

Dynamics refer to the volume and changes of volume. Listen to a recording of the piece and describe any sections as loud, soft, or somewhere in between. Then note any changes in volume, which may be sudden or gradual, and correspond with contrasts in form, text, or dramatic elements. You may also notice that a single note or beat exhibits a sharply articulated, short increase in volume, commonly called an accent.

DETERMINE AND DESCRIBE THE NOTES OF A PIECE OR SONG

Notes are minimal structural units of pitch or rhythm produced by a voice or instrument. If you transcribe the melody of a song, you can make note of its Pitch Inventory, Range, and Contours in the Community Arts Profile.

Pitch (or tonal) inventory: All the notes used in a musical piece or genre.
Range: The pitch difference between the lowest and highest notes used in a musical composition. This term is also used to describe the absolute highest and lowest notes normally sung by a certain voice (e.g., tenor, soprano) or normally played on an instrument. Languages often refer to differences in pitch frequencies with vocabulary other than "high" and "low" (these result from how Europeans began writing out notes on staves). Terms for higher frequencies may include "small," "skinny," or "low," while lower frequencies may be described as "big," "fat," or "high." Ask.
Tonal center: The pitch around which the musical piece revolves. The tonal center is often the most frequent pitch in a piece and fills prominent structural roles, but further analysis is beyond the scope of this manual.
Modulation: Change of tonal center or key within a composition.
Melody: A succession of musical notes; the horizontal aspect of pitches in music.
Contour: The characteristic (motion) shape of a melody within a musical composition. Possible shapes of a melody include the following:

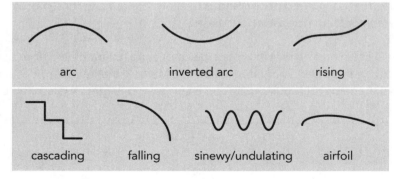

Figure 5: Contours of a Melody

CONTENT

Content refers to the subject matter in artistic activity.

SUMMARY AND RELATIONSHIP TO OTHER LENSES

Content associated with music relates primarily to song texts and speech surrogates.

EXPLORE RELATIONSHIPS BETWEEN MELODY, RHYTHM, AND OTHER FEATURES OF SUNG TEXT

A melody's shape and rhythm may be influenced by stress, linguistic tone, part of speech, discourse features, and the like.[43] To expose relationships between linguistic tone and melodic movement, do this: (1) write down the text of the song, marking tone on each syllable; (2) transcribe the melody over the text, or draw the melodic shape with curved lines; (3) note the direction of melodic movement over each syllable, and compare with the direction of linguistic tone movement. Describe your findings in the Community Arts Profile according to the following kinds of relationships:

Parallel: Tone and melody move in parallel directions.
Contrary: Tone and melody move in opposite directions.
Oblique: Tone or melody moves, while the other remains level.

Note also the term **vocable**, which refers to a syllable without lexical meaning set to music. Vocables may, however, communicate emotional or symbolic meaning.

IDENTIFY AND BRIEFLY DESCRIBE SPEECH SURROGATES

Communities sometimes mimic elements of spoken language with instruments or whistling to communicate verbal content. When used this way, these sound producers are called speech surrogates. Common instruments acting as speech surrogates include pitched drums, xylophones, and harps. To learn more about speech surrogates, ask questions like these:

- Are there instruments that can communicate messages?
- What kinds of messages can these instruments convey? Give examples.
- Who knows how to communicate in this way?

Record examples of people communicating this way, with translation to spoken language.

---

43 Paul Richards, "A Quantitative Analysis of the Relationship between Language Tone and Melody in a Hausa Song," *African Language Studies* 13 (1972): 137–61.

PREFACE

PREPARE

STEP 1

STEP 2

STEP 3

STEP 4B

STEP 5

STEP 6

STEP 7

CLOSING

PREFACE

PREPARE

STEP 1

STEP 2

STEP 3

STEP 4B

STEP 5

STEP 6

STEP 7

CLOSING

UNDERLYING SYMBOLIC SYSTEMS

Underlying Symbolic Systems refer to the grammatical and social rules and structures that guide participants' actions in artistic activity.

SUMMARY AND RELATIONSHIP TO OTHER LENSES

Systems like scale and meter provide grammatical structure for composing and understanding musical production. Though the analytical procedure to determine scale and meter are beyond the scope of this manual, the definitions below may help you get started.

SCALE

All the notes used in a genre and their functional relationships. A closed set of notes and the grammar that orders their production. Examples include the following:

Diatonic scale: In Euro-American music theory, melody or harmony confined to the pitches within a major or minor key. It consists of five whole tones and two semitones, as it is produced on the white keys of a keyboard tuned to Western pitch conventions.

Tetratonic, pentatonic, hexatonic, heptatonic, octatonic scales: These terms simply describe the number of notes a scale uses within an octave; i.e., 4, 5, 6, 7, or 8.

Raga: A term used in East Indian musicology that includes the concept of scale but also implies much more, such as the relationship of the notes and even melodic themes. Different ragas are associated with different concepts such as fire and the time of day.

METER

The underlying pattern of beats, by which the time span of a piece of music or a section thereof is organized.[44]

Divisive meter: A basic unit of time (usually a measure) is subdivided into a number of equal notes, each of which may be subdivided. Indicated by time signatures in Western notation (e.g., 2/2, 4/4, 6/8).

Additive meter: A pattern of beats that subdivide into smaller, irregular groups. Larger periods of time are constructed from sequences of smaller rhythmic units added to the end of the previous unit (e.g., 2+2+3, or 3+2).

Isometer: The use of a repeated pulse without its organization into groups.

Mixed meter: The sequential use of two or more different meters in one piece.

Polymeter: The simultaneous sounding of two or more different meters.

---

44   Cf. Apel, Harvard Dictionary of Music, 523.

Step 4B: Explore the Event's Genre(s) through Artistic Domain Categories

103

PREFACE

PREPARE

STEP 1

STEP 2

STEP 3

STEP 4B

STEP 5

STEP 6

STEP 7

CLOSING

Asymmetrical meter: A meter with beats of different lengths.
Nonmetric: No sense of underlying pulse in the music.

DRAMA IN AN EVENT

This section will help you describe more completely the ways participants recreate actions, or create a world of possible actions, in a story event. We use the same seven lenses we introduced in **Part A**, but introduce descriptive categories particularly pertinent to drama. You will gather your discoveries about the dramatic characteristics of this event and others like it in the Community Arts Profile.

We learn about dramatic features of a tradition by observing rehearsals and performances, by participating in the activities of drama groups, and by analyzing scripts, transcripts, audio recordings, or video recordings of performances.

SPACE

Space is the location, demarcation, and physical characteristics of the areas used, which can affect the form of artistic communication.

SUMMARY AND RELATIONSHIP TO OTHER LENSES

Space has two senses in relation to drama. First, **performance space** is the place where actors relate to an audience. Second, the **dramatic setting** is the imagined location of the story conveyed by the performers' use of words, space, set pieces, lighting or props to evoke an imagined place and time (see also Materials below).

DESCRIBE HOW PARTICIPANTS DESIGN SPACE

Interview some performers when they are not performing. Ask them where and when performed events occur, to whom, and why. It may be that they perform in places that are used for other purposes at other times, such as a clearing, under a tree, or someone's yard. A performance space like this is called an *arène trouvée* (found stage). Alternatively, performers may use a structured stage such as a raised platform or floor designated for performances. Ask whether performances always occur at a fixed location or at variable locations.

Ask where performers get ready before a performance. Backstage may be part of a structured stage that is not seen by the audience. Backstage may include a waiting room for actors (sometimes called a *green room*), a dressing room, prop

PREFACE

PREPARE

STEP 1

STEP 2

STEP 3

STEP 4B

STEP 5

STEP 6

STEP 7

CLOSING

storage or costume storage areas. Space in view of the audience, beside the stage, may also serve as a de facto backstage, or waiting area, for the actors.

Write down the name of each preparation space and each performance space in the local language, and any other languages used in the area. Write down what performers do in each space. For example, in Japanese theater, a raised platform walkway leads out into the audience. The raised walkway is called a *hanamichi* (flower pathway). Actors may enter or exit on the *hanamichi* to perform nearer the audience than when on the main stage. Performers sometimes freeze in particular dramatic poses that are associated with particular emotions. The poses are called *mié*. *Mié* poses on the *hanamichi* allow audiences to appreciate the poses and emotions at close range.

DESCRIBE THE PERFORMANCE SPACE CONFIGURATION AND DIRECTIONALITY

Either an *arène trouvée* or a structured stage may have different configurations. The name of the configuration is determined by where the audience is located in relation to the performers. Write down how the audience is arranged in relation to the performers.

In theater-in-the-round the audience is located on all sides of the performers, so the performers direct their performance in all directions. In a thrust theater, the audience is located on three sides of the performers, so the performers direct their performance in three directions. On a three-quarter round stage the performance space has one wall and an audience is located in a partial circle around them, so similarly, performers act to an audience in a partial circle around them. On a proscenium stage, the audience is located on one side of the stage and the other sides are hidden. The performers direct their performance in only one direction toward the audience.

After you have described the performance space configuration and performance directionality, also describe if the performance space is all on one level or has multiple levels. Describe if there are stairs, partitions, or other physical barriers. Ask performers how the shape of this space affects their performances.

MATERIALS

Materials are all of the tangible things associated with an event.

SUMMARY AND RELATIONSHIP TO OTHER LENSES

Performers use materials to help them convey other places, times, people and events. The dramatic setting is the imagined location of the story conveyed within the performance setting by performers' use of costumes, set pieces, props, instruments (sound/music), words, performing objects, or lighting.

Costumes, props, scenery, and set pieces can be categorized as realistic, impressionistic, minimalistic, improvised, or mimed.

- They are **realistic** if they aim to reproduce real life as exactly as possible.
- They are **impressionistic** if they are prepared in advance and give an idea of a thing without trying to reproduce it exactly.
- They are **minimalistic** when they are few and unassuming so attention is placed on other aspects of a performance. Minimalistic costuming, for example, uses a few representative items to designate characters; minimalistic settings use a few objects to represent a place.
- They are **improvised** if they are found on hand without being prepared in advance and made to represent things that they are not by the performer's spontaneous ingenuity.
- They are **mimed** when the actors' actions cause the audience to imagine objects that are not physically present; mime is actually an absence of materials, but it is worth noting this, so you do not influence participants to use more materials that they would normally. Similarly, actors' words or actions may portray a setting in audience's minds using **a bare stage** with no set at all. Rather than costumes actors may dress in **street clothes**, meaning regular, unaltered clothing.

The same performance may display more than one of these categories.

EXPLORE HOW PARTICIPANTS USE MATERIALS TO EVOKE AN IMAGINED STORY

Materials in the performance space may be used to evoke one or more dramatic settings, helping take the audience in their imaginations to another time and place, recreating a past world or imagining a possible world.

Attend a play and remember what you saw. If possible, record it. List and tentatively categorize types of props, set pieces, costumes, and performing objects (things used as characters, such as puppets). If these are numerous, you can list representative examples of each.

Talk about what you saw or watch your recording with one or more performers or audience members. Ask them where and when performed events occur to whom, and why. Ask them what visual signals allow them to know these things. Make notes of characteristics you learn.

PREFACE

PREPARE

STEP 1

STEP 2

STEP 3

STEP 4B

STEP 5

STEP 6

STEP 7

CLOSING

PREFACE

PREPARE

STEP 1

STEP 2

STEP 3

STEP 4B

STEP 5

STEP 6

STEP 7

CLOSING

Describe costuming: Describe the clothes and makeup the performers wear and what these signify. Clothes may indicate something about the character by color symbolism or by what type of character would wear that kind of clothing. How do the costumes make the audience think of a different place and time? Are masks used to change character? If so, which kind of character is evoked by which mask? In various Asian classical and folk theaters, makeup is very important to the character understanding, almost like a mask. Color in makeup can also be significant, as in Indian and other South Asian theater traditions.

Describe lighting: Describe the quality of light. Is it natural, or how is light generated? How does the light make the audience think of a different place and time?

Describe the set: Describe the arrangement of set pieces and objects within the performance space. Describe the set and scenery as realistic, impressionistic, minimalistic, or bare. Describe how scenery is created; for example, if there are painted flats, describe them. (A flat is a piece of wood, a hanging canvas, or a wooden frame covered by a sheet and painted to form scenery.)

Describe performing objects: Describe any performing objects or puppets that are manipulated by a performer to give the impression that the object has a life of its own. Is the real performer hidden or visible?

Describe props: Props are objects used by a performer which can change location in the course of acting. Hand props are carried by actors. Set props are pieces of the scene. Props may be realistic, as when a stick is a stick, or impressionistic when one object suggests a different object to the audience's imagination, such as when a stick represents an arrow. Props are improvised if they are found on the spot.

SUMMARIZE HOW COSTUMES, PROPS, SET PIECES, AND LIGHTING COMBINE TO SHOW DRAMATIC SETTING

Are they all realistic, impressionistic, improvised, or minimalistic? Are some in one category and others in another category?

SHAPE OF THE EVENT THROUGH TIME

Shape of an event refers to its segments, organized hierarchically.

SUMMARY AND RELATIONSHIP TO OTHER LENSES

Performances that include dramatic actions usually enact narratives, and so draw on cultural systems guiding the telling of stories, such as plot and character. Look for segment breaks. How do performed stories begin, develop and end? What characteristics signal shifts in parts of a performance? These performances also frequently include features of other arts, including song, dance, storytelling, and proverb telling.

AUDIO AND/OR VIDEO RECORD A DRAMATIC PERFORMANCE IN PREPARATION FOR STRUCTURE ANALYSIS

Create a written transcription while listening to the recording of the performance. Make either a **summary transcription** providing a concise description of the key elements, or a **transcription** of every word, or a **complete transcription** of every word, gesture, and movement. Look for segment breaks and what characterizes each segment. If in another language you do not know well, work with a bilingual person to translate the transcription into a language you know well. Note the date and place of the performance, because different performances will have different transcriptions.

Look for combinations of performance features that signal changes in parts. Your transcription may note the following kinds of things:

Line: One utterance. Do performers wait for one another to finish speaking? Are there times when performers speak at once? If the audience reacts or laughs, will performers wait to deliver the next line until the audience is quiet, or keep on going?

Gesture: One bodily movement in the same place

Cross: A performer changes positions from one part of the performance space to another part of the space. The combination of actors' changing positions in the performance space is called the performance's blocking.

Beat: One interaction between two performers. One does something or says something, and another reacts by doing something or saying something. Another meaning of the word "beat" is when a scriptwriter wants an actor to pause for a moment without saying anything. For example, a line may read, "All I have is (beat) now." This indicates the actor is thinking and adds emphasis to the word "now."

French scene: An event in the story with the same exact group of actors on stage. French scenes are shorter than scenes, because they change any time any actor enters or exits.

Scene: A series of events in one setting with the same approximate group of actors. When the imagined place changes, or the grouping of performers present changes significantly, the scene changes.

Act: A series of scenes. Often a first act situates the audience as to the place, situation, and characters; a second act develops a conflict; and a third act resolves the conflict. An act may be a single scene or a series of scenes.

Play: A full story enacted with a beginning, middle, and end. It can be a series of acts or a single act. Watch for what signals the beginning and the end, and any changes of structure in between.

Play series or play cycle: Several plays performed as one event.

Epic play cycle: A series of play cycles performed as a series of events.

PREFACE

PREPARE

STEP 1

STEP 2

STEP 3

STEP 4B

STEP 5

STEP 6

STEP 7

CLOSING

PREFACE

PREPARE

STEP 1

STEP 2

STEP 3

STEP 4B

STEP 5

STEP 6

STEP 7

CLOSING

USING A PLAY SCRIPT OR PERFORMANCE TRANSCRIPTION, WRITE A FRENCH SCENE ANALYSIS

Every time any character enters or exits, write what line is the first line spoken and the last line spoken. Number each segment as a new French scene. Go through the scene list and write down the setting (imagined place) for each French scene. Write down the names of all the characters onstage together during each French scene. Summarize in one sentence what key action takes place in each scene. Directors may use this list to know what actors to call to rehearse which scenes.

FROM YOUR FRENCH SCENE ANALYSIS, CREATE A PLOT SUMMARY

A plot summary tells the main events of a play as a story. You can turn your French scene list into a plot summary. In *Story*, Robert McKee defines Structure as "a selection of events from characters' life stories that is composed into a strategic sequence to arouse specific emotions and to express a specific view of life." [45] **Plot** is the series of events in a play and their structured arrangement in time. The ordering of events helps express the world view and meaning of the play (see the sections on "Underlying Symbolic Systems" and "Content" that follow.)

USING YOUR FRENCH SCENE ANALYSIS, WRITE A DRAMATIC INTENSITY CURVE

A dramatic intensity curve shows the rise and fall of action across the time of the play. [46] Make the line going right to left the numbers of each French scene. Make a line going up and down on the left-hand side of your page. This intersecting line shows low intensity on the bottom and high intensity on the top. Plot an approximate point for the intensity of each numbered French scene. Note the names of story events that define major turning points in the story.

PARTICIPANT ORGANIZATION

Participant Organization highlights the people involved in an event in terms of the roles they play, the ways they interact with each other through time, and how they use the space around them.

SUMMARY AND RELATIONSHIP TO OTHER LENSES

Participants who contribute to the representation of reality include one or more actors, and may also include a scriptwriter or scriptwriters, a director, set designers and builders, choreographers, light designers,

---

45   Robert McKee, *Story: Substance, Structure, Style, and the Principles of Screenwriting* (New York: HarperCollins, 1997), 33.
46   Buzz McLaughlin, *The Playwright's Process: Learning the Craft from Today's Leading Dramatists* (New York: Back Stage Books, 1997), 131–134.

PREFACE

PREPARE

STEP 1

STEP 2

STEP 3

STEP 4B

STEP 5

STEP 6

STEP 7

CLOSING

and others. People who are observing a performance may also play important roles in the development or enactment of the story.

OBSERVE OR PARTICIPATE IN A REHEARSAL OF A PERFORMANCE

Performances may be based on a written document called a script, from which every word is memorized, or on an outline of events called a scenario. The scenario may be written or may exist only in the performers' memories based on their prior oral discussions. They may memorize a few key lines and otherwise move their characters' actions in a generally agreed-upon direction, or they may memorize every word.

Discover who is responsible for the creation and execution of different aspects of the performance. Describe various participants' roles. Do performers create from a script, a written scenario, or an oral scenario? Describe how plot structure development happens. Who decides what happens in the story: a script, the director, or a collaborative effort among all actors? Who decides what the exact words will be: the actor, the director, or the scriptwriter? Are the words always the same, or do they vary from performance to performance? Who decides what gestures to use: the director, the actor, or the script? Who decides how actors position themselves in relation to one another: the script, the director, or the performer? How does characterization happen: entirely decided by the actor, the director, the script, or some combination of these? Is direction given by a single person or by consensus of the group?

DESCRIBE THE MEMBERS OF THE PERFORMANCE GROUP AND WHAT PART EACH PLAYS

Company or **ensemble** is the group performing a drama. Describe whether it is organized more *collaboratively* or more *hierarchically*. What are the different roles assigned to group members, or does everyone do everything? Is there a director giving instructions on how the actors should act (a hierarchical model), or do all the performers coach one another (a collaborative model)? Is there a prop manager or set designer, or does everyone create and set up the performance space? Is there an author, or do performers come to a group consensus about plot structure, theme, and characterization? Do they work from a memorized script, or from an outlined scenario?

An **actor** is a person who portrays a character.

A **playwright** is a person who creates scripts for plays. Many traditions do not write plays down and work without playwrights.

The **director** is the person who supervises the creative integration of all the elements of a drama and instructs the actors and crew as to their performance elements. There may be no single director in a performance, as when performers

PREFACE

PREPARE

STEP 1

STEP 2

STEP 3

STEP 4B

STEP 5

STEP 6

STEP 7

CLOSING

coach one another. **Directing** is to instruct the actors in the preparation of their performance. Some companies decide together what to do and have no director. Director William Ball advises:

> The only real reason a director is needed in rehearsal is to perform the following function: persistently to draw the actor to a more meaningful and appropriate choice of objectives, and then to persuade the actor to lend his full commitment to those objectives. This is the purpose of a director. He helps the actor choose an objective and then encourages him to play it with all his heart.[47]

Ball describes directing as helping the actor find *actionable* verbs and then coaching the actors to strengthen the action verb they are playing.

The **crew** are the people who set up, take down, change scenes, manipulate the environment during performance (e.g., lighting, sound effects), advertise, and/or manage the set, costumes, and props. These may include **set designers** who create the scenes and stage; **costume designers** who create the clothes performers wear; and a **stage manager** responsible for technical details during performance, costuming, setting, and prompting if an actor forgets a line. The **lighting designer** and **lighting operators** may deal with special lighting. In some companies the actors perform all the duties of a crew. A **nonmatrixed performer** does not show character. Stagehands in Japanese *kabuki* theater, for example, move props and the audience sees them but ignores them.[48] A **Foley artist** specializes in creating sound effects. The group you observe may not have all of these.

The **audience** may participate passively or actively in the dramatic performance. Boal coined the term **spect-actors** for the participant role when the line between spectator and actor is blurred and the audience participates actively in the performance.[49]

47   William Ball, *A Sense of Direction: Some Observations on the Art of Directing* (New York: Drama Publishers, 1984), 81.
48   Michael Kirby, "On Acting and Not-Acting," *The Drama Review: TDR* 16, No. 1 (1972), 3.
49   Augusto Boal, *The Rainbow of Desire: The Boal Method of Theatre and Therapy* (London: Routledge, 1995), 13.

DESCRIBE THE AUDIENCE'S RELATIONSHIP TO PERFORMED REALITY

Watch a play. From the interaction between the audience and the actors, what expectations would you say actors have of the audience? What expectations does the audience have of the actors? Do actors and audience interact with one another during the performance, or do they assume a wall separates them? Describe the play as presentational or representational.

A **representational** depiction of reality shapes stage action to appear as if it were happening in much the same way it would in real life. The onstage characters behave as if they are unaware of the audience's presence. Actors and audience suspend their disbelief and act as though everything in the play is happening for the first time. The onstage characters assume an invisible *fourth wall* separates them from the audience. The audience members understand they are not supposed to interact with the performers. A **presentational** play, on the other hand, knows it is a show. The characters *break the fourth wall* between actors and audience when they behave as if they are aware that the audience is watching. (We could call presentational theater in other performance spaces simply "breaking the wall.") The audience and the performers interact with one another or acknowledge each other's presence during the performance.[50] For example, at a Jula funeral wake in Côte d'Ivoire, a granddaughter imitated the actions of her deceased grandfather in a humorous way, and any of the family's visitors could address the granddaughter as if she were the grandfather.[51]

Some mainly representational plays have presentational moments when an actor briefly addresses the audience directly and then returns to the world of the play: actors may make use of **monologues** (one actor talking at length to the audience) and **asides** (brief statements or questions to the audience).

Many plays contain one or two character(s) or a chorus that have a presentational relationship with the audience and speak to them, while all the other characters have a representational relationship with the audience and do not speak to them. That one character or group serves as a bridge between the two worlds.

There are different levels of presentational theater. In a small way, whenever a performer glances directly at the audience, he or she is being a bit presentational, because he or she is acknowledging the audience's existence; an interactional play from Ghana like *Orphan Do Not Glance* is presentational to a much greater extent since performers speak directly to the audience while in character, and audience members come on the stage to feed the actor playing a hungry child, breaking the fourth wall in both directions.[52] These participants could well be described as spect-actors.

50   Buzz McLaughlin, *The Playwright's Process: Learning the Craft from Today's Leading Dramatists* (New York: Back Stage Books, 1997), 166–167.
51   Michelle Petersen, "Scripture Relevance Dramas," *Ethnodoxology* 4, no. 4 (2010):22–31.
52   Karin Barber, John Collins, and Alain Ricard, *West African Popular Theatre* (Indiana University Press, 1997), 92–116.

PREFACE

PREPARE

STEP 1

STEP 2

STEP 3

STEP 4B

STEP 5

STEP 6

STEP 7

CLOSING

PREFACE

PREPARE

STEP 1

STEP 2

STEP 3

STEP 4B

STEP 5

STEP 6

STEP 7

CLOSING

DESCRIBE HOW PARTICIPANTS USE THEIR PERFORMANCE SPACE

Watch a dramatic event, or record it and watch it again later. While watching the video, or immediately after watching the play, note answers to these questions:

- Is there always an imaginary "*fourth wall*" between performers and audience? If there is, the audience does not interact with the performers, and performers pretend they are living their lives without the audience present.
- Is there *no wall* between performers and audience, so at any time performers may interact directly with the audience, or audience members may become performers?
- Is the *wall* between performers and audience sometimes present and at other times *broken*? If it is sometimes broken, is it broken by movement, by words, or by both? If by movement, is it movement of the audience into the actors' space, or movement of the actors into the audience's space, or both? If the wall is broken verbally, do audience members speak directly to performers, or performers to audience members, or both? Is the wall broken in both directions, or only in one direction? Is it broken occasionally or frequently? Is it broken only by some characters, or by all of them?

PERFORMANCE FEATURE CATEGORIES

Performance features are observable characteristics of a performance that emerge from an event's unique combination of physical and social context and participants' actions.

SUMMARY AND RELATIONSHIP TO OTHER LENSES

Acting is to perform a role or roles by behaving in a manner suitable for a given character. Acting involves bringing to life or interpreting a character. Acting involves performing verbs. Speaking, moving, and appearance are the actor's three main observable tools. The actor's imagination is a fourth tool that is invisible.

DESCRIBE TO WHAT EXTENT ACTORS PREPARE THEIR PERFORMANCES IN ADVANCE AND TO WHAT EXTENT THEY IMPROVISE

Improvisation may refer either to making up a whole performance around a scenario without using a script, or may involve adding small elements that were not rehearsed before into a scripted performance. Different dramatic traditions accord varying importance to improvisation. Many classical Indian dramatic forms allow for very little improvisation because they value the precise reproduction of the performance tradition in the same way for every performance. Many African traditions value great amounts of improvisation for showing the versatility of the performers and for honoring interaction with the audience, so each performance is different.

PREFACE

PREPARE

STEP 1

STEP 2

STEP 3

STEP 4B

STEP 5

STEP 6

STEP 7

CLOSING

DESCRIBE THE ACTING IN A GIVEN PERFORMANCE AS REALISTIC, BRECHTIAN, OR CODIFIED

In **realistic acting** the performer models behavior on life, giving the impression of actual events occuring, and emotion is *experienced* by the actors onstage and not only *displayed*. In **Brechtian acting** the actor interprets a role but remains outside of the role and comments on the role or situation. The actor quotes the character rather than becoming the character.[53] In this and other nonrealistic acting, emotion is *displayed* rather than *experienced*. In **codified acting** a performer uses a symbol system of movements, gestures, costumes, makeup, or melodies whose meanings are set by tradition and passed down from generation to generation. Actors and audiences know the vocabulary and grammar of this symbolic system. Western mime, Chinese *jingju*, and Indian *Bharatanatyam* are codified acting systems. In Brechtian acting and codified acting, emotion is *displayed* rather than *experienced*.[54]

PREPARE FOR VOCAL FEATURE ANALYSIS

Speaking is verbal communication that has both lexical (dictionary) meaning and contextual (situational) meaning. How we understand what a character says depends on the context in which they say it.

Text is what a character says. We still call utterances text, whether they are scripted or improvised. Subtext is the implied meaning of how an actor performs the text when it is different than the plain meaning of the text. When discerning subtext, intonation carries meaning more than text. If an actor says the text, "I hate you," with the subtext "I love you," then "I love you" is what the audience understands. The audience believes the subtext more than the text. What makes intention and subtext difficult to interpret accurately cross-culturally is that different cultures convey emotions and intentions with different intonation and vocal features. The emotions we think we are picking up based on our culture's cues may actually be different in another culture until we learn the other culture's cues.

Interview a performer or audience member. Ask them to describe an instance where the text and the subtext are different. What signifies this? How does the actor or audience member know that the text and subtext differ?

---

53   Richard Schechner, *Performance Studies: An Introduction*, integrated media ed. (New York: Routledge, 2006), 180–182.
54   Ibid., 183–187.

PREFACE

PREPARE

STEP 1

STEP 2

STEP 3

STEP 4B

STEP 5

STEP 6

STEP 7

CLOSING

ASK IF CHARACTERS' WAYS OF SPEAKING INDICATE THEIR REGION(S)

Accent is a way of speaking representative of a region. Are different characters from different regions, or are all characters from the same region?

Register is the level of vocabulary and grammar that indicates the speaker's level of formality or time period. Ask if different characters have different registers or if they all use the same register. How formal is it? Is the register different in different scenes? Is this the way people speak today, or when did people speak like this?

DESCRIBE GENERAL SECTIONS OF SPEECH

Dialogue is verbal interaction between characters. **Monologue** is a speech an actor gives directly to the audience. **Soliloquy** is a speech an actor gives to himself or herself, as though thinking aloud, usually with no one else on stage. An **aside** is a line an actor gives directly to the audience while other actors are on stage, but that the other actors pretend not to hear. See which of these you can find. Do characters generally give short lines alternating rapidly back and forth? Do characters often make long speeches?

Paralinguistic vocal features involve pitch, emphasis, volume, modulation, dialect, and timbre of a performer, and the emotions, intents, or other characteristics understood by combinations of these features.

Strength or volume refers to how loudly or softly a performer speaks. Performers generally try to speak loudly enough so everyone present can hear. We can speak more loudly by breathing more deeply before we begin to let out the air we use to speak with. Explosive volume is used in shouts. Expulsive volume releases air from the lungs in a gradual way to prolong the sentence the way a singer holds out a note.[55]

Pitch refers to how high or low a performer's tone of voice is. **Quality** refers to how the performer's voice is perceived by the audience. With what adjective would someone describe the character's voice? Is it rough, scary, gentle, gravelly, squeaky, mellow, nasal, pleasing, guttural, hollow, or breathy? What kind of character speaks that way, or what does the quality of the voice say about the character? **Tempo**, **rate**, or **pace** refers to how fast or slowly a performer speaks. This can either be in regard to the duration of the words, or the length of the silences between words.[56] What does the character's use of time say about the character?

55   Jack Frakes, *Acting for Life: A Textbook on Acting* (Colorado Springs: Meriwether, 2005), 52.
56   Ibid., 48–51.

PERFORM A LINE AND GET FEEDBACK ON EMOTION AND INTENT

Choose a line from the culture's play that you are analyzing. Use different volumes, pitches, qualities, and tempos to show different emotions and different intents in the style of drama you are analyzing. Verify with a native speaker that you are communicating the intention and emotion you think you are.

IDENTIFY PARALINGUISTIC FEATURES OF EXPRESSING EMOTION

Listen back to an audio recording of a performance and verify with a native speaker what emotions are conveyed by what paralinguistic features. Do not assume that the paralinguistic features which mean certain emotions in your culture indicate the same emotions in the local culture.

DESCRIBE HOW ACTORS MODIFY THEIR APPEARANCE TO CONVEY CHARACTER

Describe the actors' **natural appearance** or inherent physique. Note how they modify their **artificial appearance**, making deliberate changes by use of masks, different hair styles, wigs, makeup, or costumes to evoke a character (see also Materials).

DESCRIBE THE EVENT'S BLOCKING

Blocking is the arrangement of all actors' movements in space in relation to one another. Blocking may be designated by a director, by improvisation, or by prior group consensus. Emotion is conveyed mainly through the face, so most blocking patterns keep actors' faces fully or partially visible to the majority of the audience. To block the scene is to tell the story through movement of the actors on stage. "Stage business" is any activity that reveals character, often using a prop. The audience's attention tends to go to the actor who is moving. Explore how participants use movement through activities like the following:

- Ask participants to tell you terms they use to describe their movements in their local language. Note how actors' movements tell you about what their characters are like and reveal the action of the story sequence.
- How do performers keep the story action visible to their audience? Try performing the same scene with different sequences of movements, and ask participants which of the blocking options shows the story events more clearly.
- How are levels or differences in height used? How do groupings of performers place emphasis on the most important places they want their audience to focus their attention? How do actors' placements at key moments help convey their emotions and intents?

PREFACE

PREPARE

STEP 1

STEP 2

STEP 3

STEP 4B

STEP 5

STEP 6

STEP 7

CLOSING

PREFACE
PREPARE
STEP 1
STEP 2
STEP 3
STEP 4B
STEP 5
STEP 6
STEP 7
CLOSING

CONTENT

Content refers to the subject matter in artistic activity.

SUMMARY AND RELATIONSHIP TO OTHER LENSES

Because drama is usually based on showing a story, its content relates integrally to almost everything else and may include elements of visual arts, music, dance, and verbal arts.

DETERMINE THE IDEA, THEME, OR DRAMATIC PREMISE

Idea, theme, and **dramatic premise** all refer to the message or main idea the play is seeking to communicate. Interview audience member(s), the director, or performer(s) to learn what they believe to be the main idea, theme, or dramatic premise of the play. Also write down your own understanding of what the main ideas of the play are. The descriptions below may help you in your exploration.

The message may be overt, as when it is stated at the beginning or end by a narrator or character, or it may require effort on the audience's part to ascertain, as when it is shown rather than stated. Episodic plots in particular emphasize idea or theme, as this idea is what links the scenes into a coherent whole.

Dramatic premise is usually revealed through plot or the structured sequence of events. In climactic plots, dramatic premise is the idea or message that the play is seeking to communicate by the string of events that unfold. It is like a theme or idea but it may be stated as *an action* that leads to a *result*. The dramatic premise determines how the play is put together structurally in terms of cause and effect, such as "greediness leads to loneliness."[57] A performance's theme, idea, or dramatic premise may choose to either support or call into question a culture's values, assumptions, and norms. Drama may change how audiences view their lives.

A **metaphor** is an image comparing something concrete with an abstract idea. In *Fiddler on the Roof*, the character of the fiddler is a metaphor for the precariousness of the Jewish way of life in Russia.

An **image system** is a visual image repeated in various ways to convey an extended metaphor. In Peter Jackson's film *The Lord of the Rings*, for example, the white tree of Gondor is a metaphor of the King's authority. The return of the King is foreshadowed or hinted at when Sam and Frodo see a toppled statue's head crowned in white flowers and Sam says, "Look, Mr. Frodo. The King has got his crown again." As the dead tree before the throne of Gondor begins to flower, this represents hope of the King's return, ironically just as Lord

---

57   Buzz McLaughlin, The Playwright's Process: Learning the Craft from Today's Leading Dramatists (New York: Back Stage Books, 1997), 31–41.

Denethor, the Guardian of the throne, loses hope and commits suicide. The white tree is in full bloom at King Aragorn's coronation. The image of the white flowers is repeated in various ways as an image system for hope and perseverance.

UNDERLYING SYMBOLIC SYSTEMS

Underlying Symbolic Systems refer to the grammatical and social rules and structures that guide participants' actions in artistic activity.

SUMMARY AND RELATIONSHIP TO OTHER LENSES

Systems like plot structure, idea, genre, character, and characterization provide grammatical structure for performing and understanding dramatic performances.

DESCRIBE AN EVENT'S PLOT STRUCTURE

Transcribe an audio or video recording of an event. If it is not in a language you know well, work with a bilingual speaker of the language to translate it for you. Describe the plot structure as climactic, episodic, or cyclic, using these descriptions:

Climactic plots are the most often found type of plot. They begin with exposition of a problem, build on a series of minor crises to a major climax or turning point, and lead to a resolution. Climactic plots may interweave subplots or secondary stories with their own smaller crises and resolutions. The basic structure is action-reaction or cause-effect.[58] Climactic plots use cause and effect to arrange events in a story. The audience wants to find out what happens next. For this type of plot, "The cornerstone of dramatic engagement is suspense."[59]

Episodic plots contain scenes linked by theme or idea more than by actions and reactions. The series of events is not necessarily linked by cause and effect. Many history plays, myths, and folk tales are episodic.

Cyclic plots contain conflicts that are intentionally unresolved. The play ends with characters in the same situation as when the play began. Cyclic plots are the rarest type of plot in the world. They are found mostly in Bali and in some modern Western theater.[60]

58   Michael L. Greenwald, Roger Schulz, and Roberto Dario Pomo, *The Longman Anthology of Drama and Theater: A Global Perspective* (New York: Longman, 2001), 25.
59   Jeffrey Hatcher, *The Art and Craft of Playwriting* (Cincinnati: Story Press, 1996), 14.
60   Michael L. Greenwald, Roger Schulz, and Roberto Dario Pomo, *The Longman Anthology of Drama and Theater*, 25.

PREFACE

PREPARE

STEP 1

STEP 2

STEP 3

STEP 4B

STEP 5

STEP 6

STEP 7

CLOSING

PREFACE

PREPARE

STEP 1

STEP 2

STEP 3

STEP 4B

STEP 5

STEP 6

STEP 7

CLOSING

DESCRIBE AN EVENT'S TEMPORAL STRUCTURE

Temporal structure is the arrangement of events in time. It can also refer to the length of the event and what length is preferred. In Liberia, a dramatic event that ran forty-five minutes was almost an insult to the people, who expected at least ninety minutes. At forty-five minutes, they were just getting settled in for the evening. Time within the play may proceed linearly (chronologically) or cyclically (repetitively), or temporal structure may make use of flashbacks or other jumps in time. From the audience's point of view, how long do they expect the full performance to last?

IDENTIFY AND DESCRIBE A PLAY'S PLOT ELEMENTS

Plot elements are parts of the plot such as back story, exposition, conflict, climax, and resolution. From the transcription you made earlier, use the definitions below to describe the play's plot elements. Ask performers or other participants when your understandings are unclear.

Back story is what happened to the characters before the play began. The audience infers what events happened earlier, and what characters are like. This helps them understand the rest of the story. In Senegal, for example, when an audience sees a play with a rabbit character, they know from prior stories that the rabbit is a clever trickster.

Exposition tells the audience the back story and situates them through performers' conversations and actions or through visual design that sets the scene.

Conflict is created within a character or between characters either by characters seeking opposing goals or by adverse circumstances a character seeks to overcome. External conflict is opposition to a character who does not doubt himself or herself. Internal conflict is struggle within a character to make a decision, control personal emotions or determine values.

The **climax** of the play occurs when the central character makes a decision which will lead to a resolution of the conflict.

The play's **dénouement** or **resolution** shows how the conflict ends.

DESCRIBE THE DEGREE OF PLOT MALLEABILITY

Participate in or observe the creation of an event to determine whether its plot is *malleable* or *fixed*. Plot structure may be found and formed by a scriptwriter or formed on the spot as a collaborative effort by performers and audience. The majority of plot elements may be decided in advance, or only the general outline may be decided in advance, and the rest of the performance may be improvised in interaction with the audience. In **literary drama**, the outcome is decided in advance, and the audience has no input into the course of events; in much **drama for development**, the audience participates in deciding the outcome of the play. The role of the audience operates along a continuum, and the audience may have a greater or lesser input into the minor or major features of structure design.

PREFACE

PREPARE

STEP 1

STEP 2

STEP 3

STEP 4B

STEP 5

STEP 6

STEP 7

CLOSING

IDENTIFY WHO HOLDS CREATIVE CONTROL IN DETERMINING THE PLAY'S STRUCTURE AND MAIN POINT

Creative control may reside with one or more participants. In dramatic traditions where performers memorize written scripts, the structure and meanings of the play come from **authorial intent**. They may also result from **directorial intent**, **performer intent**, or **audience intent**. The audience is particularly influential in participatory theater and theater for development, where they help determine the outcome of a play. To learn about creative control, ask participants questions like these:

- Who decided which idea would be the main point of the play? Was more than one person involved?
- How did you decide to show the main idea: through how the conflict resolves, through the idea that links the scenes, through images or symbols, or through some combination of these? Who determined it?

DESCRIBE EACH CHARACTER'S TYPE

A **character** is a make-believe person represented by an actor in a drama. Types of characters and their means of characterization vary according to their intended relationship to everyday reality. A play is usually about a main character that changes. A **character arc** is the progress or regress of a character as he or she changes throughout a story. Characters begin with certain viewpoints and characteristics and, through their actions and choices, their viewpoints and characteristics develop. List each character in the event and decide whether each is archetypal, individualized, stock, personified, or self-represented. Decide who the main characters are, and if they have a character arc showing change, what that change is, and what decisions signal it.

An **archetype** is the original pattern or model of a character on which later archetypal characters are based, like a cookie cutter from which the same shape of individual cookies may come. Example archetypes include the fairy godmother, the hero, the trickster, the witch, or the wise old man. Merlin is *an* archetypal wizard in the Anglo-Saxon tradition from *the* (perhaps universal) wizard archetype, but Merlin should not be described as *the* archetype for any other culture for *their* wizards.

An **individualized** or **developed character** reveals his or her individualized personality, life history, values, physical attributes, and family background. A developed character does not always do what the audience expects. The better the audience gets to know a character, the better developed that character is.

Stereotypical or **stock character** is a simplified or generalized, predictable representation of a character without subtlety. Stereotypical characters and stock characters do exactly what the audience expects them to do. Actors represent stereotypical characters by drawing on a smaller set of

PREFACE

PREPARE

STEP 1

STEP 2

STEP 3

STEP 4B

STEP 5

STEP 6

STEP 7

CLOSING

recognizable performance features than when representing individualized characters. Characters in a melodrama, for example, have exaggerated traits such as dastardliness and heroism, reducing the range of emotions and actions produced by the actor. In general, stock characters are stronger for creating humorous comedies than for creating serious dramas. "Stereotypical character" has a negative connotation if an individualized character was expected by the audience but not achieved by the actor, while "stock character" has a neutral connotation: while the actor does not give the character an individual personality, none is expected by the performance tradition. Chinese opera, for example, has expected stock characters such as the man, the woman, the white face representing an aggressive male such as a bandit or warrior, and the clown. Some would call these archetypes. In plays with developed characters, there is often not time to develop the personality of every character well, so less central characters are often stock characters. In the Western performance tradition, a good actor can make even a small stock character into an interesting individualized character.

Personifications are characters who represent abstract concepts, such as Good Deeds, Beauty, or Strength in the medieval English morality play *Everyman*.

A **self-represented character** is when the actor is playing himself or herself, but not in this moment. The actor shows himself or herself as he or she was or will be, as though that time could be brought into this moment. Storytellers telling about their day at work are self-representing their character.

DETERMINE WHAT CHARACTERS WANT

What characters want, called their **motivation, objective,** or **intention,** determines what they do during a play. What does each character want? What obstacles are standing in the way? How are they going about overcoming those obstacles to get what they want? How do they show this? How does the audience react to different characters trying to get what they want?

DETERMINE BROAD ROLES OF THE CHARACTER(S)

Reflect on each character, using the discussion below to decide whether it is a narrator, antagonist, or protagonist.

A **narrator** is a storyteller in a play. A narrator speaks directly to the audience to set the stage, provide transitional material between parts of a story, or give the moral at the end. This person may be called different things in different drama traditions; in *Therukoothu* drama in India, the narrator role is served by the stage manager (through song) and the buffoon (who humorously comments on the action). Other traditions have no narrator.

Protagonists are characters the audience identifies with and wants to succeed. A play is usually about a main protagonist who changes in some way during the play. A **focal character** is a character the audience pays attention to and with whom the audience is most emotionally concerned. It is usually the protagonist, but may sometimes be someone that the audience wants to fail. **Antagonists** are characters whose desires or efforts conflict with the protagonist. The audience does not want them to succeed. A play is usually about a conflict opposing the objectives of the antagonist(s) and protagonist(s). If the antagonist is the focal character, his or her emotions and ambitions are not meant to be empathized with by the audience. Sometimes the antagonist may be an idea, a force, or an event rather than a person.

DESCRIBE THE ACTOR'S RELATIONSHIP TO HIS OR HER CHARACTER

Interview an actor, asking questions like these:

- Do you actually feel the character's emotions, or do you imitate what it looks like to feel the character's emotions?
- Do you like the character? Is he similar to you?

DETERMINE WHETHER CHARACTERIZATION IS DIRECT OR INDIRECT

Characterization is the underlying model guiding the creation and representation of a character or set of characters. It is shown by dialogue, through action, by appearance, and by the choices the character makes. **Direct** or **explicit characterization** relies on the performers to tell the audience what the characters are like through statements a narrator makes about a character, statements another character makes about a character, and statements the character makes. **Indirect** or **implicit characterization** relies on the audience to deduce for themselves what the character's traits are through the character's actions, choice of words, clothing, appearance, and interaction with other characters.

DETERMINE THE FRAME OF THE PLAY

Frame is the overall purpose of an event and lets the audience know how to interpret it.[61] Clues early on must let the audience know in what ways they are expected to respond. The title of the performance or the first few interchanges usually let the audience know if the play is comedic or tragic, for education or for entertainment, for community change or to uphold established community values. Generally, audiences are unhappy if the beginning of a performance does not give them a clear idea of what kind of performance it is and therefore how they should respond to the performance. A play may have more than one frame, for instance, both to entertain and to educate. Differing frames include different expectations of what the audience should expect out of the story and how to interact appropriately with the performers. The audience has differing expectations if a story is about love, growing up, family problems, adventure, history, science fiction, or fantasy.

---

61   Steve Tillis, *Rethinking Folk Drama* (Westport, CT/London: Greenwood Press, 1999), 85.

PREFACE

PREPARE

STEP 1

STEP 2

STEP 3

STEP 4B

STEP 5

STEP 6

STEP 7

CLOSING

PREFACE

PREPARE

STEP 1

STEP 2

STEP 3

STEP 4B

STEP 5

STEP 6

STEP 7

CLOSING

Interview a director or actor involved in the event you watched or recorded, and ask questions like these:

- What elements does this type of play need to have?
- Ask audience members: Why did you come to the event? How well did it meet your expectations? How is it different from another type?

EXPLORE THE TYPE OF THE EVENT FURTHER

Type (often referred to as **genre** in discussions of drama) consists of a cluster of attributes that lead the audience to expect certain sets of performance features and respond in set ways. By performing any of the research activities in "Look at an Event's Forms" (**Part A**), you are already identifying this cluster of attributes. We provide here a brief discussion of insights deriving from people looking at types with a large number of dramatic features.

The first major type distinction is if the play is literary or oral. In literary drama, a scriptwriter or scriptwriters create a text to be brought to life through performance, and a director coaches performers how to bring their performances to life. In oral traditions, a group creates collectively without using a written script.

Each of these broad types may be described by more specific terms. Stories in the same type share the same kinds of characters and plots. Types of a given culture need to be understood from an **emic** (insider's) perspective through researching the categories of performance in a community. For example, the two most popular kinds of Sanskrit drama in India are *nataka* (heroic) drama drawing from history or mythology to portray stories of gods and kings, and *prakarana* (social) drama. Research the terms used to describe kinds of performances in your community.

Historical analysis of many plays will allow you to discover how traditions of drama have developed over time and influenced one another both within a given culture and cross-culturally.

Etic terms (terms from the researcher's own culture) may be used by way of comparison to describe cross-cultural performance to dramatists from the researcher's own community. In Western drama, some broad types are **comedy**, intended to cause the audience to laugh and ending happily; **drama**, in the more specific sense of a serious story; **tragedy**, evoking sadness and an unhappy ending; **tragicomedy**, involving both tragic and comedic aspects; and **morality plays**, intending to give an example how to live or how not to live.

Aristotle described drama in terms of six parameters: character, action, idea, language, music, and spectacle (what is seen). Western theater is based on Aristotle, but Indian theater is based on the *Natyasastra*, which has its own definitions of what makes up a good plot—five stages (*avasthas*)—that must be followed. If any are omitted, there are rules for what else must be omitted.

INTERACTIONS WITH OTHER DOMAINS

Dramatic elements often interact closely with musical and other sound elements.

DETERMINE THE WAYS MUSICAL ELEMENTS INTERACT WITH DRAMATIC ELEMENTS

Reflect on the dramatic and musical features of the event. Decide if any of the following occur:

- Songs may form a feature of dialogue allowing the plot to progess or showing what characters are like.
- Songs or instrumental music may comment on the plot, serve as an interlude, or provide a chance to involve the audience.
- Ambient music may be used to set a scene.
- A recognizable musical theme (*leitmotif*) may serve to refer to a certain character.
- Sound effects produced deliberately by actors or other participants may be realistic to the action or representative of it.

DANCE IN AN EVENT

This section will help you describe more completely the ways participants move in patterned ways in an event. To understand this section best, you should first work through some of the activities in "Look at an Event's Forms" (**Part A**). We use the same seven lenses here, but introduce descriptive categories particularly pertinent to dance. You will gather your discoveries about the dance characteristics of this event and others like it in the Community Arts Profile.

Dance features are recognized visually and performed viscerally with auditory and visual awareness. An observer sees the performers, the environment in which they are moving, their relationship to other dancers, their relationship to any other participants and collaborators (such as singers or musicians), their relationship to props and costumes, the use of their bodies in the space surrounding them (kinesphere), and their use of storytelling or abstract ideas in movement. A performer feels his or her own body moving in its personal kinesphere and the environment, hears the atmosphere (e.g., music, clapping, vocalizations, breathing, impact of feet on

PREFACE

PREPARE

STEP 1

STEP 2

STEP 3

STEP 4B

STEP 5

STEP 6

STEP 7

CLOSING

PREFACE

PREPARE

STEP 1

STEP 2

STEP 3

STEP 4B

STEP 5

STEP 6

STEP 7

CLOSING

floor, etc.), and responds to it. Skilled performers also understand the purposes of the genre of the event in which they are dancing and sense physical and spiritual changes in their own bodies and in the environment.

It is often a very different thing to observe a dance versus participate in a dance. A dancer may recognize that the important thing about a step is its weight and contact with the ground (quality and dynamic), while an observer may believe that the important thing about a step is its direction in space (function and aesthetic). Watching, interviewing, and doing are all important aspects of movement analysis and documentation.

SPACE

Space is the location, demarcation, and physical characteristics of the area used, which can affect the form of artistic communication.

SUMMARY AND RELATIONSHIP TO OTHER LENSES

The space allotted to human movement in an event may have profound effects on how participants move. A large space in proportion to the number of dancers, for example, allows larger movements covering more physical space. In addition, features of the space also allow or restrict certain kinds of movement, as walls permit dancers to push off or climb upward.

DRAW A FLOOR PLAN OF PART OF THE DANCE

Choose a one-minute excerpt from a video recording of the event that includes a representative movement pattern. Include the boundaries of the space, permanent objects, and "snapshots" of dancers beginning and ending a movement pattern and their pathway to get from point A to point B.

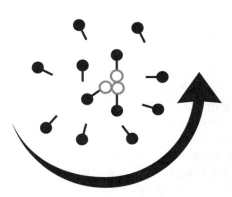

Figure 5 gives an example of a simple floor plan. It depicts eight men (shown as filled circles with a line pointing the way they are facing, e.g.,) in an outer circle facing inward, three men playing drums in the middle (drums shown as empty concentric circles), and one walking around within the circle. The large arrow shows that the outer circle of men are moving together in a counter-clockwise direction.

Figure 6: Sample Floor Plan

MATERIALS

Materials are all of the tangible things associated with an event.

SUMMARY AND RELATIONSHIP TO OTHER LENSES

Costumes and props are the most common objects associated with patterned movement. These interact primarily with dance performance features, allowing the dancer to accentuate, extend, or otherwise modify his or her movements. Floppy grass rings attached at the ankle, for example, emphasize a dancer's forceful stomps on the ground. In addition, a dancer with a cane can lean farther than one without.

IDENTIFY ALL MOVEMENT-RELATED OBJECTS AND THEIR FUNCTIONS

Look at the list of objects you created in the Materials section of "Look at an Event's Forms " (**Part A**) or make one now. Watch a video recording of the event with one of its dancers, answering questions like these:

- Which objects are in direct or indirect physical contact with a dancer? For each, describe the interaction between the dancer and object in terms of the parts of the body and object in contact, and motions of each.
- What visual effect(s) results from the dancer's interaction with each object? Does it magnify, reduce, or otherwise modify the dancer's movement?

SHAPE OF THE EVENT THROUGH TIME

Shape of an event refers primarily to its constituent segments, organized hierarchically.

SUMMARY AND RELATIONSHIP TO OTHER LENSES

In "Look at an Event's Forms" (**Part A**), you may have described an event with dance content like a concert, festival, religious service, or ritual. In this section, we focus on any concentrated periods of dance in the event, which we define as follows:

Dance: A composition consisting minimally of patterned movement.

We describe the shape of a dance in terms of its total dance form and constituent segments. Note that there is commonly an intimate link between musical and movement features in performance, so similar techniques for analyzing music will likely work with dance. This system of hierarchical segmentation is drawn from a more detailed

PREFACE

PREPARE

STEP 1

STEP 2

STEP 3

STEP 4B

STEP 5

STEP 6

STEP 7

CLOSING

expansion available in Giurchescu and Kröschlová.[62] From highest to lowest place in the hierarchy, these are the segments:

Total dance form: The highest structural level resulting in an organic and autonomous entity through the summation of all the integrated structural units.

Part: The highest structural unit within the total dance form.

Strophe: A closed higher form that is comprised of phrases and organized according to the grouping principle.

Section: An intermediate macrostructure consisting of a linking or grouping of phrases. A one-phrase section decomposes directly into motifs.

Phrase: The simplest compositional unit that has sense for the people and by which dances or dance genres are identified.

Motif: The smallest significant grammatical sequence of movements having meaning for both the dancers and their society and for the dance genre within a given dance system.

DETERMINE THE FORM OF A DANCE

You must first identify a dance. You can do this by choosing a segment you have already elicited and recorded as part of a collection. Another method is to look at a time line of an event that you created following guidelines in "Look at an Event's Forms" (**Part A**), noting the beginning and ending times of a dance. Watch a recording of this segment many times, marking repeated sections and points of change. If you can, transcribe its major movement segments.

After becoming familiar with the dance, note in the Community Arts Profile whether its form follows any of the following common patterns:

Chain forms: Movement segments are lined up one after another, and their number and relationship is not important. Subcategories include the following:

- **Homogeneous chain form**: Unlimited repetition of one segment.
- **Variation chain form**: Each repeated segment is a variation of the basic unit. **Heterogeneous chain form**: Individual segments are different and without consistent organization.
- **Rondo form**: Regular recurrence of one or more basic segments in a certain order.

Grouping forms: Movement segments have a precise number of components set in a fixed and contrastive relationship. Subcategories include the following:

- **Two-segment form**: Two equally important and contrasting segments tightly bound together in a stable balance.

---

62   Anca Giurchescu and Eva Kröschlová, "Theory and Method of Dance Form Analysis," in *Dance Structures: Perspectives on the Analysis of Human Movement*, ed. Adrienne Kaeppler and Elsi Evancich Dunin (Budapest: Akadémiai Kiadó, 2007), 21–52.

PREFACE PREPARE STEP 1 STEP 2 STEP 3 STEP 4B STEP 5 STEP 6 STEP 7 CLOSING

PREFACE

PREPARE

STEP 1

STEP 2

STEP 3

STEP 4B

STEP 5

STEP 6

STEP 7

CLOSING

- **Three-segment form**: Three equally important and contrasting segments with a fixed relation of interdependence.
- **Multisegment form**: A variable number of more or less equally important segments often framed by an introductory and closing segment.

PARTICIPANT ORGANIZATION

Participant Organization highlights the people involved in an event, in terms of the roles they play, the ways they interact with each other through time, and how they use the physical space around them.

SUMMARY AND RELATIONSHIP TO OTHER LENSES

Dancers are often set apart in some way from the rest of an event. In Western concert dance, the stage is clearly delineated from audience seating (e.g., proscenium stage, thrust stage, black box, etc.). Community ceremonial dancers may be in the center of a gathering, or the dancers may surround the community members. Recreational dancers may move in the whole space with observers surrounding them in scattered seating.

DESCRIBE THE BASIC ORGANIZATION OF DANCERS

Watch a video recording of an event, and note which of the three following categories describes the dancers:

Solo: One person is moving, whether truly alone or in the midst of a nonmoving group. This dance may be related to a rite of passage, exceptional virtuosity, social status, etc.

Ensemble: A small group of people moving either in unison, counterpoint, or in contact with one another and/or a soloist.

Corps: A large group moving in unison, canon (dancers repeating exactly the movements of a first dancer, one after the other) or other large coordinated effort.

DESCRIBE HOW DANCERS RELATE TO EACH OTHER

Watch a video recording of an event with one or more of the dancers, and observe and ask questions like these, when appropriate:

Group relationships: How do people express relationships as individuals and within groups? What does it mean for a single dancer to be broad and expansive versus minute and articulated? What similarities and contrasts exist within group movement and/or individual performances? What is the level

PREFACE

PREPARE

STEP 1

STEP 2

STEP 3

STEP 4B

STEP 5

STEP 6

STEP 7

CLOSING

of awareness and/or physical contact between performers, props, and/or an invisible/visible focal point of the performance?

Solo: Does the performer keep his or her body parts close or use the environment minimally; i.e., small extension / near-reach, such as working with a prop? Are they purposefully aware of their surroundings or are they internally focused?

Solo within an ensemble or corps: Are the performers aware of everyone, or just a few? Is the kinesphere and environment used in medium extension / mid-reach (e.g., greeting one another or in a circle dance)? Or used in large extension / far-reach (e.g., a teacher addressing students or a performer addressing the audience)?

Ensemble within a corps: Is there a main group that has more complex movement than a secondary group that may use simpler movement?

Group agreement: When does the group's movement begin? Is it dictated by a planned sound or visual cue, perhaps from a lead speaker, singer, instrument player, dancer, or community member? Or is it open-ended and determined by the performers themselves in silent agreement and awareness?

The following concepts may help you discuss these relationships more clearly:[63]

Awareness: Knowing something/someone is somewhere, demonstrating conscious perception.

Addressing: Acknowledging something/someone is somewhere, demonstrating conscious interaction.

Transient relationships: Awareness and/or addressing that comes and goes throughout the performance.

Retained relationships: Awareness and/or addressing that is maintained and sustained throughout the performance.

Canceled relationships: Awareness and/or addressing that ends at a specific time during the performance.

PERFORMANCE FEATURE CATEGORIES

Performance features are observable characteristics of a performance that emerge from an event's unique combination of physical and social context and participants' actions.

SUMMARY AND RELATIONSHIP TO OTHER LENSES

Actions that produce movement can be initiated by gravity (e.g., arm raised and then released to drop), outside forces (e.g., another dancer in contact, dancer holding part of his or her own body, body part in contact with a prop or architecture, etc.), and voluntary muscle directing the movement in specific styles (e.g., loose and free, bound and controlled, etc.).

---

63   Ann Hutchinson Guest, *Labanotation: The System of Analyzing and Recording Movement* (New York: Routledge, 2005), 296–298.

IDENTIFY PARTS OF THE BODY INVOLVED IN PATTERNED MOVEMENT

Conceptualize the body as an instrument with different parts, perhaps six "limbs": the head, the tail, the two arms, and the two legs all connected to the "center," "core," or "trunk" of the torso. Observe a dance and identify the main initiators (gravity, outside forces, voluntary muscle) and how one or multiple initiators "divide" the different body parts. Use the following as a starting point (we've included notation conventions):[64]

 Breath: All movements derive from breath, but some very small movements are initiated or guided by the breath, such as an ensemble taking a breath before commencing a particular movement phrase, then returning to stillness, and then the breath initiating the next movement phrase.

 Head-tail: A clear connection between the head and the pelvis, perhaps the head is weaving side to side, and the spine weaves as a result, culminating in a large pelvic sway.

 Core-distal: A clear connection between the "center" or "core" of the body and the limbs of the arms and legs, usually very three-dimensional and asymmetrical; often considered a "gathering," or drawing inward, motion followed by a "scattering," or releasing outward, such as a performer hunching over a focal point and then throwing himself or herself away from the focal point. Note the dot highlighting this central position.

 Homologous: A clear connection between the upper half of the body (head, arms) and the lower half of the body (pelvis, legs), usually very two-dimensional and symmetrical, such as a rhythmic, repeated bowing at the waist or a jump into the air that "scissors" the body with the legs and torso coming forward.

 Homolateral: A clear connection between the right side and left side of the body, usually very two-dimensional and symmetrical, such as the right elbow coming toward the right knee and the same motion repeated on the left side.

 Contralateral: A clear connection between the upper right (usually arm) and lower left (usually leg) of the body and vice versa, such as walking or exaggerated walking-like movements; e.g., when the left arm extends upward and the right leg contracts or lifts off the ground.

64   Peggy Hackney, *Making Connections: Total Body Integration through Bartenieff Fundamentals* (New York: Routledge, 2000), 71–218.

PREFACE

PREPARE

STEP 1

STEP 2

STEP 3

STEP 4B

STEP 5

STEP 6

STEP 7

CLOSING

PREFACE

PREPARE

STEP 1

STEP 2

STEP 3

STEP 4B

STEP 5

STEP 6

STEP 7

CLOSING

DESCRIBE BROAD CHARACTERISTICS OF PATTERNED MOVEMENT

When viewing a live performance or a video performance or imitating the movements, decide what the "big-picture" happenings are by observing the following:[65]

- Is the movement constant, or are there moments of stillness?
- Does the performer(s) travel or remain stationary? If traveling, is it in a straight path, curved or circling path, or a meandering/free-form path?
- Is the performer always facing a particular direction, or does the facing change? If facings change, does it affect the method of traveling or remaining in place?
- If there is turning, is there a pattern in how many revolutions (around a performer's own axis), or is there spiraling closer or farther away from a focal point, or does turning occur in degrees, or is the performer turning while traveling on a path?
- If there is jumping, are there gestures in the air or jumping while traveling? How many or how big are the jumps? Are they always one foot to the other, one foot to the same foot, two feet, one foot to two feet or vice versa, etc.?
- Does the whole body (or parts of the body) flex or contract and/or extend or elongate and/or fold (such as the knee or other hinge joint)?
- Are there rotations of the whole body or parts of the body? Does the body revolve around a vertical axis (like a spin while standing), a horizontal axis (like a cartwheel), a sagittal axis (moving through a vertical plane, like a somersault), or are there revolutions that occur when the body is on the floor (rolling, spinning, etc.)?
- How is the dancer supported or connected to the ground—feet, hands, torso, stilts or other props, knees, forearms? How is the sense of weight/gravity and balance treated—"on" center, "off" center, tilting, falling?
- Do the parts of the body seem to have relationships to other body parts or other performers, such as grasping, sliding, enclosing nearness, approaching, retreating, supporting?
- Are gestures (non-weight bearing) making designs or shapes in the air (or elsewhere), making paths, occurring symmetrically or asymmetrically?
- Do the performers seem to operating in an axis of physical space (e.g., "forward" is toward an audience, "backward" is away from the audience, "up" is toward the heavens, "down" is toward the ground), or do the performers operate in an axis of personal space—especially if the body has moments of being on the ground (not supported by the feet)—(e.g., "forward" is always in front of the face/chest, "backward" is always toward the back, "up" is above the head, "down" is toward the feet)?

- Check to see if the performer moves in ways relating to their personal space or kinesphere primarily (or secondarily) in one or several of the following ways:[66]
  - One-dimensional or one directional "pull": forward/backward, side/side, up/down (often a pin-like posture), as if standing within a life-size octahedron and touching the connecting points.
  - Two-dimensional or two directions "pull": forward and up/down, backward and up/down, side and up/down, forward and side/side, backward and side/side (often a wall-like posture in the vertical "door," sagittal "wheel," and horizontal "table" planes), as if standing within a life-size icosahedron (i.e., with twenty plane faces) and touching the connecting points.
  - Three-dimensional or three directions "pull": forward/side / up or down, backward/side / up or down, as if standing within a life-size cube and touching the connecting points—can include ball-like or screw-like postures.

IDENTIFY CHARACTERISTIC TYPES OF MOVEMENT PHRASING

Movements are performed with a particular quality of energy or intensity that may vary from performer to performer and which can make the same movement performed with a different phrasing both look and feel different. Identifying phrasing is a subjective interpretation but can assist in understanding phrase types that are valued, commonly used, or rarely used within a culture or performer's movement style.[67] Phrasing types may be used consecutively (one at a time) or simultaneously (multiples or overlaps).

Even: Maintaining the same level of intensity—most easily identified with slow, steady movement but quick movements can also be even if the intensity remains the same.

Increasing: Energy starting at one level and going to a more intense level, which can also end with an **impact** or sudden stop (either of strong or light accent), such as an inhale that leads to a shout or a stomp (increasing, impact), or a spin that starts slow and gets faster and faster (increasing).

Decreasing: Intensity starting at a high energy level and becoming less, which can also begin with an **impulse** or outburst (either of strong or light accent), such as a sharp gasp followed by an exhale (impulse, decreasing), or a flailing arm that gradually becomes still.

Increasing-decreasing: Builds energy up and then diminishes; the building and diminishing can be of equal time (symmetrical intensity; e.g., jogging into a run in one minute and then returning to a jog in one minute), or one may take longer or shorter than the other (asymmetrical intensity; e.g., breathing in quickly and breathing out slowly). Can also include impacts or impulses.

Decreasing-increasing: Diminishes intensity and then builds intensity; the diminishing and building can be of equal time (symmetrical intensity; e.g., kicks starting very "loose" for ten seconds and then becoming very "tight" for ten seconds), or one may take longer or shorter than the other (asymmetrical

66   See http://www.mindspark.biz/zome_platonic.shtml.
67   Vera Maletic, *Dance Dynamics: Effort and Phrasing Workbook* (Columbus, OH: Grade A Notes, 2004), 57–95.

PREFACE

PREPARE

STEP 1

STEP 2

STEP 3

STEP 4B

STEP 5

STEP 6

STEP 7

CLOSING

PREFACE

PREPARE

STEP 1

STEP 2

STEP 3

STEP 4B

STEP 5

STEP 6

STEP 7

CLOSING

intensity; e.g., a flippant gesture goes on for several measures and becomes a very firm gesture within one measure). Can also include impulses or impacts.

Accented: Spurts of intensity or energy that can be repeated with pauses or stillness in between each spurt, which can be strong (such as flamenco dancing) or light (such as typing on a keyboard).

Vibratory: A series of quick and repetitive movements that can be repeated at various "wavelengths," which can be strong (such as whole body convulsions) or light (such as a shoulder shimmy).

Resilient: Energy that plays with gravity, emphasizing the strength or heaviness and/or the lightness or "weightlessness" of a movement. Variations fall into three categories:

- **Elasticity**: Equal balance between strength and light, like bouncing a basketball down the length of a court.
- **Buoyancy**: Demonstrates the lightness more clearly and has a rebounding quality like jumping in the air and "hovering" for a moment.
- **Weight**: Demonstrates the strength of gravity and releases into the ground, like jumping in the air and spending more energy on the ground than in the air.

IDENTIFY CHARACTERISTIC TYPES OF MOVEMENT DYNAMICS OR EFFORTS

While Phrasing can be used to identify movement energy or intensity, Dynamics are used to identify movement quality or engagement of effort. It is the nature of individual performers to use multiple variations of movement quality, but it is possible for particular qualities to be highlighted and become more prominent than others, and these prominent dynamics can be used to identify existing movements and assist in creating new movements. Dynamics or Efforts deal primarily with Space, Time, and Weight (Flow will not be emphasized here, as it is easy to confuse with Phrasing).[68]

Dynamics can be categorized broadly as Efforts (Space, Time, Weight) that are **fighting** (i.e., resisting gravity, momentum, etc.) or **indulging** (i.e., giving in to gravity, momentum, etc.). Certain Efforts have affinities to other Efforts but all Efforts can be combined in a variety of ways. The pelvis is a good indicator of Dynamic or Effort because it is often the core or base of the majority of movement.

Space: Deals primarily with how the performer thinks of and uses traveling through the physical space, either **directly** (particular, planned, thought-out) or **indirectly** (meandering, allowing other factors to guide). For example, Direct Space controls ("fights"), such as crossing a room or going around an object to reach another object or person, and Indirect Space allows ("indulges") other things to occur while en route to a particular object or person. Space-related movements tend to be but are not always horizontally oriented movements.

---

68   See ibid.

Step 4B: Explore the Event's Genre(s) through Artistic Domain Categories

133

PREFACE

PREPARE

STEP 1

STEP 2

STEP 3

STEP 4B

STEP 5

STEP 6

STEP 7

CLOSING

Time: Works with a performer's intuition or decision making while moving, either **suddenly** (alert, immediate) or **sustained** (calm, lingering). For example, Sudden Time may mean a quick change ("fighting") in direction in response to a music shift, and Sustained Time may mean a change in direction in a more casual manner ("indulging") to the same music shift. Time-related movements tend to be but are not always sagittally oriented movements.

Weight: How a performer senses and uses gravity, either in a **strong** sense (firm, concentrated, grounded) or a **light** sense (delicate, refined, tender). For example, Strong Weight appears to be carrying a heavy burden and "fighting" it, while Light Weight appears to be unhindered ("indulging") by any affect of gravity. Weight-related movements tend to be but are not always vertically oriented movements.

CONTENT

Content refers to the subject matter in artistic activity.

SUMMARY AND RELATIONSHIP TO OTHER LENSES

Dance is a very interdisciplinary art form, often overlapping with music and drama but can also include vocal arts (spoken song or text is part of the dance) and visual arts (costumes, props, scenery). Since collaboration is crucial to its creation and performance, it is often difficult to dissect or separate "pure" dance from other art forms. Dances are often special events, even when they are performed frequently, and can range in content and elaboration from telling stories, parables, didactic lessons, reliving/remembering histories, to symbolizing and portraying abstract ideas or spiritual happenings.

Content can dictate how the other lenses function. For example, a mourning dance will use space, participant organization, etc., differently than a celebration dance; mourning dances may be respectful movements in a confined space, while a celebration dance may be exuberant movements in an elaborate space.

IDENTIFY EFFECTS OF DIFFERENT CONTENT ON MOVEMENT

Using multiple live performances or video recordings of multiple performances, observe and describe all of the lenses, especially Participant Organization. Notice how Phrasing, Dynamics, etc., vary depending on the content or subject matter, and articulate what are the clearest variations.

PREFACE

PREPARE

STEP 1

STEP 2

STEP 3

STEP 4B

STEP 5

STEP 6

STEP 7

CLOSING

UNDERLYING SYMBOLIC SYSTEMS

Underlying Symbolic Systems refer to the grammatical and social rules and structures that guide participants' actions in artistic activity.

SUMMARY AND RELATIONSHIP TO OTHER LENSES

The conceptual systems that performers interact with when performing these actions construct time and relationship with the music (movement phrasing sharing or counterpointing musical phrasing), weight or relation to gravity, space or relation to kinesphere and environment, and flow or relationship to performative focus and body control. Dance systems interact with music, song, text, and costume/prop systems.

Questions related to underlying systems include the following: What prescribed moves and movement combinations are allowed or disallowed? What is improvisation etiquette and dancer/audience interaction etiquette? What rules are followed in composition? How are movements controlled by the music being played, or how do the movements control the music? How does the text affect the movement? What are dance-related lexical items or moves that must be memorized to be culturally functional? What kinds of moves are clearly outsiders' moves and why?

PERFORM EMBODIED INTERVIEWS

Understanding another culture's symbolic systems requires multiple in-depth interviews with native performers to understand the movement language and its complexities. This may include using symbolic systems such as Laban's Motif and/or Labanotation to make a written and visual record of particular dance or particular movements. While this can help an observer understand the intellectual information about a dance performance, dance can often only be truly understood by actual doing and moving. Work with local performers to learn their movement language (which may raise more questions than answers) in order to understand viscerally (and sometimes spiritually) the nuances of the symbolic system.

ORAL VERBAL ARTS IN AN EVENT

This section will help you describe more completely the ways participants use words in the event you began to explore in "Look at an Event's Forms" (**Part A**). We use the same seven lenses, but introduce descriptive categories particularly pertinent to oral verbal arts. You will gather your discoveries about the verbal characteristics of this event and others like it in the Community Arts Profile.

We use the term Oral Verbal Arts to refer to special kinds of oral communication that use words. There are countless varieties of and names given to oral verbal genres of communication: anecdotes, anthems, ballads, bedtime stories, boastings, complaints, curing chants, curses, diatribes, divinations, epics, exhortations, fables, fairy tales, folktales, funeral dirges, ghost stories, greetings, heroic tales, hunting songs, hymns, jokes, jousts, legends, love songs, lullabies, magical chants, mourning songs, myths, odes, origin narratives, parables, personal narratives, poems, praises, prayers, protest songs, proverbs, puns, return songs, riddles, scatting, slam poetry, tall tales, taunting songs, tongue twisters, war songs, weeping rites, work songs, and more (see the Oral Tradition website: http://www.oraltradition.org). In this chapter we will limit our exploration to characteristics common to all oral verbal arts, and give advice about researching song texts, stories, proverbs, and oratory.

Common to all oral verbal arts are poetically modified words, and vocal modifications and gestures. These communication forms are primarily experienced through auditory channels. The essentially verbal nature of these art forms requires the hearer to understand the semantic content of what is being communicated. Oral verbal arts, however, do not simply use everyday language and patterns of speech; rather, they draw on artistically formulated words and additional levels of communication, such as expressive semantic meaning. Expressive meaning includes attitudes, feelings, sentiments, and tone. Artistic forms are also particularly apt at clarifying semantic meaning, as when particular words, phrases, themes, and actions are highlighted or brought into focus by extraordinary grammatical constructions, intonational patterns, rhythmic segmentations, or speech registers. Their oral manner of production not only intensifies expression, but can also clarify thought.

An adequate understanding of people's oral verbal art forms cannot, of course, be limited to these generalizations. We begin with such generalizations, but must gradually come to recognize and interpret them on their own local terms: similar form and use does not necessarily mean similar meaning and function. The activities

PREFACE

PREPARE

STEP 1

STEP 2

STEP 3

STEP 4B

STEP 5

STEP 6

STEP 7

CLOSING

PREFACE

PREPARE

STEP 1

STEP 2

STEP 3

STEP 4B

STEP 5

STEP 6

STEP 7

CLOSING

that we've included in this section are intended to help you begin such a process of recognition and interpretation.

Though we've stated that oral verbal arts are primarily experienced through auditory channels, visual channels play important roles in helping the experiencer understand auditory information. Hand, face, and body gestures, for example, typically complement auditory signs. Though the activities we propose in this section focus on auditory phenomena, we encourage you to expand these to include some of the complementary visual activities proposed in this manual's sections on dance and drama. Furthermore, you can extend your analyses of the sonic dimensions of oral arts—like speaking, chanting, and singing—to include many of the complementary sonic dimensions treated in the music sections of this manual. Finally, though we're focusing on oral verbal production, written arts play important roles in working toward a better future for communities. Consult the activity, "Turn Orature into Literature" (**Step 5**) and explore the relationship between existing oral and written verbal arts.

For resources that will help you investigate the forms and meanings of particular kinds of oral verbal arts more deeply, see the works by Pete Unseth[69] and Karl Franklin.[70]

GROUNDWORK

As with many of the other artistic domains, the most helpful research activities in understanding the artistic aspects of verbal performance include audiovisual recording, ethnographic interview, and participant observation. Note that the two activities we describe in this section are fundamental for the research of all oral verbal art forms. Most of the subsequent activities depend on these initial two.

ISOLATE VERBAL ELEMENTS OF AN AUDIOVISUAL RECORDING OF AN EVENT

You can't adequately research the features of an oral verbal performance without the aid of audiovisual technologies. Our natural memory cannot keep up with and retain the overwhelming stream of oral communication. Audiovisual recordings typically serve as the basis for many other research activities: text transcriptions, music transcriptions, ethnographic interviews, ethnographic analyses, discourse analyses, etc. Watch or listen to a recording that you have made of an event and identify the time segments that include verbal content. Verbally intensive genres like narrative, song, proverb, and oratory may consist of words from beginning to end. In other forms, verbal content may be less frequent. In this latter case, it may help you logistically to create new files that contain just these verbal segments.

69   Peter Unseth, "Using Local Proverbs in Christian Ministry" (prepublication draft, 2010); Unseth, "Enjoying Proverbs"; and Unseth, "Receptor Language Proverb Forms in Translation (Part 2: Application)," *Bible Translator* 57, no. 4 (2006): 161–70.
70   Karl J. Franklin, *Loosen Your Tongue: An Introduction to Storytelling* (Dallas: Graduate Institute of Applied Linguistics, 2009).

TRANSCRIBE THE VERBAL TEXTS OF A RECORDED EVENT

The first step in understanding the verbal elements of an event is text transcription. Transcribed representations of orally performed texts afford the analyst multiple alternative perspectives on complex real-time performances; these perspectives would otherwise be impossible for any individual to perceive in real-time performances. Your transcriptions should minimally include the following interlinearized fields of data:

- **Vernacular language**: The full text in its original form and language.
- **Word-for-word gloss**: A literal translation into a language of wider communication.
- **Free translation**: A translation that is natural in the language of wider communication.
- Optional: Gestural indications.
- Optional: Recording time line.
- Optional: Brief description of the linguistic and external event context.

This table presents such a transcription of one line of a song lyric in the Mono language (Democratic Republic of Congo):

Vernacular language	'bœ dœ gbolo avwara 'bœ mbœrœ anda nœ zœa
Word-for-word gloss	You are child wisdom you make house of you (question marker)
Free translation	If you are wise, how will you build your house?

Eventually you will edit this transcription to indicate larger sections of the discourse's structure.

SPACE

Space is the location, demarcation, and physical characteristics of the area used, which can affect the form of artistic communication.

SUMMARY AND RELATIONSHIP TO OTHER LENSES

There are many potential correlations between where an oral performance takes place and what and how it is verbalized. For example, national and regional specifications can help explain the use and meaning of borrowed words in the performance's text; urban and rural specifications can help to explain the decline or vitality of traditional oral performance types; indoor and outdoor specifications may correlate with the relative loudness or softness of the oral delivery, the relative distance between speakers and hearers, or the relative casual or formal tone of the performance.

PREFACE

PREPARE

STEP 1

STEP 2

STEP 3

STEP 4B

STEP 5

STEP 6

STEP 7

CLOSING

PREFACE

PREPARE

STEP 1

STEP 2

STEP 3

STEP 4B

STEP 5

STEP 6

STEP 7

CLOSING

LOCATE EACH RECORDED VERBAL ELEMENT NATIONALLY, REGIONALLY, MACROLOCALLY, AND MICROLOCALLY

For every recording or transcription that you make of oral verbal elements in an event, perform activities like the following:

- Describe in varying degrees of specificity (from national to local) the location of the performance. This can include multiple degrees of space; e.g., neighborhoods, courtyards and areas of courtyards, buildings and areas of buildings, indoors and outdoors, open and enclosed, stages and areas of stages, bodily movement into and out of any of the above, relative spatial relationship of verbalizers and hearers, etc.
- Describe how participants change the content or manner of their oral performance in response to their physical space. Do certain genres only take place in certain places? When performers move to a different location, does some aspect of their verbal performance change?
- Interview performance participants to explore if and how participants choose, design, or use that performance space to achieve particular performance goals.

EXPLORE HOW PARTICIPANTS MODIFY THEIR VERBAL ACTIONS IN RESPONSE TO THEIR PHYSICAL SPACE

Perform activities like these:

- Ask performers of verbal arts about different contexts in which they have performed. How did they change what they did in response to characteristics of each space?
- Observe a single performer of verbal arts in more than one context. Note his or her volume, distance to other participants, and other characteristics in each context. Compare.

SHAPE OF THE EVENT THROUGH TIME

Shape of an event refers primarily to its constituent segments, organized hierarchically.

SUMMARY AND RELATIONSHIP TO OTHER LENSES

Performance of a verbal form can happen very quickly—as with a proverb or curse—or move through a complex, long progression—as in a story or oration. The local genre is the biggest determiner of how longer forms are organized hierarchically through time. Narrative forms relate closely to dramatic forms.

PREFACE

PREPARE

STEP 1

STEP 2

STEP 3

STEP 4B

STEP 5

STEP 6

STEP 7

CLOSING

EXPLORE ASSOCIATIONS BETWEEN THE TEMPORAL OCCURRENCE OF A RECORDED ORAL VERBAL ELEMENT AND BROADER CULTURAL FACTORS

Write down the month, day, hour, season, and occurrence of a verbal performance in its overall social event. Many genres are socioculturally associated with particular seasons, months, days, hours of the day, and past historical events. The reasons for these associations are many, and are often taken for granted. To learn about these associations, ask a knowledgeable friend questions like these:

- When have you experienced someone producing a verbal event like this? List every time you can remember.
- Are there particular times, seasons, or events when this kind of verbal performance is more likely to occur? Why?

IDENTIFY AND DESCRIBE THE LENGTH OF EACH VERBAL ELEMENT IN THE EVENT

Write down the time in the event that every new set of words begins and ends. Use the Hierarchical Segmentation Time Line you began in "Look at an Event's Forms" (**Part A**).

DETERMINE THE TEMPORAL FORM OF THE ARTISTIC VERBAL PERFORMANCE

Oral verbal performances unfold in real time. Traditional genres are *expected* (though often subconsciously) to progress according to basic local time patterns. Exceptions to these patterns yield new effects—some desired, some undesired. Either way, all verbal discourse genres are in one way or another based on socially received formal templates.

Temporal form of narrative

If the recorded and transcribed oral discourse under investigation has narrative, or story components, describe its temporal shape in terms of the following developmental template:[71]

- the stage,
- the inciting incident,
- the mounting tension,
- the climax of tension, and
- the release of tension.

You may be able to identify these elements by noting the

- introduction and actions of characters;

---

71   Borrowed from Robert E. Longacre, *The Grammar of Discourse*, 2nd ed. (New York: Plenum, 1996), 33–50.

PREFACE

PREPARE

STEP 1

STEP 2

STEP 3

STEP 4B

STEP 5

STEP 6

STEP 7

CLOSING

- increase or decrease of rates of events in the narrative (a quicker succession of events implies a climax);
- introduction of special words to mark a climax; and
- change in a performer's vocal timbre, volume, and pitch.

Temporal form of poetry

If the recorded and transcribed oral discourse under investigation is organized poetically, such as in a song or oral poem, describe its temporal shape in terms of the following:

- **Repeated units.** E.g., lines, verses, verse segments, stanzas, strophes, refrains. You may represent these as "A, A, A, etc." or "a, a, a, etc."
- **Contrastive units.** You may represent these as "A, B, C, etc." or "a, b, c, etc."
- **Varied units.** You may represent these as "A^1, A^2, A^3, etc." or "a^1, a^2, a^3, etc."
- **Derivative units.** You may represent these as "A, B, B^a, C, C^b, etc."

You may also describe these same phenomena in conventional Western literary terminologies (e.g., poem, stanza, and line) or local terms.

Temporal form of narrative poetry

Many artistic verbal forms are constituted at multiple formal levels, as in the case of narrative poetry. Discourse scholar Robert Longacre, for example, combines the complementary structures for both the narrative and poetic forms constituting Psalm 18 as follows:

- Strophe 1, Introduction, vv. 2b–4
- Strophe 2, Episode 1, vv. 5–25
- Strophe 3, Didactic Peak, vv. 26–32
- Strophe 4, Episode 2, vv. 33–49
- Strophe 5, Conclusion vv. 50,51[72]

Temporal form of proverbs

Proverbs, riddles, and other short verbal forms have little internal shape over time; we sometimes call short forms like these distilled. They are more often woven or inserted into larger discourses, like court proceedings, games, or communal reconciliation events. Make note of how people use and respond to proverbs in their temporal context.

Temporal form of oratory

Verbal production with oratorical characteristics often is used to persuade and educate, and may be relatively long. Elements of oratory often include

- connection to listeners,
- explanation of a problem and its importance, and
- a call to action.

---

72   Robert E. Longacre, "Discourse Structure, Verb Forms, and Archaism in Psalm 18," *Journal of Translation* 2, no. 1 (2006): 17–30.

PARTICIPANT ORGANIZATION

Participant Organization highlights the people involved in an event, in terms of the roles they play, the ways they interact with each other through time, and how they use the space around them.

SUMMARY AND RELATIONSHIP TO OTHER LENSES

Participants in oral verbal arts fall broadly into roles of those who perform words and those who hear them.

IDENTIFY THE ROLES OF PARTICIPANTS PRODUCING VERBAL CONTENT

Certain genres of oral verbal art may only be performed by people with very particular roles in a community. The association of such performance genres with specific social roles may be explicit or implicit. An interview may be necessary to determine the case.

The voice of the oral verbal performance may change. Your transcription should reflect this. Further analysis may indicate a correlation between shifts in voice (who is speaking or singing) and the content, form, and delivery of the text. These correlations may be socially malleable or stable. They may follow social convention or they may be due to individual style. The patterns of multiple recordings and transcriptions will do much to clarify the nature of these correlations between the identity of the performers and the resulting form of the performance.

Note each person who produces verbal content in the event, and perform activities like the following:

- Ask knowledgeable friends if there are local names for various roles people play in the event that include verbal production. If there are, ask them to describe what these roles entail.
- Decide if any participants in the event fill roles sometimes associated with the kinds of verbal arts listed here:

  - Roles sometimes associated with narratives: Crafter, Contributor, Teller, Listener, Affirmer, Heckler
  - Roles sometimes associated with oratory: Speaker, Orator, Preacher, Listener, Crafter, Affirmer, Audience
  - Roles sometimes associated with proverbs: Speaker, Listener
  - Roles sometimes associated with poetry: Speaker, Crafter, Listener
  - Roles sometimes associated with songs: Crafter, Singer, Listener, Improviser

PREFACE

PREPARE

STEP 1

STEP 2

STEP 3

STEP 4B

STEP 5

STEP 6

STEP 7

CLOSING

MATERIALS

Materials are all of the tangible things associated with an event.

SUMMARY AND RELATIONSHIP TO OTHER LENSES

Participants in oral verbal arts use objects to emphasize points (e.g., an item referenced by a storyteller), evoke characters and places (e.g., costumes or props), or amplify or modify sound (e.g., microphones or acoustic shells). There may be close relationships between a participant's role and the objects he or she interacts with.

LIST OBJECTS AND DESCRIBE HOW PARTICIPANTS USE THEM TO EMPHASIZE OR OTHERWISE MODIFY VERBAL CONTENT

Watch a video recording of an event, list all of the objects that performers of verbal content interact with, and discuss questions like these with a knowledgeable friend:

- How does this object affect the hearers' understanding and experience of the performers' words?
- What symbolic meaning does this object evoke?

PERFORMANCE FEATURE CATEGORIES

Performance features are observable characteristics of a performance that emerge from an event's unique combination of physical and social context and participants' actions.

SUMMARY AND RELATIONSHIP TO OTHER LENSES

Performers of verbal arts make their words special through unique combinations of poetic features, gestures, and vocal modulation.

IDENTIFY THE POETIC FEATURES OF VERBAL CONTENT

Most artistically rendered verbal communication will have poetic features that influence its overall feel. Study a transcription of a short section of an event while listening to or watching the recording from which it was produced. Then, using the list of features below, note which features the event exhibits. This is just a small sample of possible poetic features, so remain open to others.

PREFACE

PREPARE

STEP 1

STEP 2

STEP 3

STEP 4B

STEP 5

STEP 6

STEP 7

CLOSING

Overall characteristics
- **Verbal play**: A highly creative act that overlaps with other features. It is often found in storytelling by means of various semantic devices, including metaphor, allegory, metonymy, puns, humor, and so on.
- **Rhythm or pulse**: This often is structured by syllables. These syllables come together in a certain number of beats or a certain pattern.
- **Text density**: Number of lines per verse, number of verses per poem or song, number of syllables per line, number of notes per syllable (in song).

Poetic devices
You may find these devices in short verbal forms like proverbs and riddles, and longer forms like song lyrics, speeches, and poems. In poems, they may be distributed between lines, within lines, or between verses.

Word-level poetic devices
- **Lexical repetition**: Use of the same word in more than one context.
- **Homonyms**: Two or more words that share the same pronunciation and spelling but with different meanings.
- **Archaic language**: Words, phrases, or grammatical structures no longer used in normal speech.
- **Borrowed words**: Words adopted from another language.

Phrase-level poetic devices
- **Phrase repetition**.
- **Subphrase repetition**.
- **Acrostic**: Arrangement in which the first letter of a phrase or line combines with other first letters to spell a word or other meaningful sequence.

Poetic devices related to sound
- **Assonance**: Rhyme referring to the same or similar vowel sounds in neighboring words.
- **Rhyme**: The same or similar vowel sounds at the end, beginning, or middle of lines.
- **Vocables**: Words without propositional meaning.
- **Ideophones**: A vivid representation of sensory imagery.
- **Consonance**: Close correspondence of sounds.
- **Alliteration**: Repetition of the same or similar sounds at the beginning of words.
- **Rhythmic speech**.

Poetic devices related to meaning
- **Semantic categories**: Examples include similes, metonymy (where a word or expression stands for another one; e.g., sweat = hard work), synecdoche (when part of something refers to the whole; e.g., set of wheels = car), personification, hyperbole, euphemism (describing something socially unpleasant in indirect terms), and symbols.
- **Rhetorical questions**: Meant to persuade rather than elicit information.
- **Ideophones**: Words that sound like the thing they refer to.

PREFACE

PREPARE

STEP 1

STEP 2

STEP 3

STEP 4B

STEP 5

STEP 6

STEP 7

CLOSING

- **Loan word synonymy**: A word in a language other than that of the verbal event.
- **Metaphors**: Figures of speech in which a word or phrase corresponds to an object or action that is not literally applicable.
- **Ellipsis**: The omission of words that one expects to be there.
- **Semantic parallelism**: Similarity of structure in the meanings of two or more words or phrases.

IDENTIFY HOW PARTICIPANTS USE PHYSICAL GESTURES TO MODIFY THEIR VERBAL PRODUCTION

Watch a video recording of part of an event with a friend who knows the genre and language(s) of the event, with a transcription and translation of the words. Whenever a speaker or singer moves a body part, stop the recording and discuss questions like the following with your friend:

- Does the gesture emphasize, contradict, add to, or otherwise modify the words being produced?
- Do participants use the same gesture in other parts of the event? If so, is the effect on meaning the same or different?
- Is this gesture codified (i.e., with a set meaning agreed upon by the group and tradition) or unique to an individual?

IDENTIFY HOW PARTICIPANTS MODIFY THEIR VOICES IN THEIR VERBAL PRODUCTION

Performers use combinations of words, gestures, and vocal modulation together to communicate in verbal arts. Vocal modulation refers primarily to changes in pitch, volume, and timbre. To explore how participants in an event enlist vocal modulation, watch a video recording of part of an event with a transcription and translation of the words in front of you. Perform activities like these:

- Along the top of each line of words, draw a line representing the pitch of what's coming out of the performer's mouth. When the pitch rises, let the line rise. When the pitch falls, let the line fall. When there are abrupt changes in pitch, write a note to that effect.
- Note significant changes in volume at points in the transcription. You may use words (e.g., "abrupt volume drop") or symbols (e.g., ">" for a drop in volume).
- Note changes in vocal timbre (also known as vocal color or voice quality) when they occur. These could include qualities like nasal, open, muffled, thin, etc.
- Discuss how these vocal modifications affect the meaning and impact of a performer's words with a friend who knows the genre and language(s) of the event.

CONTENT

Content refers to the subject matter in artistic activity.

SUMMARY AND RELATIONSHIP TO OTHER LENSES
Because Oral Verbal Arts are by definition text based, its content relates integrally to almost everything else.

IDENTIFY THE RANGE OF CONTENT EXPECTED IN A VERBAL PERFORMANCE
Watch a video recording of part of an event with a friend who knows the genre and language(s) of the event. Ask questions like these:

- What is this *verbal item* (e.g., story) about?
- Think of another performance of this kind of verbal event. What was it about? Repeat as long as possible.
- Then suggest other topics as possible content in the same kind of verbal event, asking, "Would this fit?"

UNDERLYING SYMBOLIC SYSTEMS

Underlying Symbolic Systems refer to the grammatical and social rules and structures that guide participants' actions in artistic activity.

SUMMARY AND RELATIONSHIP TO OTHER LENSES
Underlying Symbolic Systems relate to verbal arts in complex relationships between the linguistic rules that govern everyday speech and those associated with heightened verbal communication. Because of this, most of the research activities we've included require familiarity with linguistic analysis.

PREFACE

PREPARE

STEP 1

STEP 2

STEP 3

STEP 4B

STEP 5

STEP 6

STEP 7

CLOSING

PREFACE

PREPARE

STEP 1

STEP 2

STEP 3

STEP 4B

STEP 5

STEP 6

STEP 7

CLOSING

IDENTIFY BASIC ELEMENTS OF A STORY'S PLOT

The characters and their actions in a story form its central series of events, or plot. The plot may flow in a form that contains the following major sections:

- **Introduction**: The way that a story begins is of primary importance.
- **Body**: The body of a story reveals the plot (if there is one), characters, events, and main point or peak of the story.
- **Closure**: The ending of a story may draw some lesson or invite questions or speculation on the purpose of the story.

How the plot develops depends upon genre expectations and the central theme or purpose of the story. Its structure will determine how best to use the grammatical, syntactical, and semantic features inherent in the language. The structure of the language and its context will affect how and when characters are introduced, how they are described, and what actions will follow. For further discussion of plot, see activities related to plot in "Drama in an Event" (**Part B2**).

ANALYZE AN ORAL (MONOLOGUE) NARRATIVE

There are numerous kinds of narrative discourse analyses, not to mention numerous degrees of detail to which they are carried out.[73] However, we strongly suggest that you initially *describe at least four fundamental dimensions of your chosen narrative*, even if only modestly. These dimensions include (1) type of content, (2) means of production, (3) manner of production, and (4) medium of production. You will find that the type of content (genre) and manner of production (style and register) are particularly complex dimensions of analysis. Because of this complexity, seek the assistance of someone trained in discourse analysis when analyzing these two dimensions of any discourse. We recommend Dooley and Levinsohn's *Analyzing Discourse*[74] as a basic introductory methodological text.

There are two prerequisites to carrying out this research activity adequately: (1) access to a basic grammatical analysis of the language at hand; and (2) a complete text transcription of the verbal performance, including vernacular text, a word-for-word gloss, and a free translation. We recommend that you also learn the facts of the discourse; e.g., who did what to whom in the immediate context, and the relationships between their actions.[75] This means that you should have a fairly complete picture of the text world, and of the external contextualization as well.[76]

---

73   See Robert E. Longacre and Shin Ja J. Hwang, *Holistic Discourse Analysis* (Dallas: SIL International, 2012); Deborah Schiffrin, Deborah Tannen, and Heidi E. Hamilton, eds., *The Handbook of Discourse Analysis* (Oxford: Blackwell, 2001).
74   Robert A. Dooley and Stephen H. Levinsohn, *Analyzing Discourse: A Manual of Basic Concepts* (Dallas: SIL International, 2000).
75   Robert E. Longacre and Stephen H. Levinsohn, "Field Analysis of Discourse," in *Current Trends in Textlinguistics*, ed. Wolfgang U. Dressler (Berlin: Walter de Gruyter, 1978), 103–22.
76   Dooley and Levinsohn, *Analyzing Discourse*, 22.

For the narrative discourse genre in particular, we recommend that you also try to address two additional, fundamental domains of analysis: (1) narrative discourse cohesion, and (2) narrative discourse development.

1. NARRATIVE DISCOURSE COHESION
Describe some of the more common grammatical devices affecting narrative discourse cohesion. These include *substitution* (of nouns, verbs, clauses; e.g., anaphora), *ellipsis*, *reference*, *conjunction* (by addition, causality, temporality), *lexical cohesion* (through reiteration, as accomplished through repetition, synonymy, hyponymy, metonymy, antonymy, etc.), and *collocation*.[77]

2. NARRATIVE DISCOURSE DEVELOPMENT
Narrative development may take place on a number of levels. Your description of narrative development should account for the organization of various *thematic*, *grammatical*, and *schematic* phenomena.

- Describe some of the narrative's *thematic development*. For example, you may mark whether the narrative's "continuities and discontinuities" are according to one or more of the following domains: time, place, action, and/or participants.[78]
- Describe some of the narrative's *grammatical development*. First, distinguish and describe the characteristic features of the narrative's *foreground* (mainline) and *background* (supportive) material. Second, describe the marks of its *climactic development*.

  - Identify the *mainline material*; it is most often marked by "a characteristic constellation of verb forms" (i.e., tenses, aspects, and/or moods).[79]
  - Once the marks of the mainline material are determined, identify *supportive material*. Supportive material is commonly categorized according to *Participant Information*, *Setting Information*, *Explanatory Information*, *Collateral Information*, and *Evaluative Information*.[80]
  - The *expressive qualities* of oral verbal arts encode evaluative information—attitudes, feelings, opinions, beliefs—in countless ways. Artistic verbal acts may range from heightened speech forms to poetic devices to explicitly musical phenomena. More specifically, *expressive grammatical markers* may include *obligative mood*, *imperative mood*, *exclamatives*, *interjectives*, *ideophones*, *intensifiers*, *rhetorical questions*, and *vocatives*. Expressive *poetic devices* may include specially formalized *rhythms*, *syntaxes*, *phonologies*, and *semantics*. Expressive musical formalizations commonly include particular configurations of *melodic*, *harmonic*, *rhythmic*, *timbric*, *dynamic*, *formal*, and *performative features* (see "Music in an Event," **Part B1**).
  - Describe some of the narrative's *climactic development*. It is most commonly signaled by (1) *particular verb forms*, (2) *rhetorical underlining*

77   Jan Renkema, *Discourse Studies: An Introductory Textbook* (Amsterdam: Benjamins, 1993), 37.
78   Dooley and Levinsohn, *Analyzing Discourse*, 18–21.
79   Ibid., 39–48.
80   Joseph E. Grimes, *The Thread of Discourse: Janua Linguarum* (The Hague: Mouton, 1975).

PREFACE

PREPARE

STEP 1

STEP 2

STEP 3

STEP 4B

STEP 5

STEP 6

STEP 7

CLOSING

(e.g., repetition), (3) *heightened vividness*, (4) *change of pace*, and (5) *incidence of ideophones*. All of these marks are extraordinarily expressive and often achieved by the peculiar qualities of oral verbal arts. The special musico-poetic devices of oral verbal arts—whether rhythmic, syntactic, phonological (including timbre, dynamics, melody, and harmony), or semantic—are kindred marks of climactic development.

- Describe the narrative's overall (or episodic) *schematic development*, which typically reflects—though not simplistically—the following developmental template: the narrative's *stage, inciting incident, mounting tension, climax of tension, and release of tension*.[81]

MAKE A PRELIMINARY MUSICO-POETIC ANALYSIS OF A SONG

Describe some of the distinctive musico-poetic features of a single song. The analysis assumes the availability of a text transcription of the complete performance of an audio recording of the selected song. The transcription should minimally represent the vernacular text, a word-for-word gloss, and a free translation. And like the narrative activity outlined above, the transcription should include notes indicating a fairly complete picture of the text world, and of the external contextualization as well.

Your analysis should describe five basic domains of musico-poetic phenomena: rhythm, syntax, phonology, morphology, and semantics.

- **Rhythm**. First, describe the rhythmic nature of the song's poetic *line*. A song's *line* is its most fundamental poetic feature. Most *song* lines are measured *periodically* (as patterned groups of beats, or pulses). And often, but by no means always, these periodically measured lines also pattern with phonological and/or semantic patterns, or combinations thereof. Search, then, for patterns of vowel sounds, consonant sounds, accents, vowel stresses, syllable stresses, word stresses, phrase stresses, tones, and combinations of these. Simple quantifications, like typical words and/or syllables per line, should not be discounted, for whether strictly repeated or approximately repeated, their quantitative patterning does affect the performance.
- **Syntax**. Second, describe the corresponding syntactic formalizations of a song's poetic line. Multiple distinctive characteristics may constitute the syntactic nature of a song's poetic line. The syntactic ordering (versification) of morphemes, words, phrases, and clauses are segmented according to the constitutive rhythms of the song's musico-poetic line. The subsequent segmentation and ordering of these morphemes, words, phrases, and clauses give rise to a variety of syntactic poetic units conventionally identified as *verses, verse segments, stanzas*, and *repeated, contrastive*, or *varied refrains*, etc. The boundaries of lines and verses often coincide, but by no means always. This play between line (a rhythmical unit) and syntax (a grammatical unit) is yet another effect of the song's poetic function. Your present analysis

81   Longacre, *The Grammar of Discourse*, 33–50

Step 4B: Explore the Event's Genre(s) through Artistic Domain Categories

149

PREFACE

PREPARE

STEP 1

STEP 2

STEP 3

STEP 4B

STEP 5

STEP 6

STEP 7

CLOSING

need not determine the exact affective function of this play (though you could speculate); your job, for now, is to simply identify such phenomena as further potential poetic resources.

- **Phonology**. Describe a variety of distinctive phonological poetic devices. Identify, for example, the use of particular *vocables*, *ideophones*, *assonance*, *rhyme*, *consonance*, *alliteration*, etc. You may observe that certain phonological patterns appear to function rhythmically, though not exclusively so. There may be other functions, but an in-depth functional analysis is probably beyond the scope of this project. Your job, again, is to simply identify these phenomena, and thereby highlight many potential poetic resources.
- **Morphology**. Describe some of the lexical poetic devices exhibited. Identify, for example, any use of homonyms, or any number of repeated, reiterated, or reduplicated phonemes, ideophones, or words.
- **Semantics**. Describe various semantic poetic devices. Identify, for example, various uses of ideophones, similes, metaphors, metonyms, personification, meronymy, semantic parallelism, syntactic-semantic parallelism, syntagmatic-paradigmatic substitution, rhetorical questions, archaic language, loan word synonymy, ellipsis, etc. Any one of these devices may be subject to repetitive processes as well.

COMPARE THE RHYTHMIC DEVICES OF THREE OR MORE SONGS

For this activity, you will first need to record and transcribe the texts (and if you are able, the music) of three or more songs. It is best to sample songs performed by different performers and different social occasions.

Second, for each song, carry out the Rhythm step "Describe the rhythmic nature of the song's poetic *line*" above. Third, compare your descriptions of the rhythmic devices used in the performance of all the songs. Which rhythmic devices were exhibited in every song? Which were performed in most songs? Which were unique to each song? Those devices common to every song may turn out to be *systemic*; that is, they are culturally expected—consciously or unconsciously—to be in most if not all songs. We assume that every song will exhibit the general rhythmic phenomenon conventionally called a line. The length or meter of that *line*, however, may vary significantly. For example, some may be measured by particular patterns of vowel sounds, consonant sounds, accents, vowel stresses, syllable stresses, word stresses, phrase stresses, tones, or combinations of these. Some may only be described in terms of words and/or syllables per line. Whatever the case, such devices are typical indicators of underlying symbolic systems that guide what and how sung poetic discourse is *competently* performed.

PREFACE

PREPARE

STEP 1

STEP 2

STEP 3

STEP 4B

STEP 5

STEP 6

STEP 7

CLOSING

VISUAL ARTS IN AN EVENT

This section will help you describe more completely the ways participants produce visual symbols in a work or event. To understand this section best, you should first work through some of the activities in "Look at an Event's Forms" (**Part A**). We use the same seven lenses here, but introduce descriptive categories particularly pertinent to visual arts. You will gather your discoveries about the visual characteristics of this event and others like it in the Community Arts Profile.

Visual communication, like any other kind of communication, uses symbols to convey or create meaning. Each culture agrees upon relationships between its *signifiers* (an often arbitrary symbol that stands for something else) and its *signified* (the meaning that the symbol represents: a person, story, concept, etc.). The study of visual symbolism is the attempt to find the meaning behind visible signifiers. This meaning is often contained in shapes (like a *kanaga*, see below) or colors, which are culturally defined. Meanings can also be combined in specific ways through a visual grammar.

Visual features are primarily experienced through the eyes, initially at a subconscious level. Most art forms have a visual component— paintings and sculptures, the movements of the body or hands in dance, the colors and costumes in drama, the visual composition of musical instruments. Note also that some visual features may also be experienced through touch: people can feel textures and shapes. This may be especially important for visually impaired experiencers or other participants involved in an event where there is little or no light.

INTERACTIONS WITH OTHER DOMAINS

Visual messages may stand alone, as in functional design such as architecture, material cultural objects, or objects created purely for their aesthetic value. They may also be part of other expressive arts, such as accessories for rituals (costumes, masks, garments), the design and appearance of musical instruments, etc. Some visual messages are created for use at specific times or events, such as invitations, Christmas cards, or skull-shaped pastries for the *Día de los Difuntos Muertos* (Mexico). Because of this dual nature, you will notice that we apply the lenses below on artistic objects both as independently meaningful and meaningful as part of a larger event.

Among the Dogon people in Mali, when people have a quarrel, they go to "the place of words" to make peace. By sitting under a low roof, they are unable to fight. The symbols on the pillars of the peacemaking place are important to the Dogon people's identity and their understanding of peace.

This *kanaga* symbol can symbolize the peaceful intersection of heaven and earth, or a lizard, or a myth in which a man became a lizard to make peace between heaven and earth.

SPACE

Space is the location, demarcation, and physical characteristics of the area used, which can affect the form of artistic communication.

SUMMARY AND RELATIONSHIP TO OTHER LENSES

Space relates to visual artistic communication both in how it is used in an event, and how visual features are arranged in and on an object.

DESCRIBE SPATIAL RELATIONSHIPS BETWEEN AN OBJECT'S VISUAL FEATURES

Examine an object, writing in the Community Arts Profile how its features express the following spatial concepts:

Visual unity: An integrated message in which the various parts of the message are in harmony with the other parts: **proximity**, in which objects are spatially related; **repetition**, in which objects are quantitatively related; **continuation**, based on psychological principles of closure; and **controlled chaos**, to name a few.[82]

Balance: The way some elements in an image relate to other elements in that same image. This can be **symmetrical**, in which the parts are subjectively mirrored; **asymmetrical**, in which the elements have a distributed weight that is not symmetrical; or **radial**, in which the parts appear to balance outward from a point of origin.

Rhythm: The process of directing eye movement through an image, based on repetition.

Proportion: The relationships between visual elements, particularly with reference to relative size.

---

82   David A. Lauer and Stephen Pentak, *Design Basics*, 5th ed. (Stamford, CT: Wadsworth Publishing, 2002).

PREFACE

PREPARE

STEP 1

STEP 2

STEP 3

STEP 4B

STEP 5

STEP 6

STEP 7

CLOSING

PREFACE

PREPARE

STEP 1

STEP 2

STEP 3

STEP 4B

STEP 5

STEP 6

STEP 7

CLOSING

MATERIALS

Materials are all of the tangible things associated with an event.

SUMMARY AND RELATIONSHIP TO OTHER LENSES

Creators of art objects choose materials that will allow them to produce the visual features they desire. Characteristics of materials that can inform these choices include strength, plasticity, smoothness, texture, color, shape, and the like. An artist may also choose a material simply because it is available, along with the necessary tools to work it.

IDENTIFY AND DESCRIBE THE MATERIALS USED IN AN OBJECT

Obtain an example of an object that friends think is representative and of good quality. For each material it contains, ask the creator of the object questions like these:

- What is this material? What names do you know to describe it in different languages?
- Where did this material come from? How did you get it?
- How did you manipulate it to make this object?

DOCUMENT THE CREATION OF AN OBJECT

Arrange with someone who is recognized as a skilled creator of an art form to document his or her creation process. This may include payment or other forms of compensation. Videotape a representative portion of each step, photograph the object in different stages of completion, and ask the creator what he or she is doing in each step. You might decide to edit a video of the process to give to the creator and to the community, for use in passing on these skills. You could also write a short, illustrated document of the process.

SHAPE OF THE EVENT THROUGH TIME

Shape of an event refers primarily to its constituent segments, organized hierarchically.

SUMMARY AND RELATIONSHIP TO OTHER LENSES

Shape here refers primarily to change through time, which relates to visual artistic action in three important ways. First, objects generally retain their form for long periods of time, in contrast to other kinds of artistic communication that are dynamic. From this perspective, an object (unlike an event) seldom changes through time; a melting ice sculpture may be an exception. Some works are durable; others, such as Navajo sand paintings, are only intended to last for the length of a specific occasion or ceremony.

Second, as we discuss in Participant Organization below, an experiencer's interaction with an object is structured through time. We see this as a person experiences architectural features while walking through a cathedral, or when someone spends thirty minutes examining a painting in a museum. Third, at given moments in a performance event, the participants, objects, and other elements of the performance may create a series of visual snapshots, each with its own set of features.

COMPARE TWO VISUAL SNAPSHOTS OF AN EVENT

Watch a video recording of an event. Pause the recording at two moments that seem visually contrastive to you, save freeze-frame images of the moments, and describe them through Performance Features and Space lenses. Look at the two images with a participant in the event, noting what stands out to them visually in each.

WRITE THE HISTORY OF AN OBJECT

Identify the oldest example that you can of an object with artistic features, perhaps one that is well known in a community. Ask several people questions like these:

- Who created it and when?
- On what occasions and how often do you remember it being used? How has it changed over time? What events have happened to it, like being broken, repaired, lost, or stolen?
- How often and for how long is the work viewable, by whom, where, and when?

PREFACE

PREPARE

STEP 1

STEP 2

STEP 3

STEP 4B

STEP 5

STEP 6

STEP 7

CLOSING

PREFACE

PREPARE

STEP 1

STEP 2

STEP 3

STEP 4B

STEP 5

STEP 6

STEP 7

CLOSING

PARTICIPANT ORGANIZATION

Participant Organization highlights the people involved in an event, in terms of the roles they play, the ways they interact with each other through time, and how they use the space around them.

SUMMARY AND RELATIONSHIP TO OTHER LENSES

Common roles of participants in visual artistic activity are the message creators, manipulators, and experiencers.

IDENTIFY THE ROLE(S) IN VISUAL ART CREATION

One or more people will be involved in the production of objects with artistic features. **Creator** roles could include painters, sculptors, weavers, dye makers, carvers, potters, and the like. Ask friends to identify who made an object, others who make similar objects, and who is recognized as being especially skilled in doing it. Ask if there are local names for people filling these roles.

DESCRIBE HOW PEOPLE MANIPULATE ART OBJECTS

Art objects often function within larger events, as instruments, set pieces, costumes, props, and the like. In these cases, **manipulators** play, place, wear, hold, or otherwise use them. Watch a video recording of an event with people who participated. For each object you're interested in, ask questions like these:

- What is that person doing with the object? Are there restrictions on who can do it?
- How does what they're doing with the object affect how people experience it?

DESCRIBE HOW PEOPLE EXPERIENCE ART OBJECTS

Experiencers are people who receive the meanings encoded in the objects intended by their creators and manipulators. The key activity of the experiencers is **perception**—the process of decoding the visual message. The perception process is influenced by one's culture, previous experience, the expectations created by enculturation through experience, and physiological processes in the human brain.

Watch a video recording of people experiencing an object. This could include someone interacting with a sculpture in a museum, watching actors wearing costumes, walking into a specially designed building, or other event. Write down where their eyes are directed at different times. You can also watch the video with the experiencer and ask him or her to describe what they saw, felt, and thought of.

PERFORMANCE FEATURE CATEGORIES

Performance features are observable characteristics of a performance that emerge from an event's unique combination of physical and social context and participants' actions.

SUMMARY AND RELATIONSHIP TO OTHER LENSES

Though visual artistry is not always performed by participants in real time, its features are the building blocks of visual communication. We define several features that creators manipulate to create meaning and aesthetic pleasure.

DESCRIBE THE VISUAL FEATURES OF A STATIC OBJECT

Look at an object and write down its use of the following kinds of features:

Line: "The path made by a pointed instrument: a pen, a pencil, a crayon, a stick. A line implies action because work was required to make it."[83]

Shape: A two- or three-dimensional area, often formed by lines, usually with defined edges or colors.

Value: The lightness or darkness of a part of an image compared to other parts of the image. Value can be based on a gray scale, from black to white, or in tints and shades of colors.

Color: The visual response to the wavelengths of light reflected from something, identified as red, blue, green, etc. Communities may assign meanings to particular colors. For example, in a graduation ceremony, the colors of the gowns and hoods have a meaning known by those who understand such things. The color of the front of the hood identifies the discipline in which the degree was earned, while the colors of the trim and back represent the school colors of the granting institution. Related to color are the following:

a.) **Hue:** The prototypical color definition in a culture.

b.) **Shades:** Darker variants of a color formed by adding varying amounts of black to the hue.

c.) **Tints:** Lighter variants of a color formed by adding varying amounts of white to the hue.

Texture: The sense of feeling that a visual message evokes, such as roughness or softness—the message creator substitutes an imagined sense of touch by a visual representation.

---

83   Edmund B. Feldman, *Varieties of Visual Experience*, 4th ed. (New York: Adams, 1992), 207.

PREFACE

PREPARE

STEP 1

STEP 2

STEP 3

STEP 4B

STEP 5

STEP 6

STEP 7

CLOSING

PREFACE

PREPARE

STEP 1

STEP 2

STEP 3

STEP 4B

STEP 5

STEP 6

STEP 7

CLOSING

CONTENT

Content refers to the subject matter in artistic activity.

SUMMARY AND RELATIONSHIP TO OTHER LENSES

Visual art forms relate directly to content when they use symbolic symbols like language, and when they evoke ideas through other means.

ELICIT A VISUAL SYMBOL'S STORY

Research any story that goes with a given symbol or work of art in your community, such as the story and symbol that accompany the Dogon *kanaga* pictured above. Many works of visual art cannot be understood without hearing their accompanying story. Ask a local storyteller what story or concept each visual symbol conveys. Some may convey both stories and concepts. Always interpret a visual image with its oral story if there is a story associated with it.

UNDERLYING SYMBOLIC SYSTEMS

Underlying Symbolic Systems refer to the grammatical and social rules and structures that guide participants' actions in artistic activity.

SUMMARY AND RELATIONSHIP TO OTHER LENSES

The symbolic systems underlying a community's visual communication contribute to its visual literacy: the understanding that people have of the various components and elements of visual messages; the learned ability to understand and create visual images to communicate messages. Visual communication skills allow message creators to create and manipulate mental images. Every community has different rules of visual literacy.

ANALYZE THE MESSAGE OF AN IMAGE

Begin by identifying the content elements of the message:

1. Create an inventory of the content elements.
2. Notice the composition of the image—which elements are visually centered and which are marginal, at the edges.
3. List "the visual cues of color, form, depth, and movement within the image."[84]

---

84   P.M. Lester, *Visual Communication: Images with Messages*, 4th ed. (Stamford, CT: Thomson-Wadsworth Publishing Company, 2003), 112.

4. Attempt to place the image in a geographical and temporal setting, and identify its purposes.

Consider Lester's perspectives for critical analysis of visual messages:[85]

5. **Personal**: Refers to the subjective viewer response.
6. **Historical**: Attempts to place the message in a historical context.
7. **Technical**: Attempts to understand specific techniques, quality, expertise, and budget for the production of the message.
8. **Ethical**: Attempts to understand moral implications of the message for the producer, the subject, and the viewer.
9. **Cultural**: Attempts to understand cultural symbols that affect the meaning of the message by applying insights from the historical, technical, and ethical perspectives in a specific context and time. It is closely related to semiotic theory. The cultural perspective analyzes cultural values and worldviews.
10. **Critical**: Expands the viewer's perspective beyond the specific image to include medium, culture, and audience. This helps the viewer: (1) understand how this message makes a broader statement about human nature, and (2) better understand why some cultures find messages like this one acceptable or unacceptable. As the final perspective, it incorporates the results of all the other analytical perspectives.

SPECIAL ISSUES IN VISUAL ARTS

Frame is the purpose or intention of the artist. The audience needs to understand the intention of the artist to interpret a work rightly. A common Horace Knowles Bible illustration, for example, shows a bit in the mouth of a horse, designed to clarify James 3:3, "When we put bits into the mouths of horses to make them obey us, we can turn the whole animal." This illustration provides background information for cultures unfamiliar with bits. The audience will interpret the illustration's meaning wrongly if they interpret the artist's intention as storytelling. People looking for a story frame, rather than a background knowledge frame, may be confused by a "story" showing a horse's head without a body. The audience needs to know that the artist's intended frame is to provide background knowledge.

A Chinese depiction of Jesus' nativity in a Chinese context or the Jesus Mafa Association's pictures of Jesus drawn in an African

85   Ibid.

PREFACE

PREPARE

STEP 1

STEP 2

STEP 3

STEP 4B

STEP 5

STEP 6

STEP 7

CLOSING

PREFACE

PREPARE

STEP 1

STEP 2

STEP 3

STEP 4B

STEP 5

STEP 6

STEP 7

CLOSING

context have a storytelling frame, not a background knowledge frame. They are not meant to tell the audience that Jesus was Chinese or African, because the frame is not to provide background knowledge but rather to communicate that Jesus came for Chinese and African people also. Some people say this is an inappropriate approach to biblical art because the first priority should be to make it as historically accurate as possible. But for many cultures, their first question is not whether this is actually what these people looked like, but rather, "Is this story for us, or for some other culture? If it is for some other culture, we may look at it to learn about you, but we won't think it has anything to do with us. Stories for us must be drawn from our world, just as they must be told in our language."

When we hear stories, most of us are thinking more or less abstractly in images about the story. When we use a story frame to show others a series of images, the concepts behind the images are more critical for communication than the precise historical accuracy of the images. People often use visual arts as an aid to story memory or concept memory. The "time-travel" interpretive frame, where artists conduct historical research and try to make their drawings resemble as closely as possible how historical events might have actually looked, seems to have originated at about the same time as films that used huge budgets to recreate events with historical accuracy. And besides that, films are simply glorified plays. We do not know how tall or short Jesus was or if he had a particular hairstyle, let alone what his exact skin color was. But a contextualized depiction is not incorrect if the frame is to put on a play or conceptualize a story rather than to travel in time.

IDENTIFY THE FRAME OF A BIBLICAL STORY IMAGE

When you see a Bible story depicted as though it happened in a local context, ask the artist if the work is to tell a story or to provide accurate historical information. Is it framed or interpreted by the art-is-a-moment-of-a-play paradigm or art-is-a-time-traveling-photo paradigm? If we understand visual arts as languages, we should be no more surprised when Bible stories are told in local images than when they are told in local words.

ANALYZE
AN EVENT
CONTAINING THE
CHOSEN GENRE

PART C:
RELATE THE EVENT'S GENRE(S) TO ITS BROADER CULTURAL CONTEXT

Nothing you encounter in a community exists in isolation. Words, clothes, houses, food, movements, facial expressions, family—everything is interwoven, like threads in fabric. Likewise, events with artistic communication exist in relationship to other parts of a society and interact with local, regional, national, and global realities. Understanding how an event connects to its broader context allows you to enter more accurately into its creation, evaluation, integration, and celebration.

We've chosen some categories of cultural investigation that have helped other people gain insights into the workings of artistic activity. Each topic consists of the following sections: the central question or questions that should guide your investigation of the topic; and a discussion of the aspects of the topic that have proven to be relevant for others, with research activities to get you started.

A common way that communities connect an event to the rest of their lives is through *genre*. We use this term simply to refer to a type or category of artistic production. People usually perform something that connects strongly to an event they've experienced before, such as a wedding, concert, or particular ceremony. And in many places, communities have names for these types of events or kinds of communication. Never does someone create a new bit of artistic communication with no connection to something

PREFACE

PREPARE

STEP 1

STEP 2

STEP 3

STEP 4C

STEP 5

STEP 6

STEP 7

CLOSING

they've experienced before. Nothing comes from nothing. The explorations we guide you through here are centered on a particular event containing the enactment of a particular genre, but relate to broader realities. The Community Arts Profile contains a section for you to compile summaries of your discoveries about how genres in an event relate to the themes below.

Note also that you can't be sure of the reality of broader cultural themes unless you have had a detailed familiarity with actual artistic communication. Facts without themes are trivial. Themes without facts are vapors. So keep investigating genres in events, guided by activities in this step. For each topic ask, "How does this relate to the lenses and artistic domains?"

ARTISTS

People are at the core of artistic communication. They learn, perform, and pass on the skills and knowledge that make such communication effective. They add their individual skills, interests, and goals to existing traditions. They are the keepers of artistic treasure. So any plan a community makes to draw on its arts for kingdom goals must have understanding of and interaction with artists at its core. Other people will play strategic roles in the encouraging, limiting, and acceptance of a type of artistic communication. But without the artist to create and perform, plans will never succeed. They are the ones God is calling us to learn from, welcome, and encourage. They are the central actors in our cocreation activities.

The exploratory activities that will help you answer the questions in this section have to do with getting to know people: interviews, participation, and observation. In addition to the particular tasks below, you may decide to study formally or informally with a skilled artist, join artists in their personal and artistic worlds, sit with a composer and see how he or she creates, ask to watch an artist teach someone else, or share your own life and artistic gifts with him or her. These are our people.

WHO ARE THE ARTISTS RELATED TO THIS KIND OF EVENT?
Everyone in a community is likely to be involved in artistic communication in some way—by listening, watching, singing, dancing, composing, admiring, critiquing, etc. Some people, however, have more knowledge and skills related to creation, performance, and transmission; our focus is on these people. Every community categorizes and defines artists in different ways, and few use broad categories like "musician" or "artist." More often, an artist is given a role and identity in his or her language of singer, player of a particular instrument, mask maker, or other such designation.

To find artists involved in a type of event you've experienced, perform activities like these:

- Through interviews, list the roles of participants in an event. "Look at an Event's Forms" (**Part A**) will help you in this.
- Choose one of these roles and ask friends and other community members who some of the most respected fillers of that role are. Repeat this for other roles.
- Over time, ask, listen, watch, and confirm the skills and reputations of artists you get to know. Everyone will have different combinations of skills and attributes, and so will play different roles in kingdom activities. You may find, for example, an older man who knows the most songs in a genre, but is not the best singer. The community may decide to have the older man lead the choice of which songs to record on an audio product they create for wide distribution, but have someone else sing.

HOW DO ARTISTS IN THIS GENRE RELATE TO THEIR COMMUNITY?

A community may ascribe high, neutral, or low status to an artist associated with a particular genre. Though the status level may be determined by the individual character of an artist, respect or disrespect is often associated with a particular artistic role. People who play drums associated with royalty, for example, may enjoy high levels of respect and honor. Artists who perform for activities a society deems less respectable—for example, lewd dramatic entertainment in a brothel—may be merely tolerated. We need to be aware of community attitudes when encouraging artists to create for kingdom purposes, because these feelings will have a strong effect on how deeply Christians embrace their activities.

It may also be useful to investigate how a community compensates an artist, either monetarily or through some other means. In Daasanech society in northern Kenya, a man pays a woman *gaaro* specialist to compose songs relating important events of his life. Most Daasanech mothers compose songs for their babies, but are not paid.

To find out how artists involved in a type of event you've experienced relate to their society, perform activities like these:

- Through discreet and sensitive interviews, ask people their opinions of people who fill particular roles in an artistic event.
- As you get to know an artist, ask how they are treated by different segments of society, and if and how they get paid for their work.

HOW DO PEOPLE BECOME ARTISTS IN THIS GENRE?

Becoming an artist in a particular genre may be largely determined by societal patterns, achieved by individual effort and skill, or—most often—through a combination of the two. In parts of West Africa, for example, members of certain castes are expected to work

PREFACE

PREPARE

STEP 1

STEP 2

STEP 3

STEP 4C

STEP 5

STEP 6

STEP 7

CLOSING

PREFACE

PREPARE

STEP 1

STEP 2

STEP 3

STEP 4C

STEP 5

STEP 6

STEP 7

CLOSING

as professional singers and storytellers. Because of this societal expectation, children in these castes are taught musical skills and performance practices from a young age. In other cultures, people are encouraged primarily to follow individual interests and skills.

To find out how artists become involved in a particular genre, perform activities like these:

- Do a biographical study of an artist's life, using common journalists' questions: Where have you lived? How did you learn the skills associated with this role? Who has influenced you in your art? Why did you follow this path? Describe some important events in your life that impacted your artistry.
- Similarly, ask people knowledgeable in a genre to describe its history: Where did it originate? Who were important figures in its development? When did important steps in the genre's development take place?

CREATIVITY

We define artistic creativity as occurring when one or more people draw on their personal competencies, symbolic systems, and social patterns of their community to produce an event of heightened communication that has not previously existed in its exact form.[86] To find out how it works in the community you're working with, you'll need to get inside what is a very dynamic process. You can do this through asking questions, participating in creative acts, and commissioning new works and watching what happens.

WHO ARE THE CREATORS OF NEW WORKS?
Creation can be performed by an individual specialist—someone who is recognized for their abilities, or a casual "one-shot" composer who writes for a particular occasion—or a collaboration of several individuals. To find out who the creators of the artistic elements of an event are, watch a live performance or a video of a performance, or look at an artistic object with a friend and ask questions like these:

- Who made this, and when?
- Who made each element of this event, and when? Examples of elements might include a dance move, a song, a play, a poem, or a woven cloth.

HOW DO NEW EXAMPLES OF THIS FORM COME INTO BEING?
Composition can take place through deliberate and conscious effort, or be received through dreams or visions. If through conscious effort,

86   See also Csikszentmihalyi's concepts of person, symbolic domain, and field. Mihalyi Csikszentmihalyi, *Creativity: Flow and the Psychology of Discovery and Invention* (New York: HarperCollins, 1996), 23–31.

an individual may make it happen, a group may work on it together, or it could be a combined effort (several composers working on different parts or at different times).

Techniques for composition include the following: conscious creation of an element of a genre, like a song, poem, dance, or mask; taking parts of old creations and putting them together in a new way; improvisation; communal re-creation; creating out of emotional stress after a particularly meaningful or traumatic situation; and composition-in-performance. To find out how people compose new works, perform activities like these:

- Watch a live performance, a video of a performance, or look at an artistic object with a friend and ask questions like this: What did people do to make this? Who was involved?
- Commission a new work in the genre this event is a type of, then ask the creator(s) what steps they will follow. You can also ask if you could document the process by written notes, photographs, and video.

WHAT DOES "NEW" MEAN IN THIS ART FORM?

Creativity is about making something new. But each community values and defines newness in different ways. If a group values tradition and continuity more than innovation, then they may discourage changes in a tradition. If they have the opposite view, they may reward creators who depart significantly from tradition.

To find out how people involved in the creation of this art form think about newness, perform activities like these:

- Interact with a creator while he or she is making something. Ask what aspects of the new creation are different from existing creations, and which are the same. Ask if they can list any principles, wisdom, or proverbs that guide their creativity.
- Ask a group of people if they can remember an example of a work that jarred them because it was too new. Ask if they can isolate an element that displeased them.

WHERE DO THE COMPONENTS OF CREATIVITY FOR THIS GENRE LIE?

Each community performs arts that draw on a unique combination of its components of creativity—creators, language and other symbolic systems, and audience and gatekeepers. Each component, in turn, can vary in its nearness to the community, measured geographically, conceptually, and in communal identity. According to this rubric, then, a community may have composers and performers that draw on symbolic systems residing in local traditions, in traditions from another community, in a regional or national artistic genre, or in the artistic traditions of a distant culture.

Applying the questions below to this event, fill out this table.

PREFACE

PREPARE

STEP 1

STEP 2

STEP 3

STEP 4C

STEP 5

STEP 6

STEP 7

CLOSING

PREFACE

PREPARE

STEP 1

STEP 2

STEP 3

STEP 4C

STEP 5

STEP 6

STEP 7

CLOSING

Location		Creativity Components		
		Creators	Language and Other Symbolic Systems	Audience and Gatekeepers
Distant – Near	Community			
	Region or Nation			
	World			

- *Creators*: Where are the creators, the individuals and groups who compose and perform each element of this event? This may refer to singers, instrument players, lyricists, composers, playwrights, sculptors, and others.
- *Language and other symbolic systems*: In what communities do the systems and skills underlying their artistic production reside? This speaks to systems of language, melody, scale, rhythm, timbre, poetic devices, dramatic characterization, movement, repertoire, and the like. Also included are competencies such as instrument building, and means of learning performance skills, such as formal and informal educational structures.
- *Audience and gatekeepers*: Where are the individuals and groups who influence artistic production most in this context? This comprises knowledgeable audiences; highly and widely regarded performers; commercial, social, religious, or aesthetic gatekeepers; and others.

LANGUAGE

The language(s) and types of language used in an artistic event can reveal much about its relationship to its broader cultural context. Song lyrics in a regional or national language support regional or national identity. A woven tapestry with words in a minority language, using that language's unique alphabet, accentuates identity with a minority community. It's also common in artistic communication to use archaic or special registers, forms not used in everyday speech. This may reflect a sense of mystery or fear associated with the genre, or it may simply have been frozen in that form for other reasons.

WHAT LANGUAGE(S), DIALECT(S), AND REGISTER(S) ARE APPROPRIATE FOR THIS FORM?

Watch or listen to a recording of an event, or look at an object with someone who knows a lot about it. List every component containing language, and write down answers to questions like these:

- What language or dialect is this in? Are there some words in other languages?
- Can you imagine someone saying this in normal speech, or is it a special kind of language?

WHAT STATUS AND IDENTITY ARE ASSOCIATED WITH EACH LANGUAGE CHOICE?

With the same list of language types used, ask questions like these:

- When you hear this type of language, who does it make you think of?
- Why do you think the creator(s) used this type of language?

TRANSMISSION AND CHANGE

The participants in an artistic event learned its associated skills and knowledge somehow. This transmission may have happened in a socially structured way, through schools, lessons, or formal apprenticeships. It could also have happened informally, through learning by watching, or individual exploration. Methods could include aural activities like repetition of an expert's singing, playing, or acting. The process could also include written helps, like music notation or a dance score. This human-to-human transfer always includes some measure of change: the teaching process is not perfect, people remember inaccurately or forget completely, and each individual has different interests and levels of skills that affect what they learn.

HOW ARE COMPETENCIES ASSOCIATED WITH THIS FORM PASSED ON TO OTHERS?

To find out how people learn this type of event, perform activities like these:

- Ask participants in the event to tell how they learned to do what they did. Ask if you can participate in or watch that process sometime. As you watch, note the interactions between people, how more knowledgeable people are treated, and what objects are part of the process.
- If this event is part of a long tradition, ask an older person how and when people used to learn it. Then ask if they still learn it this way, and if not, what has changed to make the difference.

PREFACE

PREPARE

STEP 1

STEP 2

STEP 3

STEP 4C

STEP 5

STEP 6

STEP 7

CLOSING

PREFACE

PREPARE

STEP 1

STEP 2

STEP 3

STEP 4C

STEP 5

STEP 6

STEP 7

CLOSING

HOW HAS THIS FORM CHANGED HISTORICALLY?

To find out how this type of event has changed over time, perform activities like this:

- Find old and newer recordings or examples of an art form. Watch or listen to them with a knowledgeable person, and ask how the two differ. Ask what might have caused differences.

CULTURAL DYNAMISM

Healthy communities maintain a mix of continuity and change. Artistic genres can feed into this vitality through interactions between their stable and malleable elements. Stable elements occur regularly in time and place, and are tightly organized. More malleable elements are less predictable (perhaps marked by improvisation) and more loosely organized. Cultural dynamism happens when artists masterfully use the most malleable elements of their arts to invigorate the most stable. The chart below gives an example of malleable/stable pairs in a song genre with percussion instruments.

	Performance Organization	Song Structure	Rhythm
Malleable	Occasional performances	Changing vocal call	Improvising drum
Stable	Rehearsals	Unchanging vocal response	Unchanging percussion

Without creative, malleable structures to infuse new energy into the stable structures, the stable structures will decay and dissipate. And without stable undergirdings, the creators in malleable forms will have no dependable reference points to anchor their creativity.

Discuss these questions with artists to begin to understand the interplay between stable and malleable elements:

- *To identify stable artistic elements*: Which art forms or aspects of art forms occur most regularly, with the least amount of variability and tight organization?
- *To identify malleable artistic elements*: Which art forms or aspects of art forms occur with less predictability and are more loosely organized?
- *To identify interactions between stable and malleable elements*: See if you can find any artistic elements in the domains of rhythm, performance organization, or shape of the event through time that interact in pairs. For example,

does the rhythmic structure of a performance have some parts that never change, allowing a master percussionist to improvise?

IDENTITY AND POWER

We express who we are or who we want to be by choosing what, how, and where to communicate artistically. This means that every dance step, song, story, proverb, hairstyle, piece of jewely, and woven cloth is an act of identity affirmation. These affirmations relate to social power structures in different ways, which can cause controversy. It is important, then, to know how an art form fits into its local and wider communities, so they can make informed decisions in expanding the kingdom of God. Be cautious and humble in addressing issues of power.

WHAT KINDS OF PEOPLE IDENTIFY WITH THIS FORM AND WHAT CHARACTERIZES THEIR IDENTIFICATION?

To explore participants' identification with this type of event, perform activities like these:

- Make a list of elements associated with the event: language, dress, colors, instruments, and so on. Ask a friend which group each of these is associated with.
- Interview participants in the event to find out demographic information: age, gender, education, occupation, geographic origin, ethnic self-identification, language(s) spoken, and religion. Avoid discussing categories that may cause contention or invite danger.
- Ask participants why they are involved in this event.

HOW DOES THIS FORM RELATE TO SOCIAL STRATIFICATION, GENDER, OR OTHER DISTINCTIONS IN CULTURES THAT RELATE TO IT?

Artistic communication can affirm power structures, as with national anthems or royal pageantry. People can also use it to oppose power, as in early African-American rap and Rastafarian reggae. In terms of visibility, art forms can be expressed publicly or in hidden ways. Examples of public expressions affirming power include national anthems and West African praise songs. Less direct and visible comments on power occurred when slaves in the United States embedded antislavery messages in spirituals. To research this type of event's relationship to power, perform activities like these:

- Transcribe any texts associated with this event, like song lyrics or story content. Examine them to see if there are overt messages affirming or opposing a person, institution,

PREFACE

PREPARE

STEP 1

STEP 2

STEP 3

STEP 4C

STEP 5

STEP 6

STEP 7

CLOSING

PREFACE

PREPARE

STEP 1

STEP 2

STEP 3

STEP 4C

STEP 5

STEP 6

STEP 7

CLOSING

or other entity. Discreet discussion with a friend may help you find out if there are any hidden messages.

- Observe the event. Did people communicate messages that challenged authority in the event that you haven't seen them do elsewhere? Artistic action can provide a safe place for contestation or resolving conflict.

AESTHETICS AND EVALUATION

People find pleasure in their experience of artistic communication for many reasons: the group solidarity it may engender, the association of the experience with an enjoyable memory, or satisfaction in the attributes of an art form. This last possibility has to do with aesthetics, the study of the criteria people use to judge an artifact with respect to attributes perceived to be intrinsic to it.[87] Though there may be overlap between different communities, every society has a unique set of criteria they use to judge the intrinsic value of works of art they experience. In other words, there is no formal characteristic of artistic communication that is intrinsically pleasing, beautiful, or good.

Humans are quick to judge others' arts by their own aesthetic, but we must help ourselves and others not fall into this trap. Here are a few activities you can perform to find out how the community you're working with approaches correction and evaluation in general. Ask a friend questions like these:

- Would you correct someone older or younger, or in roles of higher or lower status than you? If so, how? The community might value direct correction in some contexts, or require indirection.
- How would these same kinds of people correct you?

Here are ways to explore evaluation specifically of the form of artistic objects:

- Ask people what makes a component of an art form good or bad.
- Observe experts teaching an art form to someone else— perhaps you—and write down what advice they give or mistakes they correct. These may point to an ideal.
- Notice items that are put in a place of prominence, spoken of with reverence, or that take special expertise and time to create. These are likely to have ideal characteristics. Ask people what makes them good or pleasing.
- Gather a small group of people to watch and listen to a recording of an event or look at an artistic object. Ask them to say what's good or bad about it.

---

87   See Joseph Margolis, *The Language of Art and Art Criticism: Analytic Questions in Aesthetics* (Detroit: Wayne State University Press, 1965), 44.

TIME

Artistic communication intersects with time in two important ways. First, because most arts provide some sort of rhythmic structure, people often experience time during performance differently than they do in other parts of life. Goodridge describes movement rhythm in performance as "a patterned energy flow of action, marked in the body by varied stress and directional change; also marked by changes in level of intensity, speed and duration."[88] Time may flow more quickly, more slowly, or in unpredictably complex ways to the experiencer of a performance. Secondly, the structure, flow, and timing of a performance may intersect with broader cultural temporal patterns. In many communities, certain events only occur at particular points in agricultural, religious, or other calendrical cycles.

To find out more about the intersection of artistic and community time, perform activities like these:

- Soon after an event, ask participants questions like these: How did you know when to do certain things? How did you experience time? Was it linear, cyclical, or flowing in waves? Did it feel sacred? When else do you experience time this way?
- Ask a small group of people to list all of the times an event of this type occurred in the last two years. Do you notice any temporal patterns? Ask why they happened when they did.
- Ask experts in a genre to describe the passage of time during performance. Do they explicitly connect this description to broader calendrical cycles?

EMOTIONS

One of the most celebrated characteristics of artistic communication is its capacity to express and evoke emotion. The arts have a way of connecting a sound, sight, movement, scent, or taste directly to potent, emotionally charged memories. They also often provide a socially accepted release for intense feelings, as lamentations and wailing do for grief. In addition, artistic communication can envelop a person's whole being, allowing gifted performers to magnify emotions in others by playing with their expectations of the art form. Finally, the arts are often associated with trance, ecstasy, and other states of overwhelming emotion.

To research an event's connections to emotion, perform activities like these:

---

88   Janet Goodridge, *Rhythm and Timing of Movement in Performance: Drama, Dance and Ceremony* (London: Kingsley, 1999), 43.

PREFACE

PREPARE

STEP 1

STEP 2

STEP 3

STEP 4C

STEP 5

STEP 6

STEP 7

CLOSING

- Watch a recording of an event and write down what emotions participants—including audience members—appear to express. Ask someone who was there if they agree with your interpretations.
- Watch a video recording of an artistic event with people who were there. Watch the observers, and when they exhibit any emotion—joy, surprise, sadness, anger, disdain, etc.—stop the recording and ask about what they're responding to. Make a list of the words they use to describe their emotions and what was going on in the performance that sparked them. Record their comments.
- Ask friends if they remember an artistic event that evoked very strong emotion in them. Have them describe the event and their reactions.

SUBJECT MATTER

The verbal content of songs, proverbs, plays, tapestries, and other arts flows from the minds, experiences, and histories of the participating individuals and communities. Sometimes artistic communication reveals information about subjects available almost nowhere else, such as spiritual actors or historical events. Other times, it communicates the values of the community in memorable form; proverbs are a strong example of this. The references of textual content may be metaphorical or cryptic, so your first understanding may not be the only one, or the deepest. To explore patterns in the subject matter addressed by artistic communication, perform activities like these:

- Make a list of the elements in an event that have verbal content, like songs, proverbs, or stories. Ask an expert to describe the messages in each. Ask: What is this about? What are they trying to communicate? Is there a lesson? If so, who is the lesson for? You may want to consult the *Outline of Cultural Materials* (OCM)[89] for examples of themes that are common to many cultures.
- As you watch a recording or read a transcription of an event, ask a small group of participants to list all of the references to people, objects, places, events, or spiritual beings. Ask them to describe each. Record or write down their answers.

---

89   George P. Murdock et al., *Outline of Cultural Materials*, 5th ed. with modifications (New Haven, CT: Human Relations Area Files, 2004), http://www.yale.edu/hraf.

COMMUNITY VALUES

Artistic communication often provides a place to challenge community authorities. However, how it is organized and performed may also reflect a community's values and social structures in important ways. Reflecting on the physical and social organization of participants may provide clues to broader community values. To research these relationships, observe an event and afterwards ask questions of participants like these:

- How do participants interact with representatives of authority within the event? How does this differ from such interactions in other contexts?
- Does the physical organization of participants show a hierarchical structure, as in the first, second, and third seats of performers in a symphony orchestra? Or are participants organized on the same physical level? Answers to these questions may reflect values of hierarchical vs. egalitarian social structures elsewhere in the community.
- In what ways, if any, are participants encouraged to express themselves individually? What signs of free vs. rigid atmosphere are there? Answers to these questions may reflect values of conformity vs. nonconformity elsewhere in the community.

COMMUNAL INVESTMENT

The amount of energy a community invests in different kinds of artistic activity varies widely. A grandfather speaking a proverb to his granddaughter involves only two people, requires no preparation, costs no money, and lasts for only a few seconds. A funeral for a king in western Cameroon, on the other hand, may last a month, include hundreds of people, and require significant finances to pay for food, transportation, and gifts. An assessment of the social, material, financial, and spiritual resources a community invests in an event provides important clues to its importance and influence.

To research a community's investment in an event, observe, ask, and write down information about the following parameters:

- length of time of performance
- status of scheduling: high status time, low status time
- amount of preparation
- cost of the performance
- location of the performance: high status, low status
- performance space: status, size, expense, exclusivity
- participants: number, status, exclusivity, level of skill or professionalism
- complexity: number of relevant features

PREFACE

PREPARE

STEP 1

STEP 2

STEP 3

STEP 4C

STEP 5

STEP 6

STEP 7

CLOSING

PREFACE

PREPARE

STEP 1

STEP 2

STEP 3

STEP 4C

STEP 5

STEP 6

STEP 7

CLOSING

ANALYZE
AN EVENT
CONTAINING THE
CHOSEN GENRE

PART D:
EXPLORE HOW A CHRISTIAN COMMUNITY RELATES ARTISTICALLY TO ITS BROADER CHURCH AND CULTURAL CONTEXT

Because we are concerned about the kingdom of God in this manual, and the church is a central component of the kingdom, we provide specialized tools to research the arts in churches. On one hand, you can treat a local church in a community like any other context where artistic communication happens—it uses particular artistic genres with unique forms and meanings, and is guided by particular social norms and patterns. This means that you can explore the arts in a church using the guides we've already presented in **Step 1** and the rest of **Step 4**. On the other hand, because we care very deeply about how God's people integrate the arts into their lives and commit to Scripture as a standard, you can treat arts in the church as a special case. The activities in this section help you do that.

In our approach, the artistic life of each Christian community need not be restricted to the artistic genres mentioned and used in the Bible. From Jesus' incarnational example of becoming a human being in a particular human culture (Phil 2), to the early spread of Christianity throughout the Roman Empire and the translation of Scripture into thousands of languages, Christianity is all about being

PREFACE

PREPARE

STEP 1

STEP 2

STEP 3

STEP 4D

STEP 5

STEP 6

STEP 7

CLOSING

born anew in every tribe and nation and language. The psalmist's charge to praise God "with timbrel and dancing" (Ps 150:4) doesn't mean we need to figure out and copy exactly what a timbrel is, its tuning, and the kinds of musical features associated with it. Rather, Psalm 150 encourages us to use every art form at our disposal to praise God.

Another unique aspect of churches is this: though every local church exists in a particular geographical location, each also connects to broader Christian communities—denominations, networks, Catholic or Orthodox orders, etc. These historical and relational ties influence a church's arts in many ways, and may change over time. The second Vatican Council's *Constitution on Liturgy* ("Sacrosanctum Concilium," no. 38), for example, resulted in musical experimentation, including the composition of indigenous masses.

The tools in this section help you learn how Christian communities function artistically in all of their social contexts, with Scripture as a guide. *The first three activities below build on each other, so you might want to do them together.* The other activities may be performed more independently. Read through them all to decide what best fits your context.

DISCOVER A CHRISTIAN COMMUNITY'S ARTS

The approach to identifying a church's artistic life is similar to that which we described for the broader community in "Take a First Glance at a Community's Arts" (**Step 1**). Put whatever you discover into the Community Arts Profile. Gather leaders and participants in various aspects of church life, and lead them through activities like these:

1. **List all of the contexts in which people act as part of this Christian community.**
   These contexts could include—but are not limited to—the following: Bible studies; home groups; Sunday school; adult education; corporate worship services; spiritual mentorships; Mass; Vacation Bible School; children's ministries; food pantry; visits to people who are sick; rites like baptism, weddings, and funerals; healing services; holiday celebrations; social outings; retreats and camps; outreach activities; festivals; concerts; prayer vigils; individual or family devotions.
2. **List any arts used in each of these contexts.**
   For each context the group has listed, write down if people use any form of artistic communication. If so, write what that form is. Common kinds of arts in Christian communities include singing, preaching, drama, storytelling, sculpting, carving, designing space, incense, dancing, making banners, drawing, reading or reciting poetry. Note also that rituals are common in Christian communities; they may be artistic

PREFACE

PREPARE

STEP 1

STEP 2

STEP 3

STEP 4D

STEP 5

STEP 6

STEP 7

CLOSING

events in themselves (e.g., as forms of drama or pageantry), and they often include artistic elements.

3. **List all of the people who have significant artistic gifts, whether they use them in the church or not.**
For each person in the Christian community with artistic training and gifts, list the kind(s) of arts they have skills in, and their particular competencies (e.g., composing, performing, drawing). Church leadership may be unaware of many of the gifts that its members have. In this case, you may want to help them perform a more thorough investigation through a simple questionnaire or oral investigation.

COMPARE A CHRISTIAN COMMUNITY'S USE OF ARTS WITH THAT OF ITS SURROUNDING COMMUNITIES

These steps will help churches decide how to better connect to the people in their geographical context. See especially "Church Life" and "Personal Spiritual Life" in **Step 2**. Remember that this is part of a broader process in which churches critically evaluate different artistic genres for potential use.

1. Consult the list you made above of all the kinds of arts that the Christian community uses in everything it does.
2. Consult the list of artistic genres used in the church's surrounding community you created in **Step 1**.
3. Mark each genre of artistic communication that exists both in the church and in its surrounding community.
4. For each genre that exists in both, discuss and write down ways in which their performance and purpose differ in each context.
5. Make a list of all the genres in the surrounding community that are not used in the church. Discuss reasons why these are not being used, and explore their potential for use.

EVALUATE HOW A CHRISTIAN COMMUNITY'S ARTS CURRENTLY FULFILL ITS PURPOSES

In **Step 2**, we highlighted a few reasons that a Christian community might act to extend the kingdom of God: to deepen corporate worship, improve spiritual formation, extend its witness, etc. A brief survey of how people used the arts in the Bible reveals a longer list: celebrate victory (Ex 15), accompany processions (2 Sam 6), adoration (2 Chr 5), cultural festivals (2 Chr 35:15), repentance (Ps 51), dancing (1 Chr 15), funerals (Matt 9:23), strengthen church (1 Cor 14:26), express happiness (Jas 5:13), express sadness (Ps 6),

PREFACE

PREPARE

STEP 1

STEP 2

STEP 3

STEP 4.0

STEP 5

STEP 6

STEP 7

CLOSING

spiritual warfare (2 Chr 20:21–23), healing (1 Sam 16). It's important to remember that not every use of the arts shown in Scripture serves as a positive example—Aaron crafted a golden calf as an idol (Ex 32), but we should not imitate him.

In addition, the Bible points to even more purposes of the church, including confession, witness, prayer, teaching, thanksgiving, discipleship, lamentation, evangelism, encouragement, exhortation, mind renewal, reconciliation, forgiveness, correction, commemoration, building solidarity, creating contextual equivalents, and testimony. Though we can't create an exhaustive list of all potential purposes, it is essential that each church identify the reasons they do things, so they can evaluate whether the arts they use help bring them about. This process may also reveal additional biblical aims that the community should adopt. The following steps can help do this:

1. Consult the list of all the contexts in which people act as part of their Christian community.
2. Choose at least one context in which artistic communication exists, and list its purposes. Refer to the paragraphs above for ideas.
3. List ways in which the form(s) of artistic communication used in each context support or detract from its purposes. You may need to go deeper into the features of these arts, beginning with Step 4, Part A's "Look at an Event's Forms."
4. Use what you've discovered…sparking activities in **Step 5**.

APPLY A HEART ARTS QUESTIONNAIRE TO A CHRISTIAN COMMUNITY

In this activity, the aim is to find out the artistic genres that most touch people's hearts in wider society and in any existing Christian congregations. The responses will provide strong indicators of artistic genres that could be used for kingdom purposes (1 Sam 16:23; 2 Kgs 3:15; Ps 81:1–3) and help you answer questions like these:

- What forms of expression in the surrounding community could be most appropriate to express joy and reverence in corporate worship? What would be the reaction of believers and nonbelievers to those? What artistic genres could you choose? How can you draw on the characteristics of this genre—the people involved, where it happens, the form of the event, the objects involved, the languages used—to deepen worship in a community?
- How could church planters and congregations evaluate the forms and symbolic meanings of the artistic genres that could be used in worship times?

- If your worship community is multicultural, how could you celebrate diversity in unity? How could each ethnic group feel equally involved, at the same time as drawing people together?
- In what ways do people communicate truth with each other in your society? How could these methods be used in penetrating ways (e.g., for preaching, evangelizing, liturgy, teaching)?
- How could you use some of these ideas when you interact with other communities (e.g., for outreach, missions, church planting, interfaith dialogue)?

Participants

Church leaders, corporate worship musicians, and someone good with forms and numbers.

Tasks

1. Define the community or community subgroup (e.g., ethnic or language groups, church) to be surveyed.
2. Based on the findings of your Community Arts Profile, draw up a list of common genres of artistic communication that are used in your church and its surroundings, along with the associated uses and meanings for each category. This may include local, national, regional, and global styles. It will also probably include a range of styles from traditional to modern and secular to religious. If this is a long list, combine similar styles and reduce it to a manageable number (ten to twenty maximum) for people you will interview.
3. Decide how large a representative interview group should be (e.g., if possible, fifty to one hundred people).
4. Decide who will conduct the interviews and how you will structure them (individually or in groups, orally or in written form). If two people conduct the interviews in person, you will be able to answer questions; one person can ask the questions and another person record the answers.
5. Devise the questionnaire:

   a. Provide interviewees with the list of common forms of arts used in your society.
   b. Ask questions about age, ethnicity, mother tongue, and reading languages.
   c. Ask what types of arts generate instant and powerful positive emotions in people's hearts, such as exceptional joy, energy, peace, or comfort.
   d. Make a way for people to rate their top four or five art styles; e.g., scoring them from one to five (if done orally,

PREFACE

PREPARE

STEP 1

STEP 2

STEP 3

STEP 4D

STEP 5

STEP 6

STEP 7

CLOSING

PREFACE

PREPARE

STEP 1

STEP 2

STEP 3

STEP 4D

STEP 5

STEP 6

STEP 7

CLOSING

maybe using the fingers of one hand). This can give a clearer result.

e. Make a space to indicate if interviewees are believers. This will help you to more easily compare and contrast the results.

6. Conduct the survey and focus in equal measure on every relevant social group and decade (aged 0–10, 11–20, etc.).
7. Collect and analyze the responses; list those with high scores in order. Take special note of the artistic preferences of minority groups.
8. Compare the results and identify differences with your current use of arts in gatherings.
9. Carefully assess each high-scoring genre in terms of its associations and its potential in worship, discipleship, evangelism, etc.
10. Make plans to further investigate each of these high-scoring genres, asking questions like: Who is gifted to develop these for kingdom purposes? What might be the response of different sectors of society? How can they be introduced?

EVALUATE WORSHIP MEETINGS USING BIBLICAL PRINCIPLES

What do you need to do to prepare yourself to encounter more of God's presence? First, there are spiritual factors, but second, we more easily draw near to God when we use the languages and cultural forms that are most familiar to us. For example, some believers sense God's presence in quiet reverence, structure, and formality. Others experience the Holy Spirit in exuberance, spontaneity, and informality. Most need a bit of both! But what forms are they? How should they be used?

This activity is a twofold study. It could be conducted in one or more workshops, or it could be spread out over several weeks. The aim is to ask questions about the whole breadth of a local congregation's communal worship experience. The purpose is to assess the appropriateness of each worship activity in the light of both Scripture and culture.

Participants

Church leaders, a representative group of believers, an ethnoarts facilitator.

Tasks

1. Define the ethnic and language groups under consideration. Then list the ways society normally expresses itself in communal life outside of church. Focus especially on values and practices common to biblical worship:

   a. When and how do people normally gather in groups?
   b. In group life, how do people show joy, contrition, respect, thankfulness, sorrow, etc. (e.g., with a dance, a song, prostration, abstinence from food, gift giving)?
   c. How do people instruct others, tell stories, rebuke others, share personal needs and griefs, give to the needy, etc.?
   d. What are the most common practices of celebration and meal sharing?
   e. What place do music or other art forms have in these activities?

2. Over several sessions, conduct a joint biblical study on the forms used in corporate and personal worship of God. Consider these passages together:

   a. worship as a daily offering of our whole lives (Luke 9:23; Rom 12:1)
   b. wholehearted and heartfelt adoration (Deut 6:5; John 4:24)
   c. the use of the voice and body in worship (e.g., 2 Sam 6:14,15; 2 Chr 5:12,13; Ps 47:1,5,6; 95:6; 134:2; 150; Luke 5:8; 1 Tim 2:8; Rev 5:8–14; 19:4)
   d. worship as a communal activity (1 Cor 14:26, Col 3:12–16)
   e. spontaneity, order, spiritual gifts, and leadership in corporate worship (1 Cor 12–14)
   f. intercessory prayer in corporate worship (1 Tim 2:1–8)
   g. Bible reading and instruction in worship (1 Tim 4:13; 2 Tim 3:14–4:5)
   h. baptism, Communion, healing, offerings (etc.) in meetings of worship
   i. the use of space, movement, music, poetry, creeds, and set texts in worship (Eph 5:18–20; Rev 7:9–12)

3. Compare each aspect of biblical worship with patterns of life you have identified in the surrounding community:

   a. In corporate worship, what community art forms might best express biblical praise, prayer, learning, and devotion? What musical instruments might be used?
   b. What physical postures are both biblically and culturally appropriate?
   c. What is a suitable physical layout of the meeting space?

PREFACE

PREPARE

STEP 1

STEP 2

STEP 3

STEP 4D

STEP 5

STEP 6

STEP 7

CLOSING

d. Who should lead corporate adoration (e.g., the preacher, priest, church leader, singer)? Should they stand, sit, or kneel?

e. In giving instruction, what is the place of Bible reading, exposition, storytelling, parables, catchphrases, memorization, group repetition, poetry, proverbs, movement, gesture, acting, chant, music, song, visual illustration, and questions from the audience?

f. What is the most culturally fitting way to do Bible reading? Should the Bible be placed on a special or dedicated desk?

g. What cultural factors are important for Communion, baptism, offerings, notices, healing prayer, etc.?

h. What will help worshipers from this community to express biblical spontaneity in expressions like prayer, song, dance, and prostration?

i. Are community members more liberated by formality or informality? Should meetings follow a regular structure? What are the roles of silence and order? Should set texts or responses be used (e.g., the Lord's Prayer, creeds, prayer formulas)?

j. Considering your answers to all of the previous questions, what helps worshipers to most easily find freedom to praise, listen, and draw near to the living God?

k. In what ways do these culturally appropriate ways of communing with God compare to the traditions of the church? How can both respect the authority and traditions of the church and promote freedom?

"Everything must be done so that the church may be built up." (1 Cor 14:26)
"Where the Spirit of the Lord is, there is freedom." (2 Cor 3:17)

EVALUATE A CHRISTIAN COMMUNITY USING THE WORSHIP WHEEL

Romans 12:1–2 shows that worship is something that flows from our whole bodies and should mark every aspect of our lives. Sometimes, however, a church's view of worship is limited to corporate gatherings with music. The "Worship Wheel" exercise helps churches see a broad range of worshipful activities in their lives that can be animated by integrating their local arts. We have divided these activities into four categories: Arts for the Lord; Arts for self; Arts for others; and Arts for celebrations and ceremonies. Note that the Holy Spirit needs to animate every action, and that we have provided some examples in each category.

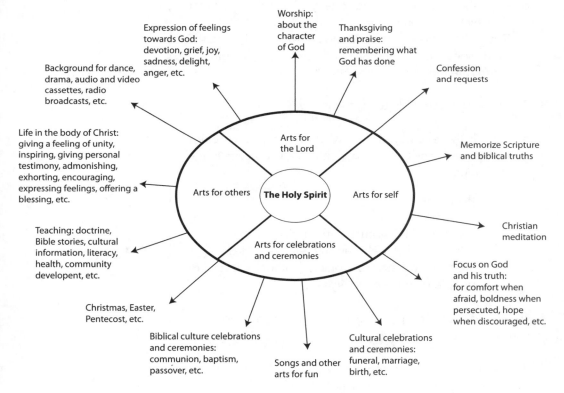

Figure 7: Worship Wheel[90]

Participants

Church leaders, musicians and other artists, a representative group of believers, an ethnoarts facilitator.

---

90   Adapted from Todd Saurman and Mary Saurman, "The Worship Wheel: Developing Culturally Appropriate Music as Expressions of Worship in the Lives of Believers," in Schrag and Neeley *All the World Will Worship*, 53–64.

PREFACE

PREPARE

STEP 1

STEP 2

STEP 3

STEP 4D

STEP 5

STEP 6

STEP 7

CLOSING

PREFACE

PREPARE

STEP 1

STEP 2

STEP 3

STEP 4D

STEP 5

STEP 6

STEP 7

CLOSING

Tasks

1. Pray for God to lead you as you use the "Worship Wheel" tool.
2. Do a group Bible study, using John 4:18–26; Romans 11:33–12:3; and Ephesians 5:14–21. Explore together what the Bible says about true worship:

   a. Do these texts give commands about the time, place, or order of service in meetings for New Testament worship?
   b. Are there any poetic texts in this passage? What does this say about the use of art forms in church life?
   c. If the Holy Spirit gives new believers new artistic messages to communicate, whose artistic styles will be used? (See 1 Cor 14:15; Eph 5:18,19.)
   d. Who should believers sing to (e.g., God, oneself, other believers, the community)?
   e. When the Bible says that we should "worship in. . .truth" and "speak to one another with. . .songs," what biblical truths are the topic of the songs?

3. Staying with these Bible texts, focus now on culture:

   a. How do these passages affirm what you are already doing?
   b. Can you see any gaps in your church arts practice in the following areas?

      i.   the range of arts
      ii.   the range of artistic styles
      iii. the range of Scripture truths in song
      iv.   arts created by believers in their own styles
      v.   arts that address God, oneself, other believers, or people in the community

4. Turning to the Worship Wheel, make a list of your regular songs or other art forms that

   a. speak to God—what topics?
   b. speak to oneself—what functions?
   c. celebrate special occasions—what occasions?
   d. speak to others—what functions?

5. Where are the gaps in your arts repertoire? What do you consider most important for the needs in your society or congregation(s)?
6. If you are holding an arts creation workshop, who can create the arts you would like to develop?

   a. Can you act on these ideas now?

b. If not, make a plan, asking these and similar questions: Which gaps can we fill? What is the best way to fill the gaps? Who can help us to do this? When could we start?

ASSESS A MULTICULTURAL CHRISTIAN COMMUNITY'S ARTS

In multiethnic churches, the church's diversity is not always reflected in its artistic expressions. The leading group often dominates artistically, to the disadvantage of others. If church leaders want their members to interact better between cultural groups and to worship as true equals, they will usually need to take intentional steps to help people cross cultural divides. This activity is designed to chart a way forward. It could be done as a workshop or as a whole church study over several weeks.

Participants
Church leaders, artistically gifted believers, an ethnoarts facilitator.

Tasks
1. Conduct a Bible study on the cultural diversity of the church of God. Explore these passages together:

    a. Genesis 1:26,27 (all are equal and made in God's image)
    b. Genesis 12:3 (God's desire is to bless all peoples)
    c. Psalm 67 (all the nations are to praise God)
    d. Isaiah 19:23–25 (former rival nations worship together)
    e. Acts 2:11 (all nations hear the Bible's message in their own languages)
    f. Romans 15:5–11, Colossians 3:11–16 (diversity and unity in love and worship)
    g. Revelation 21:26,27 (cultural diversity in the age to come)

2. Assess your current multicultural strategies in these areas:

    a. Leadership: How can the leadership become multicultural?
    b. Fellowship: How can the church help believers interact well across cultures?
    c. Pastoral care: What issues may be different for members of different cultures?
    d. Outreach: What are the natural social networks of different cultural groups?

PREFACE

PREPARE

STEP 1

STEP 2

STEP 3

STEP 4D

STEP 5

STEP 6

STEP 7

CLOSING

PREFACE

PREPARE

STEP 1

STEP 2

STEP 3

STEP 4b

STEP 5

STEP 6

STEP 7

CLOSING

3. Assess the current arts strategy of your meetings. For example, do you

    a. welcome visitors warmly but continue with your previous arts?
    b. separate believers into congregations based on language, culture, and/or age?
    c. invite members of different groups to use their own songs and other arts from time to time?
    d. rotate the arts leadership between different cultures?
    e. mix up members of different cultures in the musical or other arts team(s)?
    f. regularly and gladly sing songs all together from the cultures represented?
    g. create new art forms which blend elements from various of the members' cultures?

4. Conduct the heart arts questionnaire for your congregation (if you have not already), including one or two preliminary questions about heart language, place of birth, education, age group (0–10, 11–20, etc.), and gender. Then ask a few deeper questions:

    a. What arts are we missing if we are to be genuinely multicultural?
    b. How can we embrace different styles more?
    c. What should we make a priority?
    d. When would be a good time to introduce these ideas?

INTERPRET SCRIPTURE WELL

Before integrating Scripture into artistic creations, artists should understand the Scripture well. Biblical scholars Duvall and Hays describe the "Interpretive Journey" between the "biblical village" and "our village today."[91] According to them, a river of cultural differences separates the two villages. Christian artists need to understand this interpretive journey to create reliable messages and share Scripture accurately with their communities.

Step 1: Understand the biblical text "in the biblical town," the way the original audience would have understood the text in their context.

Step 2: Measure the width of the river to cross. What are the differences of culture, language, time, and situation between the biblical audience and us? The river between the original audience and today's audience may be narrow when many cultural aspects

---

91   J. Scott Duvall and J. Daniel Hays, *Grasping God's Word* (Grand Rapids: Zondervan, 2001), 19–25.

link us with them, or wide when the passage seems difficult to understand or apply.

Step 3: Build a principle bridge over the river. What are the key theological principles in this text? The principle(s) should be relevant to both the biblical audience and to us today. Additional biblical background knowledge may be needed to build this bridge if the river is wide. Help can be found in Bible study guides or Internet searches.

Step 4: Grasp the text in our town. Observe how the principle in the text addresses the original situation. Discover a parallel situation in the local culture today. Make your applications specific. Many applications may be drawn from the same principle. The way the application is realized may be different in different cultures, but the principle will be the same. Well-rounded Bible knowledge is needed to make good applications of Scripture to our lives today. Scripture interprets Scripture: different passages may address different aspects of a problem or topic. We can be unbalanced by looking at only one side of an issue, or balanced by considering all of the Scripture that deals with a topic.

People, including Christian artists, need to interpret Scripture according to the principle of **authorial intent** rather than **receptor intent**. If we interpret Scripture as the author meant, we are on solid ground. If we interpret what we want it to mean, we are on shaky ground.

Artists are a little bit like teachers. They need to compare the audience's point of view with Scripture's point of view on a topic, and discern what pieces of information are missing in order for their audience to understand the applications of Scripture. By understanding Scripture well, they can make their performance answer the types of questions their listeners are likely to ask.

What kinds of background information does a person need to interpret Scripture accurately? Knowledge about the original recipients' culture and historical situation and how those differ from their own; an overarching knowledge of the metanarrative of Scripture, or the big picture, to know where any given Scripture portion fits; the context of a given passage; and finally, typical questions the audience is likely to ask, to be able to answer them in the performance or recording. Make the presentation of the message specific to the people based on their assumptions. Some local assumptions may need to be affirmed as correct and true and good, and others may need to be challenged and corrected by Scripture. Bible translator Harriet Hill found that among the Adioukrou people of Côte d'Ivoire, contextual helps, whether provided orally or in writing, improved comprehension by an average of 39.2 percent.[92]

Let's look at an example. Romans 16:16 says, "Greet one another with a holy kiss." In the biblical village, this is the common way to

---

92   Harriet Hill, *Communicating Context in Bible Translation among the Adioukrou of Côte d'Ivoire* (Ann Arbor, MI: UMI), 363.

PREFACE

PREPARE

STEP 1

STEP 2

STEP 3

STEP 4D

STEP 5

STEP 6

STEP 7

CLOSING

PREFACE

PREPARE

STEP 1

STEP 2

STEP 3

STEP 40

STEP 5

STEP 6

STEP 7

CLOSING

greet someone warmly. The river of difference for some cultures today is that kissing signifies a relationship reserved for husband and wife, or kissing does not exist at all in their experience. The principle bridge is that we should greet one another warmly. When we grasp the text in our town, the way to express an appropriate greeting differs from culture to culture. Some would bow and others would hug, but the essential is the principle of greeting each other warmly. We could make a welcoming song for newcomers to our church to make them feel welcome and accepted.

ADDRESS THEOLOGICAL OBJECTIONS

The principles for addressing theological objections to unfamiliar uses of arts in Christian communities are the same as those guiding this entire manual. In short, dialogue with objectors in ways that encourage their input, show respect for and knowledge of their beliefs and practices, treat them as complete human beings, and paint a biblically based vision of a better future. We provide two tools here that can help you address common problems and misunderstandings. Many other resources exist, including Worship Resources International (http://www.worr.org) and StoneWorks (http://www.stoneworks-arts.org).

COMPARATIVE CHART OF MUSICAL INSTRUMENTS MENTIONED IN THE OLD TESTAMENT

Sometimes Christian communities have developed strong negative associations with particular artistic objects (e.g., instruments) or genres. This chart helps show how objects have no inherent moral value: it is the heart of the person using an object that determines whether God is pleased with it or not. You may follow these steps with a group:

1. Write the Scripture references along the top of a chalkboard or whiteboard.
2. Ask someone to read each passage aloud, then ask the group to say each instrument that was mentioned. Write the names of the instruments under the passage.
3. Ask the group to note instruments that occur in more than one column. Circle those.
4. Ask the group to describe the purpose of each event. Write this purpose under each passage.
5. Ask the group if they can find a correlation between certain instruments and certain purposes.
6. Ask what principles they can derive from this exercise. Then discuss how they can apply these principles to the use of arts in their Christian community.

Daniel 3:5 king's court (false worship)	Isaiah 5:12 drunken party (secular)	Psalm 150 praising God (true worship)	2 Samuel 6:5; 1 Chronicles 15:16–29 religious procession (true worship)
flute *(end-blown)*		flute *(end-blown)*	
animal horn trumpet		shofar trumpet	shofar trumpet silver trumpets
reed pipe	reed pipe		
lyre	lyre	lyre	lyre
larger lyre	larger lyre	larger lyre	larger lyre
bow harp all kinds of instruments		string and woodwind instruments	
	frame drum	frame drum	frame drum
		cymbals	cymbals
		loud cymbals	
			rattle
		dance	dance

SOME FACTS ABOUT AND BIBLICAL REFERENCES TO ARTISTIC COMMUNICATION[93]

You can use these statements and Scripture references for discussion with church leaders:

God created man in his own image.

Creativity and imagination are part of the reflection of God's image in every human being (Gen 1:27). God created *ex nihilo* (out of nothing; Gen 1), while humans create *ex creatio* (out of what God already created; Ps 96:1).

Aesthetic pleasure comes from God.

"God made. . .trees that were pleasing to the eye and good for food" (Gen 2:9). We are free to value and celebrate pleasure that comes from artistic form.

---

93   For more, see Colin Harbinson, "Redeeming the Arts," 1993, http://www.colinharbinson. com/teaching/redeemingarts.

PREFACE

PREPARE

STEP 1

STEP 2

STEP 3

STEP 4D

STEP 5

STEP 6

STEP 7

CLOSING

PREFACE

PREPARE

STEP 1

STEP 2

STEP 3

STEP 4O

STEP 5

STEP 6

STEP 7

CLOSING

Humans are culture shapers.

God put Adam in the garden to cultivate it and keep it (Gen 2:15), and has told us that we will reign with him at the end of time (Matt 24:45–47; 25:31–34; Rev 22:5). God wants humans to shape and make culture, to steward beauty.

God calls people to artistic communication.

God gave Bezalel his Spirit, understanding, knowledge, craftsmanship, and teaching abilities to make artistic designs for the building of his tabernacle (Ex 31:1–6). He will certainly give us skill, too, as we are also working to build his church, which is the body (Eph 4:11–13). We should develop our own artistic gifts and encourage others to develop theirs.

God uses diverse forms of arts for diverse purposes.

He used visual art to bring repentance (Num 21:1–8), drama to prophesy (Ezek 4), multiple arts to worship, lament, instill fear, rejoice, repent, teach, celebrate, fight battles, and other purposes.

Diverse expressions please God.

The psalmist in Psalm 150 encouraged his listeners to include as wide a range of artistic forms to worship God as possible: harp, lyre, tambourine, dancing, strings, flutes, and cymbals. We should do the same.

Most of Scripture consists of artistic forms of communication.

The Bible contains primarily proverbs, songs, stories, poetry, drama, and descriptions of visual imagery and dance; only a small proportion is propositional and didactic. Jesus' primary method of communication was parables (Matt 13:13).

Heart and allegiance are more important than the form of artistic communication.

God said, "Away with the noise of your songs!" (Amos 5:23,24) because his people were unrighteous and unjust. He also said that "those who trust in idols, who say to images, 'You are our gods,' will be turned back in utter shame" (Isa 42:17).

No one should be forced to change good parts of their culture to worship God.

In Acts 15 the early church decided that Gentiles did not need to become Jews in order to be followers of Christ.

God has opened up worship from a single earthly place to an unlimited number of places.

Jesus says that true worshipers "worship the Father in the Spirit and truth," not in a particular place (John 4:19–24). This feeds into the reality of people from every nation and language coming to gather around God's throne in heaven, worshiping in the ways they have learned (Rev 7:9,10).

One culture's music and other arts do not communicate universally to someone from a different culture.

This is a fact. Like spoken language, artistic forms communicate meaning that is assigned within a culture. In other words, artistic meaning must be learned within a community in the same way that a language is learned.

HOW TO AVOID BOTH SYNCRETISM AND IRRELEVANCE

One of the most common concerns that people have about integrating new art forms into their Christian community's life is that it will lead to syncretism. In other words, how can we know when the use of a particular artistic genre or musical instrument is syncretism—an inappropriate mixing of Christianity with another religion, or when it is simply an expression of good biblical contextualization (the wise use of culture and local context to express some aspect of biblical Christianity)?[94]

When a certain element of a community encounters Christ (e.g., artistic forms or rituals), the following situations may ensue, depending on the Christians' approach:

Christians' approach to an artistic form or ritual	Immediate effect	Ultimate effect
Total rejection	Art form goes underground	Dualism—people act as Christians in some contexts, relying on other beliefs in other contexts
	Christian community seen as foreign	Rest of community rejects Christ
Transformation	Christian community follows a process that leads to transformation of the art form	Community integrates Christian truth and actions into their lives
Total acceptance	Christian community does not "take captive every thought" (2 Cor 10:5)	Syncretism—people inappropriately mix their Christian faith with another belief system

Figure 8: Approach to Artistic Forms[95]

The only ultimate effect that we want to work towards is that resulting from transformation. In many ways, the process we describe

94   See Robin Harris, "Contextualization: Exploring the Intersections of Form and Meaning," *Connections* 9, nos. 2 and 3 (2010).
95   Adapted from Joanne Shetler, "Communicating the New Information of Scripture When It Clashes with Traditional Assumptions" (paper presented at the Evangelical Missiological

PREFACE

PREPARE

STEP 1

STEP 2

STEP 3

STEP 4D

STEP 5

STEP 6

STEP 7

CLOSING

below is a condensation of the whole Create Local Arts Together process. This brief overview should help skeptical Christians see a trustworthy way forward:

1. **Verbalize the existing form or ritual.**
   a. Describe the form or ritual.
   b. Verbalize the reasons for and consequences of performing it.
   c. List beliefs that underlie its performance.
   d. Describe the consequences of not performing it.

2. **Search Scripture.** Relate Scriptures to the reasons and consequences motivating people to perform the form or ritual, always making those reasons and consequences overt.
   a. These observations could be in the form of
      i. what we always thought (beliefs that clash with Scripture),
      ii. but what we didn't know (beliefs that align with Scripture).
   b. Identify aspects of the ritual or form that communicate any beliefs that clash with Scripture.

3. **Evaluate the existing form or ritual in light of Scripture.**
   a. Note where there is conflict between the form or ritual and Christian truths.
   b. Encourage exploration of and modifications possible that would make scriptural truths clear.

4. **Create a transformed response and unite believers.**
   a. Based on the evaluation, encourage the believers to craft a modified ritual or art form.
   b. Encourage the Christian leaders to present the transformed ritual or art form to Christian believers, explaining how and why they suggest adopting these choices.
   c. Encourage the Christian leaders to create a plan to integrate this transformed art form or ritual into the life of the Christian community.

5. **Plan to address other points of worldview conflict through the same process.**

Society Southeast Regional Meeting, Conyers, GA, 2011); Amy West, "Equipping Urban Believers to Meet Traditional Pressures" (paper presented at the Evangelical Missiological Society Southeast Regional Meeting, Conyers, GA, 2011); and Paul G. Hiebert, *Anthropological Insights for Missionaries* (Grand Rapids: Baker Book House, 1985).

PREFACE

PREPARE

STEP 1

STEP 2

STEP 3

STEP 4D

STEP 5

STEP 6

STEP 7

CLOSING

SPARK CREATIVITY

We've finally reached the climactic moment in our cocreation process. You might think of it as the point in a pregnancy when the baby is born. In **Steps 1–4**, you and the community have prepared for and nurtured the mother and the infant in the womb, and you're about to see the fruit of this preparation. New artistry is about to enter the world and you are the midwives.

Steps **6** and **7** will address how this new creation will grow in quality and influence. But in **Step 5** our goal is to help you

- design an activity
- that will result in new artistry in a genre
- which, when peformed in a community event
- will likely produce particular kinds of effects in those who experience it
- and thereby provide a chance for the community to move toward a kingdom goal.

We've already worked through all of these elements except the first. Here's the process to design a sparking activity:

- Think about what a sparking activity is.
- Identify opportunities to capitalize on and barriers to overcome.
- Decide on the type of activity.
- Design a new activity or modify an existing activity.
- Perform the activity.

PREFACE

PREPARE

STEP 1

STEP 2

STEP 3

STEP 4

STEP 5

STEP 6

STEP 7

CLOSING

Note that some activities might build on others you have done. You'll also see that many activities we describe may contribute to multiple kingdom effects. For example, you may commission an artist to create a new Scripture-based work in a traditional genre for a celebration. From this, people in the community will learn more about God, which feeds into "witness" in our "Church Life" kingdom category. But the social status of the genre will also increase, which ties into the appropriate affirmation of God's creativity we discuss in "Identity and Sustainability." This is good.

THINK ABOUT WHAT A SPARKING ACTIVITY IS

A sparking activity is anything anybody does that results in the creation of new artistry. It will require different amounts of community investment, from low to high. For example, the act could be as casual as suggesting to a friend that she respond with painting during an oration at a meeting that afternoon, or it could entail the enormous complexity of planning a festival involving scores of artists and government officials. A sparking activity may also lead to immediate fruit or provide a structure where future creativity can happen. In the Mono example, Punayima's apprentices didn't compose new *gbaguru* songs right away, but they each learned to make, tune, and play a *kundí*; this developed their capacity to compose in the future. Finally, such an activity may fold in many or all of the seven Create Local Arts Together (CLAT) steps or focus on just one. As we'll see, workshops often include times to identify kingdom goals, perform initial analysis of a genre, and create and improve works. Other kinds of activities may focus solely on the act of creating. In any case, the community needs to see the sparking activity in the context of the whole cocreation process.

With this backdrop, here are the components you need to describe in the Community Arts Profile when you design a sparking activity:

- Title and summary: A brief overview of the activity and its main purposes. Include its overall type—commissioning, workshop, showcase event, mentoring, apprenticeship, publication, creators' club, or something you make up (not more than a paragraph).
- Participants: All of the types of people who need to be involved for the activity to succeed. This may include creators and gatekeepers of various kinds. Identify actual people when possible.
- Kinds of things you'll need from the Community Arts Profile: Information someone needs to learn about the community or genre for the activity to succeed. Note which information is already in the Community Arts Profile,

and that which still needs exploration. Many of these are research activities in **Step 4** that you haven't performed yet.

- <u>Resources needed</u>: Financial, technical, logistical, formal, and other requirements to make the activity happen.
- <u>Tasks</u>: The items that someone needs to perform to carry out the activity. You may make these as detailed or broad as you like, depending on your context. The sample activities we provide below are somewhere in the middle.
- <u>Big-picture analysis</u>: In order to identify which of the seven steps are present in this activity, make three lists following this convenient graphic:

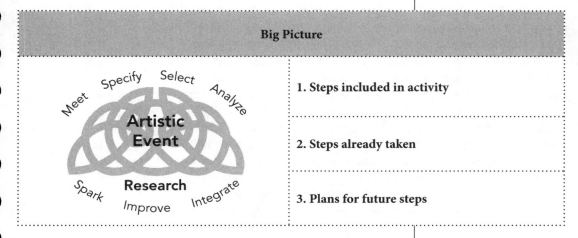

(1) CLAT steps included in the activity; (2) CLAT steps done outside the activity, such as analysis of an event (**Step 4**) that someone else already did; and (3) plans to address any missing steps in the future.

PREPARE TO DRAW ON FAMILIAR METHODS OF COMPOSITION

In "Creativity" (**Step 4, Part C**), we discussed elements of composition. Each community and especially creative individual has patterns they follow to make art, and you want to draw on those as much as possible. In the Mono example, Brian asked Punayima to compose a new example of *gbaguru* based on one of Jesus' parables. Punayima asked questions, thought awhile, started playing a repeated pattern on his *kundi*, then said he needed to be by himself to compose the song. Others may compose in a pair or group, with pencil and paper, in dreams or visions, on paid commission, with spontaneous improvisation, or use any number of methods.

As part of the preparation for the activity, perform some of the research in "Creativity." Ideally, you will be able to integrate some of these dynamics into the sparking activity; the familiarity will smooth the creation process and likely increase the quality of its products.

PREFACE

PREPARE

STEP 1

STEP 2

STEP 3

STEP 4

STEP 5

STEP 6

STEP 7

CLOSING

PREFACE

PREPARE

STEP 1

STEP 2

STEP 3

STEP 4

STEP 5

STEP 6

STEP 7

CLOSING

On the other hand, all people are primed to create because they carry God's image, and so are usually agile in adopting new methods. The activity you and the community design will likely include both familiar and new kinds of invention.

THINK CAREFULLY ABOUT THE MERISTEM

A meristem is the region in a plant in which new cells are created—the growth point. Likewise, the growth point in artistic production usually consists of one or a few key people from whose mind and body the art actually emerges. We want to love, protect, and encourage this person. Like every other human, she reflects God's image and so is inherently valuable. But in our sparking activities, she is also the crux of creativity. The hub. The nub. The one person we cannot do without. Her skill and reputation may also exert the most influence on how others respond to her new art. It's important, then, to include the people who will create the best artistry and have the social credentials that help it spread in the community.

So when the community chooses the composers (we include everyone who creates something, including painters, weavers, and the like), they should look for people who are already recognized as having experience and skill in creating within a genre. There may be many such qualified people to choose from, or only a few. Note that the choice of certain artistic genres will automatically determine the gender of the composer and performer. Local people will be able to make a list of potential experienced composers.

If you are working in a Christian community, it may be difficult to find someone who is both a Christian and an experienced composer in certain artistic genres. In this case, you can consider commissioning the work from a non-Christian composer. Questions to ask in this case: Are they interested? Are they respected by their community? If their name is made known, will that be a help or hindrance to acceptance of the work? What do local Christians think of the idea? There have been situations where commissioning Scripture-based art from non-Christian composers worked well. For example, among the Akyode of Ghana, the community's most respected and popular musician was not a Christian. However, he had a good reputation within the society, his name would actually help the song's acceptance, he was interested in the idea, and the local church saw nothing wrong in approaching him.[96] In Ghana's Nkonya culture, however, the most famous composer was viewed as a drunkard, and the local church decided to not approach him.

In some cultures, there is already an established role for composers who create arts for other people. In West Africa, especially in areas influenced by Islam, there may be a local form

---

96   Paul Neeley, "A Case Study: Commissioning Scripture Songs among the Akyode of Ghana," *Research Review* (Legon, Ghana), supplementary issue no. 10 (1997), 118–129.

of *griot* (praise singer). There are examples from Nigeria, Benin, and Ghana where such a Muslim praise singer agreed to work with a biblical text and compose and record a Scripture song.[97] Find out if an institutionalized form of composing for patrons is already in place. Note that such professional composers are used to working for some form of compensation.

IDENTIFY OPPORTUNITIES TO MAXIMIZE AND BARRIERS TO OVERCOME

Identify barriers and opportunities in the community associated with creativity in the genre. Here are a few common examples of each:

OPPORTUNITIES

- talented artists eager to use their gifts in new contexts
- government interest in promoting local art forms
- growing recognition of the value of local arts and fear for their loss in the wider community
- a respected champion of local arts in the community who could lead innovation

BARRIERS

- negative attitudes toward use of local language and art forms in some domains
- lack of knowledge and skills associated with a genre (this was the barrier that Punayima's apprenticeship program was designed to overcome)
- apathy toward change or the community
- weakening of interest in local cultural forms due to urbanization and globalization

After discussing these examples with members of the community, ask questions like these:

- What might help us spark a rich flowering of new works in this genre? How could we draw on these opportunities when designing a sparking activity?
- What might stop us from achieving this flowering? How could we overcome these barriers when designing a sparking activity?

Put the results of this conversation in the Community Arts Profile.

---

97   Paul Neeley, "Reflections of a Gatekeeper," *EM News* 6, no. 1 (1997); Klaus Wedekind, "The Praise Singers," *Bible Translator* 26, no. 2 (1975): 245–47.

PREFACE

PREPARE

STEP 1

STEP 2

STEP 3

STEP 4

STEP 5

STEP 6

STEP 7

CLOSING

PREFACE

PREPARE

STEP 1

STEP 2

STEP 3

STEP 4

STEP 5

STEP 6

STEP 7

CLOSING

DECIDE ON THE TYPE OF ACTIVITY

In this section, we present overviews and helps for several different types of activities that spark creativity. We also point you to more resources when available.

COMMISSIONING

We define **commission** as follows: to charge an artist or group of artists with the task of creating a new instance of an artistic genre for an agreed-upon purpose. Consider commissioning in almost all circumstances. It's often the most direct way to spark creativity because it requires as few as two people in dialogue.

    Commissioning commonly consists of these steps:

1. With the community, identify

- the event for which the item will be created
- the purpose(s) for the created item (e.g., literacy, church worship, or community development)
- the genre(s) of creation (e.g., *haiku*, *olonkho*, or Broadway musical)
- the content
- the creator(s)

2. Then:

- Work with the maker(s) in the creative process, including evaluation and revision of the work(s).
- Prepare the rest of the community and the event organizers for a public presentation.
- Explore other distribution means, including recordings.
- Explore ways that this work, and others like it, can enter into other domains of the community's life.

Respect and trust in your relationship with the creators are crucial to the commissioning process. Ask confidants what sort of compensation is appropriate for the artist, genre, and event. Compensation may be in the form of money, services, goods, social capital, or goodwill borne of friendship.

    It's also important to think through the commissioner's roles during the composition process. Who will decide what's good and what needs to be changed? How much freedom to innovate will the artist have? As much as possible, the commissioner and artist should agree on these things before the composition process begins.

One other curious case arises: Can you commission yourself to create something? Spark yourself? Certainly people decide to compose new things on their own. We encourage this, but insist that you should always act in relationship to a community. Too often individual artists make something new without any conversation with the community it's meant for, and present it to them timidly or defiantly for acceptance. It's much better to include gatekeepers early in the making of new things so everyone has a stake in its success.

WORKSHOPS

Workshops are short events—typically one or two weeks—that gather people to make progress together on a particular task. Consider a workshop when there is an organization in a community that can provide logistics and goals that will motivate participants to set aside the rest of their lives for a while; examples of such organizations include cultural associations, churches, and nongovernmental organizations. Workshops produce a ferment of productivity when participants interact with each other in a concentrated way.

There are many potential goals for workshops that draw on artistic communication: produce excellent translations of certain biblical Psalms, compose songs for church worship, create and record works with dramatic content to be distributed through radio or other media, weave cloths communicating health messages—the possibilities are endless.

PLANNING AN ARTS WORKSHOP

This workshop gathers a community's artists, spiritual and social leaders, and content experts to: (1) reflect on their local artistic resources; (2) specify community needs; (3) imagine how they can use their artistic resources to help respond to some of these needs; (4) produce samples of artistic performance that may meet these needs; and (5) plan for the integration of these creations into community life and contexts for continued artistic creativity.

The long-term impact we work and pray toward

We hope that this workshop would help spark the emergence or improvement (i.e., solidification, enhancement, deepening, broadening) of a sustainable tradition of biblically infused artistic composition and performance that responds to a community's spiritual, social, and physical needs.

PREFACE

PREPARE

STEP 1

STEP 2

STEP 3

STEP 4

STEP 5

STEP 6

STEP 7

CLOSING

PREFACE

PREPARE

STEP 1

STEP 2

STEP 3

STEP 4

STEP 5

STEP 6

STEP 7

CLOSING

People to invite

- Community leaders and gatekeepers. Participation of community leaders makes it more likely that innovations resulting from the workshop will be accepted. In addition, participation of values leaders like pastors and theologians helps ensure the theological soundness of creations, allows these spiritual leaders to grow in understanding and respect for people with artistic gifts, and makes it more likely that these leaders will encourage continued creativity for kingdom purposes.
- Artistic experts. Participation of composers, performers, and other gifted people helps ensure artistic excellence.
- Content experts. Participation of people knowledgeable in whatever content is going to be communicated helps ensure the trustworthiness of artistic messages produced. Bible translators, linguists, medical professionals, agriculturalists, and others may also help the artists to move from written forms of knowledge to oral artistic expression.

Notes on invitees

- One person may play more than one of these roles, though it's usually better to include more people.
- Not everyone needs to participate in every aspect of the workshop. It may be appropriate, for example, to invite a government leader just to opening and closing ceremonies.
- When possible, it is good to incorporate appropriate diversity in gender, dialect, age, denomination, region, clans.
- It may also be appropriate to invite other types of people for all or parts of the workshop: invite media people, recordists, NGO representatives, government representatives, cooks, and note takers.

Outcomes

At the end of this workshop, participants should have:

- written descriptions of kinds of artistic genres in their community
- audio, video, or photographic recordings of at least one new artistic work that draws directly on their local artistic systems
- an example of any new object that was produced, like a painting, mask, or tapestry
- written plans for expanded and sustained artistic creativity that responds to community needs

Methodologies

Whenever possible, leaders should use teaching methods that require high engagement by participants—such as those found in the Learning that Lasts approach (http://learningthatlasts.org).

Elements

Workshop group cohesion

We want to create a context of conviviality, mutual aid and support, common vision and mission, in accordance with local social norms.

Theological or ideological grounding

When appropriate to the workshop, we want participants to know biblical foundations for use of the arts and be able to communicate these to others in compelling ways when needed. If the community does not recognize the Bible as authoritative, you may use other books or ideas to provide conceptual foundations.

Spiritual transformation

When done in a Christian context, we want to help participants and instructors understand this work as ministry, to be open to God's conviction and anointing, and to leave with a new or renewed sense of their gifts and roles in the expansion of God's kingdom.

Research artistic resources

- Refer to or add to the Community Arts Profile, helping participants find this kind of information about events: settings, occasions, participants, material culture, social meanings, formal features.
- For each genre in this initial list, audio or video record an example in its traditional form.

Specify kingdom goal

If the exact purpose of the workshop has not already been determined, perform the participatory activity in **Step 2**: specify kingdom goals.

Spark creativity

- Help participants evaluate the list of artistic genres according to their capacity to communicate the desired content clearly, memorably, and reproductively; and to the existence, location, and availability of experts (composers, performers, educated audiences, etc.) in the genre. Choose one genre to communicate the desired message.
- Describe this genre more deeply using "Take a First Glance at an Event" (**Step 4, Part A**).
- Discuss and identify content that speaks to the community need identified.

PREFACE

PREPARE

STEP 1

STEP 2

STEP 3

STEP 4

STEP 5

STEP 6

STEP 7

CLOSING

PREFACE

PREPARE

STEP 1

STEP 2

STEP 3

STEP 4

STEP 5

STEP 6

STEP 7

CLOSING

- Compose an event (or series of events) that contains all of the elements of the genre you've described most fully in "Take a First Glance at an Event." State the goals of this event clearly. This composition will contain some new and modified elements to accomplish its goals.
- Audio or video record elements of the event that can be isolated for memory and evaluation.
- Describe the composed event.

Improve creations

As recorded, described, and/or performed for workshop participants, compare to researched description of traditional performance: Is it performed well? Is the message clear? Is the message true? Refer to **Step 6**.

Integrate

Plan for the dissemination of works created in the workshop. Then plan for continued creativity, perhaps through the formation of composition groups.

Celebrate

If possible and appropriate, perform the composed event for a local occasion at the end of the workshop.

Notes on the workshop

- First Saturday: arrival and registration of workshop participants
- Sunday at end of workshop: presentations in different churches
- Staff meeting every day at 14:00

Possible additional topics for a two-week workshop

- How to help your people make more arts
- Further notes on checking your artistic creations and how to make them better
- How to record your artistic creations
- History of arts in the church
- Instruments in the Bible
- Considerations in making a song book
- More on what the Bible says about worship and arts

SAMPLE WORKSHOP SCHEDULE

This is a week-long workshop schedule that has been used successfully:[98]

---

98   Adapted from Mary Beth and Todd Saurman, "Some Principles for Leading Ethnomusicology Workshops: Encouraging the Development of New Songs in the Lives of Believers," (paper presented at the Global Consultation on Music and Missions, St. Paul, MN, 2006).

	08:00	08:30	10:00	10:30	12:30	14:30	15:30	16:30
Sunday				Opening Ceremony	Meal	Opening Ceremony		Meal
Monday	Prayer and arts	01 Intro to the workshop	Break	02 Artistic genres	Meal	03 Formal charactistics of a genre	04 Evaluation of artistic genres for use in church worship	Meal
Tuesday	Prayer and arts	05 Biblical teaching about worship	Break	06 Diversity of gifts Bible study	Meal	07 Intro to composition	08 In groups: compose/ record	Meal
Wednesday	Prayer and arts	09 Methods of creating new works	Break	10 Worship Wheel — Choose a theme and Scripture verses for a composition	Meal	11 In groups: compose/ record		Meal
Thursday	Prayer and arts	12 Using instruments — Fusions	Break	13 Improve our creations — Poetic form, critiquing songs	Meal	14 In groups: critique and improve your creations; record		Meal
Friday	Prayer and arts	15 Plan for integration	Break	16 In groups: select new works and prepare for recording	Meal	17 Final recording/ evaluation		Meal
Saturday	Prayer and arts	18 Final recording, workshop evaluations		Collect evaluations, distribute travel money (per diem)	Closing ceremony			

SHOWCASE EVENTS

You may help a community plan or run a festival or competition that highlights creativity in local artistic genres.[99] Festivals are events designed to showcase a community's cultural identity and creative output. Many ethnic or religious groups already have celebratory gatherings that may be open to including new works of art produced by Christians. It may also be possible to start a new festival tradition

99   See, for example, *kwaya* contests in Tanzania, described in Gregory Barz, *Performing Religion: Negotiating Past and Present in Kwaya Music of Tanzania* (Amsterdam: Rodopi, 2003).

PREFACE

PREPARE

STEP 1

STEP 2

STEP 3

STEP 4

STEP 5

STEP 6

STEP 7

CLOSING

fueled by Christians' celebration of their God-given artistic gifts. Prizes for the best new works add the energy and excitement that events like these produce. Festivals also provide great opportunities for cooperation between different Christian, cultural, religious, and other groups within a community.

Showcase events normally emerge from a five-phase process:

1. **Imagining and planning**. How will we get from here to there? The larger the event, the more planning it requires. Some communities excel in creating detailed schedules and goals. Other communities excel in pulling together fabulous celebrations through organic social dynamics. Contribute ideas, but don't impose a system.
2. **Promotion and networking**. How can we ensure the participation of key artists and a wide public? Festivals sometimes incorporate contests or prizes to motivate artists. Make sure to clearly communicate the kinds of arts that will be rewarded and how they will be evaluated.
3. **Composition and preparation**. Will artists have time and resources to create and practice their performance?
4. **Running the event**.
5. **Evaluation and planning**. A big event requires a dedicated time afterward to graciously evaluate with key people how it went. It's also a great moment to see how the event relates to all of the seven CLAT steps and discuss the possibility of similar future events.

MENTORING

Sometimes because of your age, education, or social position you may enter a long-term relationship that benefits an individual artist or group of artists. This relationship usually develops over time from personal rapport and common goals. Mentors may help influence a mentee's professional, spiritual, and character growth, opening doors to new opportunities and sharing instructive stories from their own lives. Mentorship includes reciprocal learning as well; especially if the relationship crosses cultures, the mentee will teach the mentor skills and cultural insights. Over time, this bond often grows increasingly deep and satisfying.

APPRENTICESHIP

Apprenticeship consists of providing a structure consistent with existing cultural forms where artistic experts can transfer their skills and knowledge to other members of their community. Structured apprenticeship makes sense when experts in the genre exist, contexts for transfer of competencies in the genre are declining, but community members value it.

A community may institute such a program in this way:

1. Choose the genre to be taught.
2. Choose a master of the genre.
3. Choose the apprentices.
4. Design a training context that: (a) draws on familiar educational forms; (b) includes a place, time, and frequency that the master and apprentices can commit to; (c) covers the knowledge, skills, and attitudes crucial to the genre; and (d) lasts long enough for apprentices to reach a sustainable level of competency.
5. Implement the program.
6. During the program, explore how participants can continue to develop their skills and perform in various contexts.

PUBLICATIONS

Almost any activity will have more long-term success if it turns thoughts and artistic production into media other than live performance. Paper, recordings, and electronic data of all kinds allow ideas and artistry to live beyond a single moment and reach people beyond a single place. Periodicals and websites make it possible to disseminate information and inspire discussion on a wide range of topics. Audio and video products can be used to provide content for training programs and entertainment. And publications become repositories of history and biography when people begin to forget what came before them.

General aspects to planning a publication include the following:

1. Determine the target audience.
2. Identify editors, advisors, and contributors.
3. Solicit, select, and prepare the materials to be published.
4. Determine a scheme for the distribution of the publication.
5. Determine a schedule for ongoing publication.
6. Carry out the publication and distribution.
7. Develop and use feedback tools (e.g., electronic comments, letters to the editor, surveys, etc.) to help determine past effectiveness and plan for future developments.

In the 1990s, I and Sumatran colleagues (Indonesia) came to an understanding of issues surrounding the incorporation of Batak traditional music into the worship of the Batak church. To provide a forum for discussion of these issues, we formed an advisory panel and created a quarterly church news and information periodical, *Nada Dasar*. In the Batak language, *nada dasar* is the central tone around which melody and harmony revolve and to

PREFACE

PREPARE

STEP 1

STEP 2

STEP 3

STEP 4

STEP 5

STEP 6

STEP 7

CLOSING

PREFACE

PREPARE

STEP 1

STEP 2

STEP 3

STEP 4

STEP 5

STEP 6

STEP 7

CLOSING

which they ultimately resolve—analogous to the place held by Jesus Christ in the life of the Christian. It has allowed readers and leaders to address questions related to choral festival criteria, choir rehearsal technique, vocal technique, music theory, the function of music in the liturgy, and the like. – *Rob Hodges*[100]

CREATORS' CLUBS

Artists form associations, clubs, and fellowships to encourage each other, critique each others' work, share resources and ideas, perform, and collaborate on products. Groups like these meet regularly in certain places and times, have expectations—however modest—of each other, and often center on a particular art form and purpose. In Western Cameroon, scores of Ngiemboon associations meet each week to practice and improve songs in one of a dozen traditional dance genres. Roberta King has coined the phrase "new song fellowship" to describe a group that meets to compose new Scripture songs in sub-Saharan Africa.[101]

Each group will look different, but you should consider the following subjects when starting or modifying a new group:

- A meeting place and time that accommodates the members and allows for artistic activity.
- A discussion of the goals for the group and expectations of its members. This could vary from fluid and informal to strict and explicit, depending on the group's wishes.
- If the group forms part of a church or wants to create things for Christian communities, then it's essential to integrate spiritual formation into its activities. Artists act like God in their creativity (except that he does it out of nothing) and sometimes get drawn into unhealthy applications of the power they yield. Prayer, Bible study, accountability, and other disciplines need to provide a spiritual anchor for all artists' creative directions and performance.

---

100   For further information, see Rob Hodges, "Church Music New & Information Periodical," in Schrag and Neeley, *All the World Will Worship*, 25–27.
101   Roberta King, *A Time to Sing: A Manual for the African Church* (Nairobi: Evangel Publishing House, 1999), 5.

PREFACE

PREPARE

STEP 1

STEP 2

STEP 3

STEP 4

STEP 5

STEP 6

STEP 7

CLOSING

DESIGN A NEW OR MODIFY AN EXISTING ACTIVITY

In this section, we describe a number of sparking activities that you can use as models, organized according to the kingdom goals in **Step 2**. They are all distilled from actual experience but leave most of the details for you to complete for your context; in particular, we seldom include resources you need, since they are so often dependent on the local context. You may also choose to design a new activity, making sure to address each of the components we describe above: title and summary, participants, kinds of things you'll need from the Community Arts Profile, resources needed, tasks, and big-picture analysis. Or you might skip all this and do what seems right. It might work.

Refer often to the Big Picture graphic below to help you note the place of the activity in the seven-step CLAT process. Finally, we plan to post reports of implemented sparking activities on the manual's website (www.ethnodoxologyhandbook.com/manual).

Big Picture	
Meet Specify Select Analyze **Artistic Event** Spark **Research** Improve Integrate	**1. Steps included in activity**
	2. Steps already taken
	3. Plans for future steps

IDENTITY AND SUSTAINABILITY

Communities can promote positive cultural identity through local arts by organizing cultural celebrations (such as concerts, festivals, contests, etc.), documenting (through written descriptions, audio recordings, photography, and video), and publishing (on locally distributable media, websites, etc.). These activities should always be done with the leading and input of key community members and artists, and always in a way that will be appreciated by the community itself.

PREFACE

PREPARE

STEP 1

STEP 2

STEP 3

STEP 4

STEP 5

STEP 6

STEP 7

CLOSING

MEET A COMMUNITY AND ITS ARTS AGAIN

Your activities in gathering information about a community's arts that we describe in **Step 1** may in themselves increase a positive sense of identity. Go back and fill in some gaps.

HELP ORGANIZE A FESTIVAL CELEBRATING COMMUNITY ART FORMS

The purpose of this activity is to encourage and invigorate the use of local arts in a community. A festival can raise the status of the local arts, aid in their preservation, encourage innovation, and bring about positive changes.

Participants

Invite individuals from as many different social, age, and economic groups as possible, including community leaders, church leaders, skilled artists, members of older generations, and younger people with a passion for their culture. By including all of these groups, the festival will be more likely to bring about lasting artistic change, particularly if younger people are engaged. Note that a church's involvement in the organization and implementation of the festival could result in deepened relationships and witness.

Kinds of things you'll need from the Community Arts Profile

A list of artistic genres ("Take a First Glance at a Community's Arts," **Step 1**), and event descriptions ("Take a First Glance at an Event," **Step 4, Part A**) that include as many genres as possible.

Resources needed

Dependent on the local context.

Tasks

1. Initial community meeting. Meet with community representatives to discuss the list of artistic genres, ask and offer reasons why they are valuable, and explain the benefits a festival celebrating these arts could provide.
2. Logistics. After initial commitment to a festival, discuss goals and plans through questions like these:

   a. Who will organize the festival? Work toward broad inclusion and unity.
   b. What items need to be in the budget and how much will it be? Who will underwrite the budget?
   c. Which arts will be promoted? Who are the influential and respected artists that should be included? Who is in charge of inviting them?
   d. Shall the festival include competitions for new works in traditional forms?
   e. When should the festival take place? Should it be included as part of another regular cultural event, ritual, or festival?
   f. How do we want to use audio and video recordings? The organizing group should plan to obtain any necessary government or local permissions from authorities, and permissions from artists for the future use of recordings (see "Sample Permission Form," **Step 1**).

3. Implement the plans.
4. Evaluate. After the festival, meet with the organizers or a larger community forum.

   a. Evaluate community involvement, quality of the artistic works, and overall successful and unsuccessful aspects of the event. What parts of the festival are the community excited about? Did anything catch their attention?
   b. Decide whether the festival should become a regular event.
   c. Explore how the community can draw on the excitement and new works for other purposes. Did new purposes for traditional arts emerge? For example, it might be more possible after the festival to promote local arts for use in Christians' spiritual lives or in health education. Plan for more activities that feed into signs of the kingdom.
   d. Plan to create products from recordings of aspects of the festival and their distribution, such as DVDs, a website, storybook, collection of poetry, or song books. There also might be interest in developing a Community Arts Archive housed locally or in a government or educational organization. (See the activity "Help Develop Multimedia Collections of Local Arts" below.)

Your roles as an arts advocate will vary according to the skills and needs of the community. You may be able to contribute through making and organizing audio and video recordings, obtaining authorizations for use, and in providing international perspective on the value of their arts. You could also publish an article about the festival, an artist, or a particular tradition. If you are an outsider to an artistic tradition, you might lend prestige by learning to perform one of the showcased genres. Approach this humbly, though, to ensure that your efforts to learn and perform are viewed positively.

COMMISSION A NEW WORK IN AN OLDER GENRE FOR AN EXISTING SHOWCASE EVENT

Older artistic traditions lose value in communities in part because social changes make them less common, so less visible. One way to counteract this is by commissioning new works that are shown or performed in contexts like festivals, church services, radio and TV programs, or concerts. It's important to ensure that the new work is of high quality, and that people are able to connect practically and emotionally with it.

Participants
Expert(s) in an older artistic genre, and organizers of a community event.

Kinds of things you'll need from the Community Arts Profile
Description of an event in the commissioning genre using "Take a First Glance at an Event" (**Step 4, Part A**). You can follow other research paths that seem relevant in "Look at an Event's Forms" (**Step 4, Part A**) and "Explore the Event's Genre(s) through Artistic Domain Categories" (**Step 4, Part B**). You will also want to explore a few subjects like Artists, Creativity, Aesthetics and Evaluation, Emotions, and Community Values shown in "Relate the Event's Genre(s) to Its Broader Cultural Context" (**Step 4, Part C**).

PREFACE · PREPARE · STEP 1 · STEP 2 · STEP 3 · STEP 4 · STEP 5 · STEP 6 · STEP 7 · CLOSING

PREFACE

PREPARE

STEP 1

STEP 2

STEP 3

STEP 4

STEP 5

STEP 6

STEP 7

CLOSING

Resources needed
Dependent on the local context.

Tasks
1. With friends and colleagues, identify an influential community event that would provide a natural setting for new kinds of arts. Then explore what artistic genre and artist(s) would be most likely to result in positive emotions and excitement.
2. Conversely, you might know an artist well and decide to look for an event where a work in his or her genre could be showcased.
3. Work with the artist(s) in the creation of a prototype of something new.
4. Communicate with the event organizer(s) in locally appropriate ways. Explain that you and others hope to increase the profile and positive identity associated with the community's heritage. Bring an audio, video, or photographic recording of what the artist created. Invite the organizer(s) to help shape the content or form to better meet community goals.
5. Follow procedures associated with the event in preparations, rehearsal, payment, and other logistics.
6. After the event, meet with the artist(s) and organizer(s). Review how everything went and discuss whether this type of commissioning could become integrated into future events.

HELP DEVELOP MULTIMEDIA COLLECTIONS OF LOCAL ARTS
This activity is intended to raise the status and visibility of a community's arts by showcasing them in a multimedia collection. This collection will allow the community access to past performances, help them teach new artists, innovate for the future, and encourage the continued use of their arts.[102]

Participants
Recordists, secretarial help, artists, and people with technical expertise and access to technical resources.

Kinds of things you'll need from the Community Arts Profile
A list of artistic genres ("Take a First Glance at a Community's Arts," **Step 1**), event descriptions ("Take a First Glance at an Event," **Step 4, Part A**) that include as many genres as possible, and a list of key artists associated with each genre.

Resources needed
Multimedia collections are often expensive and require technical skills and equipment. Before beginning a project like this, consider whether

---

102   See also Anthony Seeger and Shubha Chaudhuri, editors, *Archives for the Future: Global Perspectives on Audiovisual Artchives in the 21ˢᵗ Century* (Calcutta: Seagull Books, 2004); "Education and Training in Audiovisual Archiving and Preservation," http://www.arsc-audio.org/etresources.html; "SIL Language and Culture Documentation and Description," http://www.sil.org/silepubs/index.asp?series=947.

- there is already someone with the needed skills and equipment (computer training, recording training, etc.), or else someone will need to be trained in how to create and maintain the collection.
- there is equipment available, such as computers, speakers, projectors, and recording devices.
- there are partners (individual or organization) with access to technical resources and training.
- there is ongoing funding and availability of personnel for maintaining and developing the collection.

You will also need to consider where the collection will be kept: is there an existing building or organization in the area or will a building and/or infrastructure need to be created?

These items are essential to plan for because this is not a cheap or easy project to create and maintain; many critical archives have disintegrated due to lack of continued funding and training resources. However, this activity can be incredibly beneficial to a community; even a very limited collection is better than no collection at all.

Tasks

1. Identify the purpose(s). Before beginning, the collection needs to have a purpose. Is this going to be a collection of local genres of stories, songs, stools, or rite of passage dances created by community members? Is this an archive for audio and video recordings of ceremonies? If we are going to include physical items such as clothing or sculptures or musical instruments, do we need a large space to store and/or display them? Are the items in the collection loanable or shareable?

   The community's felt needs and desires are very important to the creation of a multimedia collection. They may, for example, want digital audio files to put on their mobile devices. Or they may be interested in having a place where groups of people could come watch videos of ceremonies being performed by the experts. It could be a paper-based library, with photographs and local-language books, stories, folktales, and poetry. They may want a place to store and display important items while they are not being used—instead of the community's special attire and ceremonial musical instruments sitting packed away in between uses, why not have them on display?

   This is a very important item because if the final product (collection) does not meet their desires and needs, the community won't have much use for it. The community *must* see value in this project for it to be anything more than an unused, dusty archive.

2. Identify the users. If this collection is to benefit the community, it needs to be easily accessible and usable. The audience needs to be identified.
3. Identify who will maintain the collection. Multimedia devices and formats are constantly changing, and the collection will always need someone

PREFACE

PREPARE

STEP 1

STEP 2

STEP 3

STEP 4

STEP 5

STEP 6

STEP 7

CLOSING

PREFACE

PREPARE

STEP 1

STEP 2

STEP 3

STEP 4

STEP 5

STEP 6

STEP 7

CLOSING

who is informed about technology and can keep the files available in the latest formats. The collection will quickly become useless to the community otherwise. Before beginning, either a person or an organization (government, library, NGO, etc.) needs to be identified that will become a partner in keeping this collection running and up to date.

4. Identify a location for the collection. Even in the digital age, a physical location is still needed. There is the possibility of housing the entire collection on a website, but that requires lots of funding and expertise. In addition, a web-only collection may not be very accessible to a community in a country with limited Internet access. The location could be something as simple as a desktop computer in a room.

5. Identify the media. Identify what devices people use to listen to audio and to watch videos. Do they own computers? Do they know how to use a computer? Do they have mobile devices that can play audio and video files? Do they use CDs or tapes? DVDs or VCDs? Do they have their own tape, CD, and DVD players, or do they need to be available so people can watch and listen right there? Would it be better to have a projector set up so that lots of people can watch a video at the same time, or is a computer monitor enough? Once the media is known, it is possible to set up the collection in the most accessible way possible.

6. Acquire recordings. Plan for and record or collect the artistry of key artists in the community.

Throughout research, constantly provide the community with products of research (audio and video recordings, photographs, etc.). If you have the technical skills needed, providing the community with small "products" all throughout your work can really help them to understand the benefits of your work, and to see how a central collection for all these things could be a great benefit to them. For instance, as you make field recordings, burn a CD or make a tape and give it to the person you just recorded. If you record a formal event or ceremony, burn a DVD/VCD and give it to the community leaders as a gift. Sometimes these sorts of gifts can create a powerful motivation from within the community itself.

PUBLISH RECORDINGS AND RESEARCH IN VARIOUS FORMS AND CONTEXTS

Publishing helps people identify and promote what they value to local, regional, national, and international communities. Though here we discuss presentations through booklets, websites, and academic articles, media could also include books, CDs, DVDs, concerts, social media, etc. This activity dovetails well with the "Help Develop Multimedia Collections of Local Arts" activity above. When presented as one equal voice among thousands of the world's artistic expressions, the community learns that each voice has something unique and special to contribute.

Participants

Depending on the publishing format, you may need to include a web designer, recordist, photographer, printer, editor, or others. Involve community leaders and artists.

Kinds of things you'll need from the Community Arts Profile
A list of artistic genres ("Take a First Glance at a Community's Arts," **Step 1**), event descriptions ("Take a First Glance at an Event," **Step 4, Part A**) that include as many genres as possible, and a list of key artists associated with each genre.

Resources needed
Dependent on the local context.

Tasks
Website. With artists and community leaders:
1. Create a prototype site with these sections: Meet *Name* Communities; Contexts for *Name* Artistic Communication; Cultural and Spiritual Initiatives Using *Name* Arts; Conversations about *Name* Arts; Other Resources Related to *Name* Arts.
2. Discuss the site and its social context with community stakeholders. Show prototype to a small group of primary stakeholders, discussing issues like these:

   a. Should the community's arts be shown to a wider group through a website like this? If so, who are target audiences and purposes?
   b. Who should control the website's content? Process of publishing? Management of the site? Technical implementation?
   c. What personal and legal permissions are needed to publish the website?
   d. How should the presentation change?

3. Create a plan in which the community takes control of the website.

Booklet. With artists and community leaders:

1. List the art forms that they would most like to share with others.
2. Choose overall booklet design, visual representations of each art form (e.g., sketch or photograph), writers of texts explaining each art form.
3. Identity publisher, funding, number to print, and distribution plan.

Academic article.
1. Identify audience as regional, national, or international.
2. Identify several organizations likely to publish information about the community's arts.
3. Identify one or two people who are capable of writing an article satisfying the standards of the organization's publication. If no one within the community has these skills, a trusted outside researcher may fill this role. It may be appropriate to cowrite the article with a community expert.
4. Write the article, modifying it according to the suggestions of important community stakeholders.
5. Submit the article according to the organization's and publication's requirements.

PREFACE

PREPARE

STEP 1

STEP 2

STEP 3

STEP 4

STEP 5

STEP 6

STEP 7

CLOSING

PREFACE

PREPARE

STEP 1

STEP 2

STEP 3

STEP 4

STEP 5

STEP 6

STEP 7

CLOSING

IDENTIFY AND MEND RUPTURES IN TRANSMISSION FROM OLDER TO YOUNGER PEOPLE

Participants
Include people from as many segments of the community as possible, including older and younger, urban and rural, leaders, local artists of many kinds, and teachers.

Kinds of things you'll need from the Community Arts Profile
A list of artistic genres ("Take a First Glance at a Community's Arts," **Step 1**), and an understanding of transmission (see "Transmission and Change," **Step 4, Part C**).

Resources needed
Dependent on the local context.

Tasks[103]

1. Using participatory methods, mediate a discussion of topics like these (see "Steps to Specifying Kingdom Goals" in **Step 2**):

    a. What kinds of local wisdom and arts do you have in your communities?
    b. What is still strong? Why?
    c. What is being lost? Why?
    d. What do you want to protect from being lost?
    e. How have wisdom and arts been passed on in the past? What caused the process to stop?

2. With this discussion as background, explore actions the community might take to help pass this information on to the youth and children of the community. These could include modifying older education systems (such as initiation schools), or tying into newer community channels (like government schools). They may also establish new systems like community groups or public opportunities where older adults teach younger adults and children about playing instruments, storytelling styles, dances, poetry creation, etc.
3. Make an action plan and discuss who will take responsibility for carrying it out.

---

103   For further discussion of this kind of task, see Mary Beth and Todd Saurman, "Applied Ethnomusicology: The Benefits of Approaching Music as a Heart Language," *Journal of Language and Culture* 23, no. 2 (Institute of Language and Culture for Rural Development, Mahidol University, 2004), 15–29.

SHALOM

ORGANIZE A TRAUMA HEALING WORKSHOP

Participants
Include church leaders, Bible translators, victims of any kind of trauma, and experienced facilitators where possible.

Kinds of things you'll need from the Community Arts Profile
A list of artistic genres ("Take a First Glance at a Community's Arts," **Step 1**), and an understanding of emotional connections to artistry (see "Emotions," **Step 4, Part C**). Explore in more depth how people in the community mourn, express strong emotions through various arts, and use rituals to pass through difficult times.

Resources needed
Healing the Wounds of Trauma,[104] which has been translated into scores of languages.

Tasks
These are broad kinds of tasks. Use *Healing the Wounds of Trauma* for concrete directions.

1. Gather people traumatized by war, disease, fears, or anything else.
2. Lead participants through Bible studies addressing suffering, forgiveness, God's power, and other relevant topics.
3. Lead participants through arts-based healing exercises.
4. Help Christian leaders translate lessons into their community's language, if necessary.
5. Train community members to facilitate trauma healing workshops for others.

COMMISSION LOCAL ARTISTS TO ADDRESS COMMUNITY HEALTH PROBLEMS[105]

Participants
When possible, partner with existing nongovernmental organizations and local groups and artists already addressing serious health needs in their communities. Include expert creators of the artistic genres chosen and experts in the health information they wish to communicate.

Kinds of things you'll need from the Community Arts Profile
Refer to a list of artistic genres ("Take a First Glance at a Community's Arts," **Step 1**) and how people create in the chosen genre ("Creativity," **Step 4, Part**

---

104 Harriet Hill, Richard Bagge, Pat Miersma, and Margaret Hill, *Healing the Wounds of Trauma* (Nairobi: Paulines Publications Africa, 2004).
105 See also, Katie Noss, medical ethnomusicology encyclopedia, and Barz.

PREFACE

PREPARE

STEP 1

STEP 2

STEP 3

STEP 4

STEP 5

STEP 6

STEP 7

CLOSING

C). Explore in more depth how people in the community use art forms to pass on trustworthy and important information and types of content associated with a genre ("Subject Matter," **Step 4, Part C**).

Resources needed
Dependent on the local context.

Tasks
1. Gather artists, community leaders, and health experts who are concerned about the health problem.
2. Decide together who should create the new artistry, what the content should be, and how it should be disseminated.
3. Have the creator(s) make a prototype of the new thing in a comfortable setting and time frame, and present it to the advocacy group. Evaluate and improve the artistry according to helps in **Step 6**.
4. Implement the events in which the artistry will be expressed.
5. Plan for continued methods of creating arts to address physical and social needs.

ORGANIZE A SPECIAL EVENT TO PLAY TRADITIONAL GAMES
Though the focus of this activity is on play and recreation, games and sporting events also feed into increasing a community's sense of identity and value; developing solidarity; and transmitting language, values, and history to more people.

Participants
Include experts in the game genre, children, parents, community leaders, and good organizers.

Kinds of things you'll need from the Community Arts Profile
The community has chosen an artistic genre that includes competition or communal play. Analyze a whole event to identify its artistry. This may exist in the form itself, in costumes or equipment, or special artistic communication that participants and others perform before, during, or after an event. Also ask friends about how they view play, leisure, and competition.

Resources needed
Dependent on the local context.

Tasks
1. Gather a small group to organize the special event.
2. Decide the date, time, location, order of events, celebration of those who excel (if appropriate).
3. Decide who to invite and how to spread the word. If this is a new kind of event, start with a smaller group. If it catches on, such events could become bigger.
4. If many people who attend are unfamiliar with the game, explain its history and rules.

PREFACE

PREPARE

STEP 1

STEP 2

STEP 3

STEP 4

STEP 5

STEP 6

STEP 7

CLOSING

HOLD AN ALTERNATIVES TO VIOLENCE WORKSHOP

A key element of avoiding violence where there is hurt is preemptive conflict resolution. The aim is to creatively transform unhealthy relationships through sharing, caring, improved communication skills, and sometimes even surprise and humor.

Participants

Focus on people who live in communities where conflict is strong, but who want to avoid violence. A trained Alternatives to Violence facilitator could organize such a workshop.

Kinds of things you'll need from the Community Arts Profile

Information on genres containing storytelling and dramatic elements.

Resources needed

Alternatives to Violence is a network of volunteers who run workshops to teach people how to keep conflict from turning into violence. Learn more here: http://avpinternational.org.

Tasks

Role plays and other forms of drama allow persons to explore possible approaches to different forms of conflict. Important insights are gained through the role plays, which are flexibly adapted and debriefed as they run, helping those involved to assess and digest whatever is learned.

JUSTICE

HOLD WORKSHOPS THAT ALLOW MARGINALIZED PEOPLE TO BE HEARD[106]

Questioning power relationships can be dangerous. This activity should be carried out with much patience and as widespread community involvement as possible.

Participants

Work with a group of people in a community who suffer from being outside social power structures. Common categories include women, members of minority ethnic groups, children, handicapped, or poor people.

Kinds of things you'll need from the Community Arts Profile

A list of artistic genres ("Take a First Glance at a Community's Arts," **Step 1**), a general understanding of power relationships between different community

---

106 See also, Mlama.

PREFACE

PREPARE

STEP 1

STEP 2

STEP 3

STEP 4

STEP 5

STEP 6

STEP 7

CLOSING

subgroups, and a specific understanding of how certain artistic genres are used to promote or circumvent power relationships ("Identity and Power," **Step 4, Part C**).

Resources needed
Dependent on the local context.

Tasks
1. Talk individually to people who represent marginalized groups in the community, exploring how they are treated by others. If they have already organized themselves, offer your services in helping integrate arts into their activities. Decide together how, when, and where to meet for a workshop.
2. Review the artistic genres that exist in the wider community and within their own subcommunity.
3. Evaluate each genre in terms of its potential to safely communicate grievances to those in power. During church services, women in the African Apostolic Church in southern Africa are allowed to admonish men for abusing them, without fear of retaliation.[107] If such forms exist, discuss what messages the group wants to communicate, and when they could communicate it. Then commission someone in the group to compose it.
4. Evaluate each genre in terms of its potential to provide a sense of solidarity among people in the group. Local genres with song, dance, drama, or visual messages could provide appropriate fodder.
5. Plan for continued creativity and community-building activities.

COMMISSION AN ALPHABET SONG
Songs help people remember new information. This activity shows you how to help a local composer create a new song in a familiar style that lists the building blocks of literacy skills—letters.

Participants
Work with one or several teachers, songwriters, and/or poets who know a local style appropriate for teaching. At least one of these people needs to know how to write the language well, in order to write the composition down for others to learn.

Kinds of things you'll need from the Community Arts Profile
Look at artistic genres of song that can have lots of repetition. Also consider the kinds of songs, riddles, or poems people use to teach children or adults.

Resources needed
You will need a recorder and means to distribute copies in the format you choose to help people learn the new song.

107   Bennetta Jules-Rosette, "Ecstatic Singing: Music and Social Integration in an African Church," in *More than Drumming: Essays on African and Afro-Latin American Music and Musicians*, ed. Irene V. Jackson (Westport, CT: Greenwood, 1985), 119–44 .

Tasks

1. Decide who your intended audience is. You may choose to make one alphabet song for everyone, or one for adults and another for children.
2. List all of the symbols in the alphabet on a sheet of paper. Choose words that begin with each of these sounds.
3. Discuss what kind of a song would best help people learn these symbols. If there is a call-and-response form, you may want to imitate that to ask questions and give answers that teach the letters with words or sentences. You could associate a word with each sound, or a sentence with each sound.
4. Ask someone talented in the song genre to make a song that matches the words or sentences with a melody. The tune must be an appropriate kind of song for teaching your intended audience.
5. Test the new song with a few literacy students and literacy program leaders to make sure it is easy to remember, fun, and accepted. Revise it if you think of ways to make it better.
6. Make a plan how to teach teachers the new song so they in turn can teach it to their students. Ask students to teach it to friends or family.

In the Waodoni language of Peru, for example, animals make vowel sounds, so the Waodani made a call-and-response song to teach the vowels. The song gives questions and answers like, "What does the wild pig say? The wild pig says 'æ.'" You might want to ask if birds make consonant sounds. Other people, like the Quechua Ambo-Pasco, taught each letter of the alphabet with a word that begins with that letter. Their song says, "What are we going to learn today? We're going to learn our letters today. With A we say *algu* [dog]. With B we say *bandera* [flag]. With C we say *cuchi* [pig]." After every four letters, they repeat the question, "What are we going to learn today?" Others, like the Sango in Central Africa, created an alliterative poem associating each letter with a sentence that uses that letter many times. Each line of the poem repeats a new letter many times. The poem became the words to "The Sango Alphabet Song." – *Pat Kelley and Michelle Petersen*

COMMISSION LOCAL VISUAL ART FOR BOOKS AND LITERACY MATERIALS

Participants
Work with local visual artists, book makers, literacy specialists, people from the community to check the illustrations with, and respected leaders.

Kinds of things you'll need from the Community Arts Profile
Since each culture follows unique visual rules, perform the activity "Analyze the Message of an Image" in **Step 4, Part B5**. For example, in some cultures "big" means "near" and "small" means "far," but in other cultures "big" means "important" and "small" means "less important." The more you can learn about local visual rules and how people show stories, the better. Do people portray one event per image, or do they portray many events in the same image? Maybe people find a key moment to illustrate instead of a series of events like

PREFACE

PREPARE

STEP 1

STEP 2

STEP 3

STEP 4

STEP 5

STEP 6

STEP 7

CLOSING

PREFACE

PREPARE

STEP 1

STEP 2

STEP 3

STEP 4

STEP 5

STEP 6

STEP 7

CLOSING

a comic strip, or maybe they put many events all in one picture. How does their art reflect how they depict events in life? That helps decide content in literacy materials and illustrations.

Resources needed

Have available the texts you want illustrated, perhaps sample illustrations from other works.

Tasks

1. Gather a group of literacy specialists, visual artists, and respected leaders. Decide the goals of what you would like to illustrate. Illustrations may be needed for local language calendars, wall hangings, educational materials, Scripture portions, and Bible studies.
2. Find local artists. Agree to pay normal local wages as appropriate for similar work.
3. Tell the local artist the story you would like illustrated. He or she needs to understand it well enough to tell it back to you before he or she can draw it well. Talk together about the main characters, actions, emotion, and main point of each illustration before the artist begins to draw. You may want to ask the artist to put a member of the intended audience somewhere in the picture to help with audience identification so the audience will learn well from the illustration. Women tend to identify with women, men with men, and children with children. Agree about characters to be illustrated, their actions, and their emotions.
4. Ask the artist to create three or four rough drafts. Ask him or her not to put too much time into rough drafts; these are just to give ideas.
5. Look at the rough drafts together. For each illustration ask questions like, "Why is the jaguar so big and the man so little?" The artist may tell you that the jaguar is more important to the story, or more dangerous, so you should not impose your rule that relative size indicates relative distance. Make sure all the people or animals and objects needed to understand the story well are in the picture and no key people are left out. Make sure that the correct action is shown happening, and that characters' emotions are what the story calls for. If you find changes are needed so that complete information is communicated, then ask the artist to revise the rough draft. Be aware that the local culture may portray things in ways you do not expect, and emotion may be shown differently than you expect. Rather than telling the artist to change something, there may be times when you want to wait and see what people say in the next step.
6. Together, decide which of the drafts the artist should develop further.
7. Ask three or more members of the intended audience to look at the next rough draft illustration(s). Ask what they see, what they think the artist is trying to say, what they like, what they don't like, and if anything offends them. Find out if the illustration communicates the story's action, intent, and emotion accurately to them or not. Tell their ideas to the artist to help the artist make a good final illustration.
8. Check with community leaders before finalizing the illustrations(s). If the illustration is of a historical event, the choice to contextualize or not

(whether to make participants more local or more historical) should be made and checked with local community leaders. If another revision is needed, make changes.

PROMOTE LITERACY THROUGH LOCAL ARTS PRESENTATIONS

People will be more likely to integrate literacy into their lives if they connect it to other domains of their lives. This activity describes how to commission literacy-promoting visual, musical, dramatic, or other performances associated with normal community events like dances or celebrations.

Participants

Work with literacy experts, artists in genres chosen for activities, and community leaders.

Kinds of things you'll need from the Community Arts Profile

The kind of art you choose to carry your message needs to be in use already in the community for carrying similar types of messages. You need to know what kinds of messages carry what kinds of meaning, and make the form match the content.

Resources needed

Dependent on the local context.

Tasks

1. Choose a community event that would provide a good forum for promoting literacy. These could be festivals, church gatherings, sporting events, or other contexts.
2. Together, list possible problems for someone who doesn't know how to read. For example, the person (1) can't read instructions on medicine; (2) misses a bus because he or she couldn't read the schedule; (3) needs legal government paperwork done; or (4) needs to know something written but there's no one around who can read it to them, so they don't know what to do and go home without accomplishing what they needed to do. Choose one of these problems as the story idea.
3. Discuss the different artistic genres of communication that exist in the community. Imagine benefits and drawbacks of using each to communicate the story. Choose one or more genres.
4. Have experts in the chosen genre(s) lead the process of creating a new work, which may include drama, poetry, song, illustration, comic, or picture to connect with people. When they have told what happens without knowing how to read, add a verse or another act to the skit or another picture showing an alternate case where someone has learned to read and the situation plays differently. The person's self-esteem comes up because they can do paperwork at the government office, give the medicine correctly, take the right bus, or otherwise not be dependent on someone else.

PREFACE

PREPARE

STEP 1

STEP 2

STEP 3

STEP 4

STEP 5

STEP 6

STEP 7

CLOSING

5. Discuss the possibility of presenting the promotional art to the leaders of the community.
6. Show the work to a few people from your intended audience, and ask for their feedback on how to make it better before you show it to many people.
7. Present the artistry.
8. In addition to performing works to directly show the value of reading, performances that have another goal—such as presenting Scripture or health information—also provide motivation for reading since they require reading indirectly as a skill to make them. Among the Supyire of Mali, the possibility of being chosen to act in radio dramas was a major motivation to attend literacy classes, so as to be able to read scripts. Also, many people want to learn how to read so they will be able to read song books and participate more fully in choirs.

INTEGRATE LOCAL ARTS INTO METHODS FOR TEACHING READING

Arts can help people move from the known (e.g., orally communicated words in local songs or proverbs) to the unknown (visual representations of those same words). This activity shows you how to work with people involved in teaching literacy in a community to show the best ways to use local arts in their work.

Participants

Include community leaders, literacy experts, and gifted and creative teachers and artists.

Kinds of things you'll need from the Community Arts Profile

Focus on genres that have verbal ("Oral Verbal Arts in an Event," **Step 4, Part B4**) and visual ("Visual Arts in an Event," **Step 4, Part B5**) components. Every culture has some kinds of art forms that can lead toward literacy by helping them make conceptual associations between visual arts and letter shapes or movements used in making the letters. Woodburning and carving on gourds can tell a story in pictures in the Huanca Quechua area of Peru. Symbols woven or printed on cloth, scarves, or rugs carry meaning in the Middle East. Henna designs on hands carry meaning in India.

Resources needed

Dependent on the local context.

Tasks

Literacy and other community leaders meet to list artistic resources that may help them teach more people to read. Following are a few possible ways to connect known arts to reading and writing:

1. Use movements people know to teach them how to write similar movements. Help people make the conceptual jump from three-dimensional, concrete objects and movements to two-dimensional symbols by relating the two-dimensional symbols to similar three-dimensional objects and known movements. For example, if you are teaching an Arabic letter that looks like

a hand cupping three stones, have students make this motion and say the letter name.

2. Use the lyrics of songs, proverbs, stories, riddles, or other verbal arts as texts to learn to read. If using a genre with song, put the lyrics to a song on a wall in a classroom and have students sing as they follow the words. Some people learn to read by following along with songs as they are sung in church.

3. Performance provides content for teaching reading. If participants act out something that's happened, such as, "Show us how old Weepy went out and speared the wild pig," the teacher can ask what words Weepy used, such as "Let's spear! Wild pig!" Then the teacher can use the vocabulary that comes out of the performance to teach reading. Teachers can write these statements on a board and ask people to read them back. This teaches well how reading has meaning.

4. Ask local artists to illustrate a picture book or posters of community activities such as planting, growing, harvesting a crop, visiting a friend, knitting, or making a meal. Ask literacy students to tell you the steps needed to complete the activity, or the recipe for the food. Ask them to read the board back to you together. This connects literacy with life.

5. Ask students to draw pictures of community activities and write a simple sentence about the picture.

6. Ask students to write a song to go with pictures, events, or stories. Ask the students to read the song's words while you all sing the new song together.

TURN ORATURE INTO LITERATURE
People need literature in their local language on a wide range of topics to motivate them to become literate. This activity shows you how to transcribe the texts of oral arts like songs, stories, or riddles to provide motivation for reading and to broaden the range of available reading materials in the local language.

Participants
Work with literacy specialists, experts in genres with high verbal content, and visual artists.

Kinds of things you'll need from the Community Arts Profile
Familiarity with genres containing significant elements of oral verbal arts.

Resources needed
Dependent on the local context.

Tasks
1. To make the easiest reading materials, transcribe local folktales, songs, and proverbs people already know. It is important to record our cultural heritage so the next generation does not forget our wisdom.

2. Make a second level of literacy materials by recording personal stories and writing them down, or else train local authors to write their own experience stories. We can learn from one another's experiences. A calendar showing an

PREFACE

PREPARE

STEP 1

STEP 2

STEP 3

STEP 4

STEP 5

STEP 6

STEP 7

CLOSING

PREFACE

PREPARE

STEP 1

STEP 2

STEP 3

STEP 4

STEP 5

STEP 6

STEP 7

CLOSING

important event that takes place each month would be a good communal experience story; e.g., in March the rains come [or whatever happens in that month], so we. . .[whatever we do in that month]. A song could be created to go with this too.

3. Make a third level of literacy materials by asking local authors to teach new content in local terms, and also by training creative authors to imagine stories that have not happened. People want to know many different kinds of things and imagine many different kinds of stories, so different types of materials need to be created to interest as wide an audience as possible. We can learn by imagining how things can change, and by learning new information from outside our culture, expressed by local authors in our culture's ways. We can also create new songs and dramas and write them down for performance. What community events need new songs and dramas whose words we can write down and teach?

4. Make a fourth level of reading materials by asking local translators to translate important works such as Scripture or health information that comes from another culture.

5. Ask a local illustrator to illustrate all of these kinds of materials, using visual rules of the community.

6. Test all materials with a small audience of at least three people before teaching them to a larger audience. Make sure literacy materials are clear, accurate, natural, acceptable, and interesting. After testing, revise the material before presenting it to a larger audience.

7. Distribute the finished materials to literacy programs and community leaders. Make sure important people know where the materials are available for purchase. Advertise materials via performances or media.

PREFACE

PREPARE

STEP 1

STEP 2

STEP 3

STEP 4

STEP 5

STEP 6

STEP 7

CLOSING

INTEGRATE LOCAL ARTS INTO EDUCATIONAL CURRICULA[108]

Participants
Work with mother-tongue teachers, local arts experts, and school directors.

Kinds of things you'll need from the Community Arts Profile
A list of artistic genres ("Take a First Glance at a Community's Arts," **Step 1**).

Resources needed
Dependent on the local context.

Tasks
1. Look together at the school's curriculum.
2. Look together at the local art forms that carry meaning within various cultural contexts.
3. Discuss and plan ways to integrate cultural knowledge and materials into specific parts of the curriculum. Here are some examples of integrating a local genre that uses stitching into existing school classes:

   a. Cultural studies: traditional stitching patterns and their meaning.
   b. Reading: a story about a mother stitching a traditional outfit for her daughter to wear for New Year's Day.
   c. Writing: have a community expert come into class and talk about the traditional dress and stitching patterns; then have students write a creative story about this experience.
   d. Science: take the students to collect leaves and berries, then demonstrate how to color cotton through traditional dying techniques.
   e. Math: cut various lengths of died string used for stitching and have children measure the lengths.

4. Evaluate the success of these methods with teachers and other school personnel.

SCRIPTURE

Local artistic forms of communication feed into Bible translation in two primary ways. First, many (perhaps most) biblical source texts have strong characteristics of artistic forms of communication, such as songs, stories, poems, and proverbs. Attending to these artistic genres during the translation process can help make the final written

---

108   Mary Beth Saurman, "Culturally Relevant Songs: Teaching Tools in Education Programs," (paper presented at the joint conference of the Sixth Symposium of the International Council for Traditional Music Study Group on Music and Minorities and the Second Symposium of the International Council for Traditional Music Study Group on Applied Ethnomusicology, Hanoi, Vietnam, July 19–30, 2010).

translation communicate more like the original did. Second, it's also possible to draw on local art forms to produce oral translations of the Bible.

HOLD A SCRIPTURE TRANSLATION WORKSHOP

The purpose of this workshop is to produce high-quality translations of selected Bible portions by drawing on characteristics of local art forms. Such a workshop is helpful when a community is ready to translate Scripture that has significant artistic characteristics in the original languages, such as songs (e.g., Psalms, Mary's song, Moses' and Miriam's songs), parables, and proverbs. The community gathers participants for one to two weeks to (1) evaluate their song and poetry genres as potential guides for target poetic forms of translations, and (2) render certain passages with characteristics of these local genres.

Participants

Include Bible translators, experts in song and poetic artistic genres, and spiritual leaders.

Kinds of things you'll need from the Community Arts Profile

You can prepare to integrate the arts into a Scripture Translation Workshop by performing the research described in "Oral Verbal Arts in an Event" (**Step 4, Part B4**).

Resources needed

Dependent on the local context.

Tasks

You will contribute to both the planning and execution of such a workshop.

Planning. During the planning phase, you will help

1. Identify artistic features of the biblical source text(s). A good place to start is by noting how biblical languages mark parallel lines—parts of a text related to each other by similarity, building one on the other, or contrast.
2. Evaluate local artistic genres that exist in the target language for significant overlap of connotations, functions, and content with the biblical source genres.
3. Find artists who have skills in the local genres with the most potential to inform translation. In simplified terms, poets should be part of the team that translates poetic sections of Scripture, storytellers for stories, and skilled users of proverbs for translating proverbs. It's important for leaders to invite these artists so they can provide skilled, knowledgeable input.

Execution. During the workshop, you will

1. Study and describe the features of the target artistic genres. Co-occurring boundaries between text and tune are the most common poetic features in the world. So the first thing to do is find functional equivalents of the line between biblical and target poetic features. Meter is very common.
2. Lead a process by which participants decide how these features should best inform target forms of the written Bible translation.
3. You may also work with the artists to commission new works based on the translated Scripture that they can integrate into their communities' lives.

Like all workshops, leaders should plan for activities that enhance group unity, and provide theological grounding and chances for spiritual transformation. You may enter into any of these other aspects of the workshop according to your gifts and the leaders' needs.

Note that you can also apply these same principles in contributing to a translation team in their daily work. So when a team begins to translate orally based passages like Psalms or Proverbs, you can serve as a resource. You can help them look at the poetic features of the biblical language, examine poetic features of local art forms, and help them figure out how to connect the two. Often the best method of connecting the two is to record, listen, and re-record as improvements are suggested. Once a good oral draft is made, it can be written down.

An additional benefit to making full use of artistic features in Bible translation is this: if translators create written translations of the Scripture that have characteristics of local artistic genres, the steps to creating additional Scripture products will be shorter and clearer. Composers with the task of creating Scripture songs will bless you.

COMMISSION AN ORAL NARRATIVE PERFORMANCE OF SCRIPTURE

Participants
Include trusted Christian leaders and Bible expositors and experts in the oral narrative genre you choose.

Kinds of things you'll need from the Community Arts Profile
You will want to know as much as you can about genres that include significant verbal content. Refer to "Oral Verbal Arts in an Event" (**Step 4, Part B4**).

Resources needed
Dependent on the local context.

Tasks
1. Choose a biblical story.
2. Choose a local oral narrative genre.

PREFACE

PREPARE

STEP 1

STEP 2

STEP 3

STEP 4

STEP 5

STEP 6

STEP 7

CLOSING

3. Identify a local oral narrative genre expert.
4. Describe features of the genre, guided by "Look at an Event's Forms" (**Step 4, Part A**), and "Oral Verbal Arts in an Event" (**Step 4, Part B4**).
5. Commission an expert to create a new story. Discuss the biblical text with the composer in detail, and ask him or her to communicate that same story in the local oral narrative genre you've identified.
6. Critique and improve the new work, especially in terms of aesthetic quality, clarity, and accuracy of the message.
7. Integrate into existing performance venues.

CHURCH LIFE

Local churches usually relate to people in their geographical surroundings and to larger, historically connected Christian movements. It's therefore crucial to gain an understanding of the art forms used to communicate in both contexts. With this background understanding, the church can decide which forms they should use to work toward various kingdom goals. "Explore How a Christian Community Relates Artistically to Its Broader Church and Cultural Context" (**Step 4, Part D**) outlines these kinds of exploration.

In a vibrant Christian community in Cameroon, distrust had developed between pastors and worship leaders. Neither group believed the other understood or respected the importance of its ministry. Pastor and musician Roch Ntankeh, a man respected by both groups, orchestrated a service of crying out to God, repentance, forgiveness, and reconciliation. Pastors and worship leaders kneeled and cried in front of their brothers and sisters, granting forgiveness and restoring relationships.

HOLD A CORPORATE WORSHIP WORKSHOP
In this activity, artists and leaders in a local congregation or group of congregations meet to figure out how to worship better together. This could happen during a week-long gathering, a series of weekly meetings, or other time frame that meets the community's needs. In the case of multiple congregations, the workshop includes sessions when everyone is gathered together, and times when delegations meet separately to discuss issues, create, and plan for their unique contexts.

Participants
Make sure you include experts in local artistic genres, respected church leaders, representatives of as many age and ethnic groups in the community as possible, and others with spiritual and organizational influence in the church.

Kinds of things you'll need from the Community Arts Profile

These activities will have you drawing on and adding to the list and descriptions of genres in the church, as well as those used in the surrounding community. A good goal would be to fill out a "Take a First Glance at an Event" sheet (**Step 4, Part A**) for each genre, and "Discover a Christian Community's Arts" for the church (**Step 4, Part D**). The more of this information you have before the workshop, the less time you'll need to devote to basic data gathering while it's happening.

Resources needed

Dependent on the local context.

Tasks

1. Plan the event. A team that includes church leaders, artists, and an arts advocate (someone like you) should plan the event. Use "Planning an Arts Workshop" and "Sample Workshop Schedule" (above) to guide your planning. This team will choose the people best suited to perform each task. The rest of these steps occur during the workshop.
2. Orient the participants. With the participants, discuss logistics, finances, transport, schedule, and the workshop's purposes, outcomes, products, and guidelines for evaluation and improvement (**Step 6**).
3. Explore biblical foundations.[109] Describe biblical and conceptual foundations of arts in the kingdom of God, choosing from the following and/or developing your own:

   a. "All the Arts, From All the World, For All of God's Kingdom" (from the "Prepare Yourself" chapter at the beginning of the manual).
   b. "Interpret Scripture Well" and "Address Theological Objections" (**Step 4, Part D**).

4. Address any disruptive community problems. There may be a history of miscommunication and misunderstanding between artists, missionaries, pastors, or others in this community. If so, pray, confess to each other, and forgive one another.
5. Identify the church's arts. Make a list of each Christian community's arts using "Discover a Christian Community's Arts" (**Step 4, Part D**).
6. Identify the surrounding community's arts. Consult a list of artistic genres in the surrounding community, or create it using "Take a First Glance at a Community's Arts" (**Step 1**).
7. Evaluate the church's arts. Follow the guide, "Evaluate How a Christian Community's Arts Currently Fulfill Its Purposes" (**Step 4, Part D**). Also, examine each art according to the origins of its elements, using the table in "Creativity" (**Step 4, Part C**). Focus on questions like these:
8. How could the church's purposes in corporate gatherings be improved through better use of its arts? Does the meeting communicate clearly to each group within the community? Are people's hearts, souls, minds, and bodies deeply engaged and moved in corporate adoration?
9. Choose a purpose. Choose one or more of these purposes to focus on for the rest of the workshop.

---

109 See also *Handbook*, Foundations and Stories sections.

10. Choose an art form. Decide whether some artistic forms could be added, removed, or modified to better meet the purposes of your gatherings. Choose one or more of these for further development.
11. Create. Have groups of artists and spiritual leaders create or adapt works in these forms to accomplish the purposes identified earlier.
12. Celebrate and integrate. Discuss local and wider community authority structures, and decide the best ways to integrate these innovations into church life. These plans should include specific media and dates and locations for performance and distribution. **Step 7** will be helpful in this process. If possible, introduce the new works at a larger community event at the end of the workshop. Implement the plans for further integration and celebration, underlining the importance of humility.

HELP PREACHERS AND TEACHERS INCORPORATE MORE LOCAL ARTS INTO WHAT THEY DO

In this activity, trainers and motivators in a Christian community gather. They explore how they can integrate more of their community's arts into their preaching and teaching.

Participants

Experts in local artistic genres, pastors, preachers, teachers, and larger community gatekeepers.

Kinds of things you'll need from the Community Arts Profile

You will want to know as much as you can about genres that include significant verbal content. Refer to "Oral Verbal Arts in an Event" (**Step 4, Part B4**).

Resources needed

Dependent on the local context.

Tasks

1. Gather everyone in a Christian community involved in teaching and preaching at any level. This could be an informal meeting confined to a local congregation.
2. Show the list of local artistic genres you prepared in **Step 1**. Add any previously forgotten ones to the Community Arts Profile. Note especially those with strong verbal content, such as genres that tell stories, enact dramas, or present oratory or proverbs.
3. Have each participant tell which, if any, of these genres they have integrated into their preaching or teaching. How did it work?
4. Discuss which of the genres seem to be most promising in communicating scriptural truths in memorable, penetrating ways.
5. Together, help each other plan to incorporate one new genre into their preaching or teaching within a reasonable time frame.
6. Gather after participants have had a chance to try their innovation, and discuss difficulties, successes, and ideas for further use.
7. Plan to discuss the use of local genres in training the church at regular community meetings.

HOLD AN ARTISTIC GENRE WORKSHOP

In this activity, Christian leaders choose a particular artistic genre they want to help develop for kingdom purposes. They then gather creators and performers in this genre to produce new, Scripture-infused examples of the genre and explore potential purposes for them. In some ways, this activity ignores the **Step 1**, **Step 2**, . . . **Step 7** approach and leads you to just start making stuff and see where it goes. Arts can spread in ways you never imagine.

Participants

Include experts in the artistic genre, respected church leaders, representatives from a church congregation, and facilitators of the workshop.

Kinds of things you'll need from the Community Arts Profile

It would be great to have a Corporate Worship Workshop (above) before this workshop for a community. In the Corporate Worship Workshop, participants identify the artistic genres that are currently used in the church and list the arts of the community. They also evaluate the church's arts and to decide together which artistic genres they want to develop more for the corporate worship of the church. To identify potential purposes of the arts, there needs to be preliminary research to find what purposes the current arts in the church are fulfilling and what purposes are not being fulfilled by arts.

Resources needed

Dependent on the local context.

Tasks

These tasks are derived from "Planning an Arts Workshop" above.

1. Preparation meeting: Church leaders and facilitators meet to choose one or more artistic genres they want to develop based on the evaluation of the church's arts and discuss potential purposes for new arts that will be created in the workshop.
2. Plan the workshop: Facilitators of the workshop set the dates and place that key leaders and artists can come for the workshop and communicate the purpose of the workshop to those who are invited in advance.
3. Orient the participants: With the participants, discuss logistics, finances, transport, schedule, the workshop's purposes, outcomes, products, and guidelines for evaluation.
4. Explore potential purposes of this artistic genre: In small groups or open discussions, (a) discuss what purposes this art form has been used for in the church, (b) evaluate the present use of the art form, and (c) discuss what kind of new materials the participants need to develop or what other purposes can be fulfilled through this art form.
5. Choose purposes: Decide one purpose or more depending on the number of participants. If there is a big number of participants, divide the group into small groups to work for various purposes of this art form.

PREFACE
PREPARE
STEP 1
STEP 2
STEP 3
STEP 4
STEP 5
STEP 6
STEP 7
CLOSING

6. Create together: Artists can bring their unfinished works if they already have an idea or have started to create before the workshop, and they can work together with other artists to cocreate new materials. They can consult church leaders and congregation representatives on deciding Scripture verses that are the basis for the creation.

7. Presentation and evaluation: If it is a big group, each small group can present what they created and invite evaluation and feedback. If it is a small group, they can present it to the church leaders and congregation representatives and get feedback from them. Evaluate together if the new materials will fulfill the purposes they decided together. Revise the works based on the feedback.

8. Plan for integration and celebration: Discuss how these new arts can best be integrated in church services. Discuss what kind of church events can be a good channel to introduce the new materials, and share them with the rest of the congregation. Decide when, where, and how they will perform the new creations.

HOLD A SONG (OR OTHER ART FORM) COMPOSITION WORKSHOP ON WORLDVIEW THEMES

The purpose of this activity is to employ artistic communication to address difficult issues at the intersection of Christian truths and local community beliefs and practices. We're using genres containing songs as an example. However, genres containing other elements like proverbs, storytelling, drama, and visual communication could speak to such problems just as well.

Participants

Include composers, pastors, and denominational leaders.

Kinds of things you'll need from the Community Arts Profile

1. Choose genres containing song from the Community Arts Profile.
2. Through observation and discussions with various levels of the community, ask the question, "In our community, what areas are the most difficult to live out as a follower of Christ?" We have chosen four areas for this example. In light of these, ask, "What do community members believe about birth, death, how to make a living, and male and female relationships?" Record answers.

Resources needed

Dependent on the local context.

Tasks

1. Discuss with church leaders that the purpose of the workshop is to compose Scripture-based songs in traditional and church styles that address non-Christian worldview issues. Ask for their authorization and for their ideas concerning location and dates to hold the workshop.
2. With these church leaders, identify song genres participants will be composing in, and form a team of local artists gifted in those genres.

3. Form a planning team to prepare for promotion, costs, travel information,the formation of a local organization team, and other logistics.
4. Write up a flyer explaining about the workshop and distribute it.
5. Send a letter to central church leaders with a schedule for travel and the workshop.
6. One month before the workshop, contact the central church leader for a list of names of those attending.
7. Make travel arrangements, prepare materials, and practice lessons with team teachers.
8. One week before the workshop, contact the local organizing director to make sure all is in order (lodging, food arrangements, teaching area, blackboard, etc.).
9. Travel with the team to workshop destination, arriving the Sunday before the workshop is scheduled to begin.
10. Present the goals of the workshop in the Sunday morning worship service to elicit prayer and encourage participation.
11. Sunday afternoon before the workshop, hold a time of prayer with local church leaders for the workshop, discuss the schedule and general plans for the workshop, and make adjustments as needed after receiving local input.
12. Present workshop (six days plus Sunday morning presentation):

   a. Remind participants that God uses Scripture to affirm some parts of every culture and challenge others. This workshop is about beliefs and practices in our community that need to be addressed scripturally and through prayer.
   b. Discuss local community worldview on issues of birth, death, making a living, and male and female relationships.
   c. Follow "How to Avoid Both Syncretism and Irrelevance" in **Step 4, Part D**.
   d. Divide the entire group into four groups and compose one song on each of the four categories each day (alternate categories each day among the groups).
   e. Each evening, include a time of critique (self, community) around the fire as songs are sung and taught.
   f. Perform a consultant critique before recording songs on Saturday afternoon.
   g. Sunday morning in church, present the new songs and celebrate them!

ORGANIZE AN ALL ARTS CELEBRATION
Plan a concert, festival, or other big event that showcases all of the artistic gifts represented by members of a Christian community.

Participants
Include Christian artists, pastors, organizers, and the Christian community.

Kinds of things you'll need from the Community Arts Profile
In addition to the list of artistic genres, arts appropriate for communication in the church should be identified. Also identify who in the church can participate in these arts.

PREFACE

PREPARE

STEP 1

STEP 2

STEP 3

STEP 4

STEP 5

STEP 6

STEP 7

CLOSING

PREFACE

PREPARE

STEP 1

STEP 2

STEP 3

STEP 4

STEP 5

STEP 6

STEP 7

CLOSING

Resources needed

Dependent on the local context.

Tasks

1. Church community members work together to discover what artistic genres and styles are known within the church.
2. Local pastors, Christian artists, and organizers meet to discuss and plan the event: location, time, day, and who will be involved.
3. Artistic works may be commissioned specifically for this event.
4. If culturally appropriate, some arts could involve the whole community (i.e., improvised dramas with spect-actors, sing-alongs, dancing, dress).
5. Make the event a celebration of God's creativity and the gifts he's given this community.

STUDY THE BIBLE IN MORE THAN ONE FORM AS A GROUP[110]

We remember Scripture better when we study the message in more than one format. This activity describes how to lead a Bible study that includes multiple formats, including print Scripture; song, poetry, drama, and other types of Scripture-infused performances; and audio or visual recordings of Scripture.

Participants

Choose a wise, respected leader with Bible knowledge. Also include people gifted in local art forms and people who want to study Scripture.

Kinds of things you'll need from the Community Arts Profile

This activity requires a list of genres of artistic communication to evaluate for use in a Bible study.

Resources needed

Dependent on the local context.

Tasks

1. Decide how often, when, and where the group will meet. This activity assumes a weekly meeting, but this could vary widely.
2. Introduce how this type of group Bible study functions socially.[111] Leading a Bible study group is much different than preaching a sermon. Being part of a Bible study is more like playing together on a soccer team. The leader is like a coach who helps people train regularly without exhausting or injuring

---

110   See also, Margeret and Harriet Hill, *Translating the Bible into Action* (United Kingdom: Piquant Editions, 2010).

111   For discussions of related study groups, see Robert L. Kohls and Herbert L. Brussow, *Training Know-How for Cross-Cultural and Diversity Trainers* (Duncanville, TX: Adult Learning Systems, 1995); and Timothy Reagan, *Non-Western Educational Traditions: Alternative Approaches to Educational Thought and Theory* (Mahwah, NJ: Lawrence Erlbaum Associates, 1996).

themselves. He works to strengthen his team's muscles. A Bible study leader works to strengthen the group's spiritual muscles by helping them remember Scripture and think about how to apply it to their own lives.

3. The leader gathers existing resources on the Scripture passage the group will study. These could be printed versions in local or regional languages, concordances, songs that contain the Scripture, etc.

4. Week 1: Study the passage with available resources.

5. Week 2: List the artistic genres that exist in the church and surrounding community, using "Take a First Glance at a Community's Arts" (**Step 1**). Evaluate each of these genres for possible use in the study "Take a First Glance at an Event" and "Take a First Glance at an Event's Genre" (**Step 4, Part A**). Choose one genre that could relate the Scripture passage, and commission one or more people within the group to create such a new work. The genre could be one that includes musical, dramatic, visual, oral verbal (e.g., storytelling), or dance elements.

6. Week 3: Participants share their creations, teach them to the others when possible, and tell how the process has impacted them. Discuss ways that they could be improved (see **Step 6**).

7. Other weeks: Choose genres with different kinds of arts in them, especially dramatic, storytelling, and visual. Again, participants create new works inspired by the Scripture, share them the following week, teach them to the others when possible, and tell how the process has impacted them.

8. Explore occasions for performance or presentation of the new works together. Who else may benefit from the new works? Discuss together different ways that everyone can share what they have created with their neighbors, a school, or the wider church community.

9. As long as the Bible study continues, remember to ask these kinds of questions:

   a. What Scripture means a lot to us, and what purpose does it have in our community? How can our (wider) community learn what we've learned?

   b. Who is our audience for this performance? How much do they already know about our message? Is our presentation of Scripture clear, accurate, and natural for them? We don't want to change the meaning of Scripture. We may need to change elements of how we communicate Scripture so people will understand it better or feel more keenly attuned to the importance of God's message.

   c. What forms fit our purpose well? Remember, people will retain more if they experience the message in more than one way.

   d. What is the main idea we hope people understand? Is this the main idea emphasized by the performance?

PREFACE

PREPARE

STEP 1

STEP 2

STEP 3

STEP 4

STEP 5

STEP 6

STEP 7

CLOSING

IMPROVE A CURRENT CHURCH CEREMONY, RITUAL, OR PRACTICE

This activity was developed with a particular Central African church community's baptism practices in mind. You may adapt it to other church activities such as weddings, communion, funerals, and others.

Participants

Inlude church leaders, those desiring to receive baptism, parents and family members, and church members.

Kinds of things you'll need from the Community Arts Profile

Analyze current practices of baptism as larger events containing subevents, performing the research in "Shape of the Event through Time" (**Step 4, Part A**). In particular, explore catechism training (who teaches, how they teach, what materials are available for teaching and for the students to use to learn, physical labor and gifts required of the candidates, the role of the arts, other activities done during their training), any exam at the end of training, preparations for the celebration, the actual baptismal service, and any other services.

List the genres of local arts used during the current baptism practices (song, marching and dancing, musical instruments, clothing, etc.). Explore the ritual nature of the event: importance of carefully following particular actions, the place of the baptism, the march to the water source and the return, who participates and how.

Resources needed

Dependent on the local context.

Tasks

1. With a small group of various levels of church leaders and qualified lay people (both men and women), specify the kingdom goals that the event really is supposed to represent. Ask questions like these: What strengths are there in the present ceremony? What weaknesses? Examine traditional circumcision practices as well as traditional birth and burial celebrations to see if any parallels can be made to the baptism experience. Discuss the current teaching program to determine what results it produces.
2. At regional church leaders' meetings, discuss the pros and cons of the present baptism practice using the results of the small group discussions as a springboard.
3. Select a commission to study the issue; include at least one senior pastor, one trained theologian, one Bible school teacher, a leader of a women's group, and pastors from both rural and town churches. Ask questions like these of the commission (refer to "Evaluate How a Christian Community's Arts Currently Fulfill Its Purposes," **Step 4, Part D**):

   a. What kingdom goal is reached through a baptism service?
   b. How well is the present practice meeting that goal?

PREFACE   PREPARE   STEP 1   STEP 2   STEP 3   STEP 4   STEP 5   STEP 6   STEP 7   CLOSING

    c. How effective is the material being taught?

    d. How effective is the teaching method?

    e. What percentage of the newly baptized are still active in the church after one year? After two years? Why do those who are no longer active fall away?

    f. What are the most important biblical principles that need to be taught to the new converts?

    g. What recommendations does the commission have for changes in the program?

    h. How could artistic forms of communication (e.g., local types of song, dance, storytelling, and proverbs) be used to make the process of learning the catechism and celebrating baptism more effective and the message better understood?

4. At the next regional church leaders' meetings, present the commission's findings. Delegate the responsibility to this commission to revise the baptism rite in the following ways:

    a. Develop a catechism program based on Bible teaching lessons through local storytelling: candidates memorize Bible stories, proverbs, and verses for each main lesson in the current catechism; candidates compose new Scripture-based songs for each main lesson; female candidates learn to embroider a key word for each main lesson onto a scarf; male candidates learn how to wood burn a key word for each main lesson into a mortar or chair or plaque.

    b. Seek approval for the new program from leaders at all levels of church hierarchy.

    c. Produce a catechism guide in languages used in the community and wider church community, briefly detailing each point of each main lesson. Use sketches, pictures, and diagrams to supplement and clarify the text.

    d. Plan workshops for pastors, catechists, deacons, and women's group leaders to teach them the new material in a way that they will be able to repeat in their home churches.

    e. Pray for and find funding to assist with food at workshops and for printing new catechism guides.

    f. At workshops, determine which local art forms will help exemplify the true meaning of baptism at the actual ceremony and how that can be done well (drama, instrumental music, vocal music, marching to the water and back again, clothing the candidates wear, the receiving line when they come out of the water, etc.).

    g. Help the pastors and catechists draw up plans as to when and how they are going to begin to incorporate these new teachings into their catechism program and to teach it to their church members.

    h. At the end of the workshop, include a time of commissioning/dedicating those who will be teaching the new program.

5. With the commission members, determine evaluation procedures.

6. Pray that it will all come together to bring about a change in the spiritual life of the church!

PREFACE

PREPARE

STEP 1

STEP 2

STEP 3

STEP 4

STEP 5

STEP 6

STEP 7

CLOSING

PREFACE

PREPARE

STEP 1

STEP 2

STEP 3

STEP 4

STEP 5

STEP 6

STEP 7

CLOSING

HOLD A CONTEST FOR NEW WAYS TO MEMORIZE SCRIPTURE[112]

Institute a competition for the best new work communicating a given Scripture passage in a local artistic genre. The process will include explorations on how to create, to what degree texts can be modified to fit the form, and other issues relevant to the creative process.

Participants
In the planning phase, include Christian leaders and competent performers of several local artistic genres. The competition phase could be opened to the entire community. The judges will include spiritual and artistic leaders.

Kinds of things you'll need from the Community Arts Profile
The survey of artistic genres produced in **Step 1**, and "Creativity" (**Step 4, Part C**).

Resources needed
Dependent on the local context.

Tasks

1. With a planning team:

    a. List the artistic genres known to be available in the community.
    b. Discuss the importance of integrating Scripture into all aspects of people's lives, studying the biblical texts in "Studying and Remembering Scripture" (**Step 2**).
    c. Design the competition according to community approaches to critique, based on research you've performed in "Aesthetics and Evaluation" (**Step 4, Part C**) and on authority structures. Choose judges prayerfully and carefully, making sure to include people who are acknowledged experts in Scripture and local artistic genres. Choose prizes and figure out finances.

2. Communicate through available media (posters, radio, texts, local artistic genres, Internet, etc.):

    a. Purposes of the event (including to find new ways to remember Scripture, and to raise awareness of God's artistic gifts to the community)
    b. Participants' tasks: Choose a need or dream that the community has now, Scripture in the community's language that addresses that need or dream, and a kind of traditional art form (at least their grandparents' generation created in it). Make something new in the genre with the Scripture as its content.
    c. Date, time, and other logistics.
    d. Judging criteria:

---

112 See, Barz, and Hill and Hill, *Translating the Bible into Action.*

i. Is the content and importance of the Scripture maintained? Some incidental words may be changed to fit the form of the genre, but not the core message.
ii. How well does the chosen Scripture speak to a need, problem, or dream of the community?
iii. Has the genre existed in the community for at least two generations? (If you are not focusing on deeply rooted genres, you can omit this stipulation.)
iv. Is the creative output an excellent example of the genre?

3. Execute the plan. This will need to coincide with community norms and calendrical cycles.

COMMISSION ARTS FOR COMMUNITY EVENTS
The goal of this activity is to commission an excellent example of a local artistic genre that (1) carries scriptural content that speaks to community needs, and (2) can be performed at a familiar community event.

Participants
Choose wise Christians, expert composers, and performers.

Kinds of things you'll need from the Community Arts Profile
This activity requires having a list of artistic genres within a community, and knowing how people create new works within them.

Resources needed
Dependent on the local context.

Tasks

1. With a group of Christ-followers and people experienced in local artistic traditions, evaluate existing artistic genres according to their potential for communicating scriptural truth. Guided by the list of artistic genres in the Community Arts Profile, start asking questions like these about each genre: Does it have spiritual, social, or sexual connotations? What kind of content does it communicate? How many people know how to create new examples in this genre?
2. List and discuss upcoming events according to their potential for connecting with many and/or influential people, and possibilities for entering their planning and execution.
3. Reflect on biblical truths and stories most likely to connect with community concerns. Decide on a concern and a Scripture passage that speaks to that concern.
4. Decide on an artistic genre that could carry this message well.
5. Explore how new works are created within this genre, based on research you've performed in "Creativity" (**Step 4, Part C**).

PREFACE

PREPARE

STEP 1

STEP 2

STEP 3

STEP 4

STEP 5

STEP 6

STEP 7

CLOSING

PREFACE

PREPARE

STEP 1

STEP 2

STEP 3

STEP 4

STEP 5

STEP 6

STEP 7

CLOSING

6. Identify an expert composer or group of composers within the genre. Meet and ask him or her to create a new example of the genre. Enter into their normal processes of creation.
7. Through live performance or audio or video recording, present the new work to spiritual leaders and experts in the genre for critique and improvement. Evaluate according to biblical correctness, communicational clarity, and meeting standards of the genre derived through the seven lenses (**Step 4, Part A**).
8. Work with the composer to improve any shortcomings.
9. Perform at the event.

PERSONAL SPIRITUAL LIFE

ENCOURAGE CHRISTIANS TO COMMUNE WITH GOD THROUGH MULTIPLE ARTS
Many Christians tend to communicate with God primarily by sitting and reading Scripture. Others are unsure how to incorporate times of reflection and communication with God into their lives at all. This activity introduces people to other forms of communication at a prayer retreat, and helps participants plan to integrate arts into their times with God.

Participants
Gather members of a Christian congregation, pastors, and church leaders.

Kinds of things you'll need from the Community Arts Profile
Perform "Discover a Christian Community's Arts" (**Step 4, Part D**).

Resources needed
Dependent on the local context.

Tasks

1. Have pastors and church leaders choose a theme for the prayer retreat that will encourage the church in relevant ways.
2. Plan logistics of the retreat: location, time, etc.
3. Consult artistic church members to create activities or prayer stations where the attendees can pray and meditate using arts that are familiar and meaningful to the culture. These could include art forms with special vocal features, dance, poetry, storytelling, acting, song, and others.
4. Invite church members to come to the retreat.
5. As a final activity, have participants plan one way they will enliven their communion with God with some form of artistry.

MENTOR SOMEONE IN INTEGRATING LONG CHURCH TRADITIONS OF ARTS INTO THEIR RELATIONSHIP WITH GOD

Participants

Bring together someone who is mature and still eager to learn, and someone younger in the faith. Encourage mentoring relationships between people only after much prayer and discussion.

Kinds of things you'll need from the Community Arts Profile

Investigate community patterns of mentoring relationships.

Resources needed

Dependent on the local context.

Tasks

As part of the mentoring relationship, explore some of the following practices together, adapting them to fit local art forms. Pastor Adele Calhoun's *Spiritual Disciplines Handbook* provides excellent, practical introductions to these and more.[113] Also, St. Mary's Press has published a series called *Companions for the Journey* with practices from many noted Christians.

1. Follow liturgical calendars. Many larger church communities have developed yearly patterns of readings, poetry, and prayer. The Episcopal Church's *The Book of Common Prayer* is one example.
2. Integrate singing into fixed-hour prayers. Some traditions identify certain times of the day as appropriate for certain kinds of prayer and meditation. *The Divine Hours,* by renowned editor and author Phyllis Tickle, has made this accessible to many people.[114] Create your own chants or melodies for the psalms and hymns.
3. Use imaginative contemplation in Bible study. Often influenced by the life and writings of Ignatius of Loyola (1491–1556), some Christians integrate their imaginations into the study of Scripture. They read a story about Jesus and then imagine themselves in the scene, seeing, smelling, tasting, hearing the actions, and waiting for what Jesus might say to them.
4. Encourage the mentee to experiment with other forms of artistry while communing with God, including those that contain dance, journaling, story writing, drawing, singing, painting, and anything else that the individual can use to express himself or herself to God.

---

113 Adele Ahlberg Calhoun, *Spiritual Disciplines Handbook: Practices that Transform Us* (Downers Grove, IL: InterVarsity Press, 2005).
114 Phyllis Tickle, *The Divine Hours*, pocket ed. (Oxford: Oxford University Press, 2007).

PREFACE

PREPARE

STEP 1

STEP 2

STEP 3

STEP 4

STEP 5

STEP 6

STEP 7

CLOSING

PREFACE

PREPARE

STEP 1

STEP 2

STEP 3

STEP 4

STEP 5

STEP 6

STEP 7

CLOSING

COMMISSION A VERBAL ART FORM OF RESOLVE THAT WILL HELP PEOPLE APPLY SCRIPTURAL TRUTHS TO THEIR LIVES

Artistic forms of communication help us remember truth, but they can also help people move us to act on that truth. "I Am Determined to Walk with Jesus" is a song in African-American churches that fills this role.

Participants

Include both artists and spiritual leaders.

Kinds of things you'll need from the Community Arts Profile

Refer to a list of genres that exist in the community.

Tasks

1. Examine each genre for how well it can communicate resolve, fortitude, determination, and similar emotions. Choose one.
2. Commission an excellent composer in that genre to create a new work that encourages people to love and obey Jesus no matter what.
3. Have the composer present his or her creation to a small group of spiritual and artistic leaders in the community for affirmation and improvement (see **Step 6**).
4. Introduce and teach the new composition to the wider community, asking God to bring it to people's minds when they are losing their focus on Jesus.

PERFORM THE ACTIVITY AND DESCRIBE THE RESULTS

Do what you planned. Hold your plans lightly. Listen to God. Learn from mistakes. Enjoy the process. Describe what happened in the Community Arts Profile. Enough said.

IMPROVE NEW WORKS

We want communities to integrate creativity into their lives in such a way that their spiritual, social, and physical goals are not only met, but truly exceeded. Evaluating according to agreed-upon criteria helps them make their imperfect artistic communication more effective. Remember that the goal of evaluating is construction, not destruction; building up, not tearing down (Eph 4:29). Note, too, that the community can greatly reduce the need for critique by including the right people from the beginning of the cocreative process: social and religious leaders, expert creators, and expert performers.

Improvement is a key point at which the community benefits from the research performed in **Step 4**. The more we understand and can talk about an art form, the more we can identify elements that hinder positive effects from happening. Each of the processes below should include frequent reference to the Community Arts Profile (or its contents, stored in people's minds).

In **Step 6** we help you reach these goals:

- Follow comforting guidelines for deciding what's good and bad.
- Design an evaluative process using a conceptual approach.
- Design a recurring cycle of evaluation.
- Evaluate Scripture-infused arts.

FOLLOW COMFORTING GUIDELINES FOR DECIDING WHAT'S GOOD AND BAD

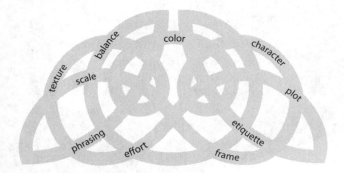

Figure 3: Sample Intertwined Artistic Features in an Event

How do you decide what's good or bad? When, for example, someone says, "I never liked the Beatles' music," do they mean they didn't like their tunes, they didn't like their lyrics, or they didn't like their long hair? People are seldom able to articulate what exactly they like or don't like about an art work. This is not surprising, because artistic communication works through the production and reception of a staggering number of possible signs and their associated meanings. If you glance through all of the research activities in **Step 4**, you'll see that people could be evaluating arts according to any of these kinds of signs: line; syntax; enjambment; rhyme; assonance; alliteration; metaphor; simile; verses; stanzas; refrains; pulse; tempo; meter; accents; figures; motifs; phrases; tonal center; keys; intervals; modes; scales; range; tessitura; themes; contours; cadences; parallel, chordal, or polyphonic relationships between concurrent pitches; formulas; progressions; tonality; strophes; iterations; through-composition; theme variation; solo; duo; trio; choir; unison; vibrato; accompaniment; use of space; characterization; number and location of participants; blocking; plot structure; idea; dramatic premise; frames; improvisation; movements; gestures; movement phrasing; dynamics; efforts; spatial relationships; visual unity; balance; rhythm; proportion; line; shape; value; color; hue; shade; tint; texture. And so on. And so on.

But there's more. Not only are the kinds of signs seemingly endless, but each group and individual may have diverse associations with any given sign. One person may smile whenever he hears Latin percussion because he met the woman who would become his wife at a party where they danced the samba. Another man may detest samba because his fiancée broke up with him at a similar event. There could be zillions of signs multiplied by zillions of associations at an artistic event, any one of which could make it fail.

But, unbelievably, our predicament is even more dire. Not only does productive evaluation require us to perceive an infinite number of signs, their combinations, and their meanings, but we need to be aware of personal relationships and social dynamics. An epic poet might perform brilliantly, but if an influential audience member is holding a grudge against him, the community might ultimately dismiss the artist's skill.

Take a deep breath. The complexity of artistic communication should keep us humble, but there are several factors that make identifying criteria for improvement possible. We here present these factors as guidelines for designing evaluation and improvement exercises.

TRUST THE LOCAL SYSTEM

Groups usually share a sense of when an art work is good or not and have ways of communicating what needs to be fixed. Perform the research in "Aesthetics and Evaluation" (**Step 4, Part C**) to find out how correction normally works in the community. In some situations they may get rid of inferior products by blocking them from future presentation and letting them die.

EVALUATE ACCORDING TO EFFECTS

In **Step 3** you identified the effects that new artistry should have on people in order to move them toward kingdom goals. Observe and ask about experiencers' responses to the new bits of artistry. Did it have the effects you wanted? If an orator's performance is meant to motivate people to join a parade celebrating their ethnic identity, but participants watch distractedly and then disperse to their homes, then the oration failed.

RELAX, BUT KEEP LEARNING

You can't study all of the possible signs, so do this: watch people's reactions and listen to what they say, and dip into the research activities in **Step 4** related to the genres you're working with regularly—maybe one activity a week or month. For example, if you're getting to know people who carve fruit, schedule these research activities: "Describe Spatial Relationships between an Object's Visual Features," "Document the Creation of an Object," and "Identify the Role(s) in Visual Art Creation" (**Step 4, Part B5**). Then start learning to carve the fruit yourself. This education will sensitize you to factors that may prove important in the improvement of new artistry.

IDENTIFY WHAT KINDS OF EVALUATION SHOULD HAPPEN WHEN

Artistic activity can benefit from evaluation at two points in the cocreative process. First, when you are helping people during the act of creation, everyone can evaluate intermediate versions of the

PREFACE

PREPARE

STEP 1

STEP 2

STEP 3

STEP 4

STEP 5

STEP 6

STEP 7

CLOSING

PREFACE

PREPARE

STEP 1

STEP 2

STEP 3

STEP 4

STEP 5

STEP 6

STEP 7

CLOSING

works. Second, you may help people reflect on a work after it has been presented.

Keep these bits of advice in mind as you and the community decide how to improve the artistry produced by the sparking activities in **Step 5**. Following are three approaches to designing such processes. The first, "Design an Evaluative Process Using a Conceptual Approach," provides basic principles you can draw on to create to your own system. The other two approaches give you more specific steps to follow. Read all three and decide which fits your context best, and modify them as necessary.[115]

In the initial process of setting Scripture portions to local Baka song forms in Cameroon, I collaborated with two Baka men—Tombombo, who normally helped me with translation, and Mai, a well-known musician and composer. Together we worked daily to translate and versify certain selected verses according to prototypical Baka song-text features. One day the two men set off to compose a Scripture song based on a text from Exodus 15—"The Song of Moses." A couple of days later, the duo returned with harp and voices, ready to perform their new composition. However, while they performed, on the outside I beamed with approval, but on the inside I sighed with disappointment. Many things about the song obviously "worked," but certain other features did not; revisions would need to be made.

Because of my music research and long experience living among the Baka, I was able to critically examine—even as a cultural outsider—a new Baka song composition. In particular, I gradually noticed that one sequence of the melodic intervals in one phrase of the melody of the song intuitively sounded "unnatural." As it turns out, in the Baka music tradition, there are certain sequences of melodic intervals that have never occurred in any of the hundreds of songs that I had recorded. My preliminary melodic analysis was also suggesting that there were certain grammatical restrictions on which interval types may follow others and for how long.

To illustrate, it is not, for example, uncommon for a melodic phrase in the modern Western music tradition to descend stepwise five to seven steps in succession before reversing melodic direction (for example, "Joy to the World" or "Twinkle Twinkle Little Star"). Most people with wide exposure to popular Western music can comfortably sing melodic sequences like these. An average Baka, on the other hand, cannot (with ease) sing such a prolonged succession of stepwise intervals; it exceeds the traditionally and subconsciously accepted limit of successive steps (that is, major or minor seconds) allowed in typical Baka intervallic syntax. So, just as certain grammatical patterns must be respected to facilitate effective speech, so it is with patterns of musical tones.

Left unrevised, the original melody, as composed by Tombombo, was never heard sung by anyone other than him. Since the song was composed with the specific *purpose* of being sung by *any* assembly of Baka Christians, it would need to be changed. Therefore, the

115   A further resource is this classic manual on pretesting with many examples: Ane Haaland, *Pretesting Communication Materials: With Special Emphasis on Child Health and Nutrition Education: A Manual for Trainers and Supervisors* (Rangoon: UNICEF, 1984).

melody *was* tactfully criticized—with all the culturally appropriate attending strategies of politeness—and then revised to employ only those melodic features truly characteristic of the Baka song tradition. In this way the melody posed no problem in *effecting its purpose*, given that now *any* Baka person would be able to naturally participate in singing the song.
– Dan Fitzgerald

DESIGN AN EVALUATIVE PROCESS USING A CONCEPTUAL APPROACH

Here is a process you can follow that will increase the likelihood of useful evaluation results:

1. Identify and work through **local social structures**, and help everyone involved provide correction in locally appropriate ways (using standards of politeness, respect, indirection, roles within a social hierarchy, etc.).
2. Define together the **criteria** for deciding how good a work is and how it could be improved. We have found this standard helpful: a created work is good insofar as its features work together to effect the purposes demanded by the context of its performance and experience. These purposes could include the work's theological correctness, accuracy of information communicated, ability to communicate, ability to touch people through its aesthetic quality, ability to motivate to action, etc.
3. Identify the **elements** of an artistic communication event (see "Take a First Glance at an Event," **Step 4, Part A**). These should include how the work utilizes space, materials, participants, shape through time, performance features, feeling, content, themes, and community values.
4. Identify the **purpose(s)** of the artistic communication event. These could include to educate, motivate to action, etc.
5. Identify **people** to include in the process of evaluation. These people need to have the knowledge, skills, and respect necessary to critique various elements.
6. Identify **objects** that can provide a focal point and reference for discussion, so that you don't have to rely exclusively on memory for critique. These could include song texts, drama scripts, musical notation, masks, dance moves, and video and audio recordings.
7. Together **affirm** the aspects of the creation that work well, and encourage the creators to **do something even better** based on the evaluation.

PREFACE

PREPARE

STEP 1

STEP 2

STEP 3

STEP 4

STEP 5

STEP 6

STEP 7

CLOSING

This table lists examples of evaluation in several creative contexts:

Kinds of Elements to Evaluate	Examples of Such Elements	Qualified Evaluaters	Example Methods of Evaluation
Space/location, time, participants, etc.	Storytelling around a fire at night, with all ages	Genre experts, traditional leaders	With written summary of the event description: Discuss relationship to genre.
Performance features (music, dance, verbal arts, drama, visual, etc.)	Proverb choice, movement characteristics, melody shape	Expert performers	With audio and video recordings: Review for aesthetic/technical successses, weaknesses of performance. Transcribe melody, lyrics, movements, poetic features, colors, etc., for analysis.
Message(s)	Theological content	Church leaders	With transcriptions of texts: Analyze texts of songs, dramas, stories (with back-translation if critiquer doesn't know language) according to clarity, truth. Comprehension testing: ask experiencers what they understood.
	Medical content	Health worker	
Purpose(s)	Church use: education, worship, evangelism AIDS education	Agenda setters for the communication event	With a summary of all aspects of the event, discuss degrees that the event fulfilled its intended purposes and other purposes, and how the event could be improved; may use a focus group or exit interviews.

DESIGN A RECURRING CYCLE OF EVALUATION[116]

We need to check art forms in order to know if the created product is meaningful to our target audience. So, for example, if we draw a picture for children, we need to know if the symbols and colors in the picture are meaningful, if the overall message of the picture is clear, if the image(s) are natural for them to both understand and imitate (as best they can), if they can easily absorb and restate the meaning of the visual image if the image clearly comes from their

116   Mary Beth and Todd Saurman, "Song Checking," in *All the World Will Worship: Helps for Developing Indigenous Hymns*, 3rd ed. (Duncanville, TX: EthnoDoxology/ACT, 2005), 179–185.

cultural context, etc. We also want to check with some experts in the community in order to know if the art forms relate meaningfully to the community as a whole.

Here are some ideas for checking an art form, but the approach should be designed appropriately for each cultural context.

WHO SHOULD HELP WITH THE CHECKING?

1. four or five target audience members
2. at least two older experts in the community

USE ALL OF THE FOLLOWING TESTS WITH EACH OF THE ABOVE PEOPLE

It is important to write down anything you learn about the art form so that improvements can be made. Checking with each person can take anywhere from five minutes to about twenty minutes. It is important to take time and learn as much you can about what needs to be improved.

Test for meaning

1. Show or demonstrate the art work.
2. Ask them to tell you what the art work communicates to them.
3. Listen to them and see if they seem to understand the meaning. If the work includes biblical texts, make sure that people understand it accurately.
4. If not, show them the art work again and ask them for the meaning once again.
5. Write down their response, and write down what parts of the art work are clear and what parts are unclear (this could be words, phrases, themes, colors, patterns, actions, etc.).

Test for naturalness

1. Show or demonstrate the art work.
2. Ask them if they can reproduce some portion of the art work back to you. Let them do this on their own and see what they can remember.
3. If they are having some difficulty remembering, show or demonstrate the art work again.
4. Ask them again to reproduce some portion of the art work.
5. If they are having some difficulty, you can prompt them a little, but it is wise to not prompt much.
6. Write down parts that are difficult to replicate.

PREFACE

PREPARE

STEP 1

STEP 2

STEP 3

STEP 4

STEP 5

STEP 6

STEP 7

CLOSING

PREFACE

PREPARE

STEP 1

STEP 2

STEP 3

STEP 4

STEP 5

STEP 6

STEP 7

CLOSING

Test for ownership and accuracy

Does the form parallel the form used by the target audience?

1. Ask them how they feel about the art work?
2. Would they use it? How would they use it? Would they enjoy hearing, seeing, or experiencing the art work? When?
3. What do they not like? What would they change? What would make the art better or more meaningful for them?
4. Does it feel to them as though it's their own? Does it feel as though it belongs to their community?
5. Is this form consistent with

   a. the listener's learning or education level?
   b. local teaching methods?
   c. the appropriate language and symbol or sound?

Correct the art work

Take the results from the arts checking to the art work creator or meet with the creation committee and change or adjust its unclear portions.

Test for effectiveness

Test again to see if you hit the target audience.

DESIGN AN EVALUATIVE PROCESS THAT FOCUSES ON SCRIPTURAL FIDELITY

There are three kinds of checks to help make Scripture-infused arts better. For all three, ask open-ended questions that lend themselves to exploratory answers, not yes-no short answers.

1. SELF-CHECK

Ask the artist to think of ways to make the work communicate more clearly to the desired audience. Encourage the artist to think about the work from the audience's point of view, taking into consideration the prevalent background knowledge and worldview assumptions of the local area. What could we change that would make the work clearer? To what extent is the most important thing the artist wants to communicate the most important thing the audience is likely to grasp from this performance?

2. CONSULTANT CHECK

When the text of an artistic work is based closely on Scripture, the need for evaluation and improvement is especially important. In these cases, experts in Scripture and the arts should be consulted.

When consultants don't speak the local language, they need a translation into a language they know well.

Two types of translation are important for evaluation. First, a word-for-word translation reveals poetic and discourse features of the text. Although slight adjustments of word order may be made, it follows the original text almost exactly. Second, a free translation attempts to convey the original meaning naturally in the target language. This helps the consultant understand the overall importance of the text. Translations will be better if they result from following these guidelines: the translator should be a mother-tongue speaker of the source language; the translator should not already be familiar with the text; the translation could be oral and audio recorded, or written; if the translator doesn't understand what the artist meant, they should discuss it together; if there are unintended misunderstandings, the artist should strongly consider changing the text.

With these translations in hand, check whether the material has these characteristics:

- relates Scripture meaningfully to the local worldview
- the rate of information flow is neither too fast nor too slow
- meaning, form, style, and emotion go together
- not insulting to any particular group
- nonoffensive portrayal of sensitive issues, like violence
- believable portrayal of interesting characters
- balance of character development and actions
- biblical background knowledge is either already generally known or provided
- follows the discourse rules of similar materials in the genre
- the way the material opens and closes (greetings and leave-takings, for example) is culturally appropriate
- time frame is clear

3. COMMUNITY CHECK

The third check tests the material with a small audience of the target group before the material is presented to a larger audience. In general, the same person who made a translation and the artist should not check the work with the community.

Record the work, play it back for the focus group, and ask questions like these:

- What was it about? What else was it about? *For an illustration or visual artwork*: What do you see? What else do you see? *After a dance*: What did you see? What else did you see? *After a song*: What did you hear? What else did you hear? *After a drama*: What happened? And then what happened? And then what happened? Do not tell people the answers.

PREFACE

PREPARE

STEP 1

STEP 2

STEP 3

STEP 4

STEP 5

STEP 6

STEP 7

CLOSING

- What do you think the author/artist/storyteller/actors/ dancers wanted to communicate? What did you learn? Do not explain the intended meaning to them; if you do, you will not get a valid impression of their comprehension.
- What did you like? What did you appreciate?
- What did you not like? Did anything offend you?

Testers should talk with the creator(s) and work together to revise the work accordingly.

PREFACE

PREPARE

STEP 1

STEP 2

STEP 3

STEP 4

STEP 5

STEP 6

STEP 7

CLOSING

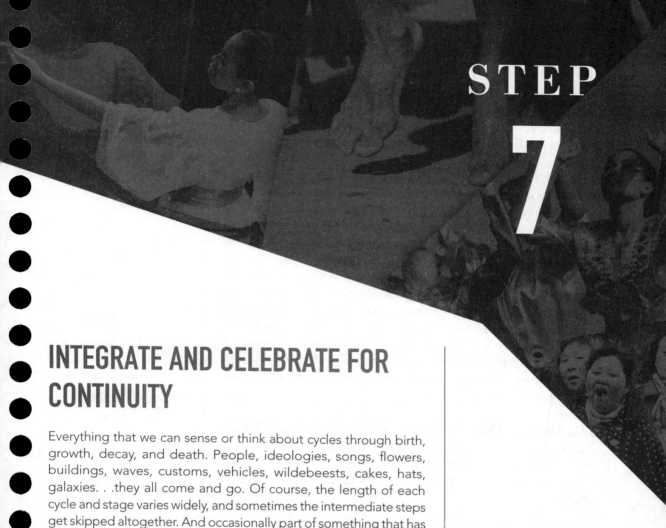

INTEGRATE AND CELEBRATE FOR CONTINUITY

Everything that we can sense or think about cycles through birth, growth, decay, and death. People, ideologies, songs, flowers, buildings, waves, customs, vehicles, wildebeests, cakes, hats, galaxies. . .they all come and go. Of course, the length of each cycle and stage varies widely, and sometimes the intermediate steps get skipped altogether. And occasionally part of something that has died gets resurrected, as when the forgotten works of a sixteenth-century painter are found and inspire artists centuries later. So why don't we just join the ebb and flow, the wax and wane of history? Why do we try to make some things last longer and others not? How do we know when to integrate and celebrate for continuity, and when to fold our hands and rest?

In **Step 7** we'll provide a few ideas that will help you wrestle with these daunting questions in your cocreative context. Specifically, we'll give some pointers on how to

- choose what to integrate and celebrate
- act to keep good things going
- understand more about how continuity works
- know when to let go[117]

---

117 See Schrag's chapters in the *Handbook*, "Planning an Arts Showcase Event" and "Evaluating and Improving Local Arts", chpts. 144 and 145.

PREFACE

PREPARE

STEP 1

STEP 2

STEP 3

STEP 4

STEP 5

STEP 6

STEP 7

CLOSING

CHOOSE WHAT TO INTEGRATE AND CELEBRATE

Your first choice here is simple: integrate and celebrate the arts that you have been engaging with in **Steps 2–6**. With a community, you've identified goals consistent with the kingdom of God, decided on certain kinds of artistry that can move the community closer to these goals, and implemented actions that resulted in new bits of this artistry and then improved them. And all along the way you've been listening to God and trying to discern what he's up to. This process has ensured as much as possible that the creative processes and people you've been engaging with are the ones that should take root and flourish.

But all situations change all the time. This invigorating (or frustrating, depending on your personality) fact means that communities need to regularly reassess their present and think about the future. The constituency of a community will alter, new modes of communication will enter, government policies will evolve—so the kinds of artistic communication best suited for growth toward a better future will change. Here are some suggestions for initiatives in the months and years ahead.

ENCOURAGE THE COMMUNITY TO MAKE INTENTIONAL CREATIVITY A HABIT
Go through the cocreative cycle in this manual again: **Steps 1–7**. The more a community does this, the more it will become a familiar, institutionalized process that flows naturally and efficiently through members' lives.

ENCOURAGE CONTINUITY IN ARTS THAT MAKE THE MOST UNIQUE CONTRIBUTIONS TO THE KINGDOM OF HEAVEN
Globalization, urbanization, missionary activity, wars, and other factors often (though certainly not always) lead to the devaluation of and declining interest in the art forms of minority communities. The end of Revelation 21 suggests that elements of every culture will last into heaven. When we all sing, dance, act, paint, and tell truth in similar ways, we impoverish the global church on earth and in heaven (at least at the beginning). So don't assume that global trends are necessarily God's plans. Every bit of God-created diversity we can experience helps us know God better.

This value on uniqueness extends to multicultural communities, especially churches. No two churches embracing more than one community is like another. This means that each church that is profoundly multicultural has the chance to craft utterly unique combinations of artistry.

ENCOURAGE CONTINUITY IN ARTS THAT ARE MOST FRAGILE
Diversity and fragility are closely connected. UNESCO states than nearly 2,500 of the world's approximately 7,000 languages are in

one of five levels of endangerment: unsafe, definitely endangered, severely endangered, critically endangered, and extinct.[118] Other aspects of these communities—including artistic forms of communication—normally experience similar fragility. We should take special note of the artists and their art forms that are most in the world's margins. God's image is there.

ENCOURAGE CONTINUITY IN ARTS THAT ARE MOST LIKELY TO FLOURISH

We want new artistry to make positive differences in a community, so innovations that spread like wildfire can be great things.

As you reflect on these guidelines, you'll realize that they sometimes work counter to each other. Well, that's the way life is. If the community listens to God and grows in wisdom, they'll do fine.

ACT TO KEEP GOOD THINGS GOING

Your first task here is also simple: if you've followed the cocreation cycle, you've already done what's most important for sustainability. The best way to keep something good going is to start it in the right way. We've encouraged you to make relationships, encourage others to create, get to know and value artists, include all of the important artists and decision makers in sparking activities, and help make artistic products and their presentation better. These activities make it more likely that a critical mass of key community members will champion this new thing, resulting in persistent momentum into the future.

However, you might still need to plan activities that inject energy into strategic points. Following are a few ideas.

INTEGRATE

Integrating has to do with making artistic practice part of normal patterns of community life. A good place to start is to reflect with the community on the ways that they teach each other things like new songs, dances, and carving skills. If possible, their plans should include these means of transmission. In order to keep creativity going, the community may decide to repeat sparking activities like workshops or commissioning. Existing social groups like dance associations or literacy clubs may also have motivation to keep creating. Or communities might decide to form new groups that meet regularly to help members create for kingdom purposes, like the creators' clubs we described in **Step 5**. Each of these ideas feeds into repeated parts of community life, so the engines of creativity keep running.

---

118 Christopher Moseley, ed., *Atlas of the World's Languages in Danger*, 3rd ed. (Paris: UNESCO Publishing, 2010), http://www.unesco.org/culture/languages-atlas/.

PREFACE

PREPARE

STEP 1

STEP 2

STEP 3

STEP 4

STEP 5

STEP 6

STEP 7

CLOSING

PREFACE

PREPARE

STEP 1

STEP 2

STEP 3

STEP 4

STEP 5

STEP 6

STEP 7

CLOSING

CELEBRATE

Good things happen when you celebrate the intrinsic value of artistic expression and share it with the wider community and the outside world. Celebrating the positive and redemptive aspects of local art thus serves to strengthen the cultural esteem of a community, and protect an invaluable cultural heritage. By affirming the local arts, you serve as an advocate for a community's unique expressions and foster conditions for further artistic flowering. You also help a community's voice (their unique stories, perceptions of the world, and values) to be heard and understood by others.

Ways to celebrate new and older art forms include

- presenting them to community officials and leaders
- disseminating recordings
- performing at festive social events
- entering contests

The "Identity and Sustainability" goals and activities (**Steps 2, 5**) offer more detailed suggestions for celebration.

EVALUATE

Every so often, look at the community's cocreative activities and see what the results are. Try to develop a milieu in which everyone recognizes that everything can be improved and everything has a life cycle. This will help in planning.

A PLANNING METHOD: RESULTS BASED MANAGEMENT

Our seven-step cocreative cycle is in itself a planning and management method. But sometimes you will work with organizations who use other systems. Results Based Management (RBM) is a very effective tool and in use in a number of successful government and religious organizations; RBM also shares many characteristics of the CLAT approach.

Results Based Management is a participatory and team-based approach to planning and management that focuses on achieving defined results. It is a way of viewing what we do by first looking at the hoped-for impacts and working back in time and levels of detail.

Imagine dropping a stone in a pond. The ripples spread out from the point the stone first hit the water, eventually lapping up on the pond's shoreline. RBM leads you through a process of imagining the impacts a community wants to see happen (the shoreline), thinking logically about what would need to occur backwards in time to reach that impact (the ripples), and planning activities to make those things happen (dropping the stone in the water). RBM has developed a particular vocabulary to describe this, depicted on the next page:

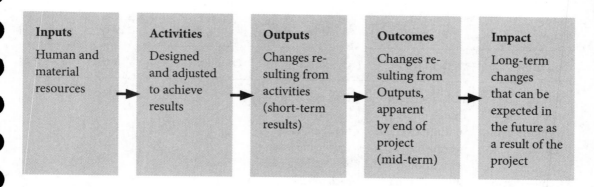

When you use RBM to plan, you create a results chain (like the ripples in a pond) based on cause-and-effect relationships:

- Carrying out Activities causes short-term results (Outputs)
- Outputs cause mid-term results (Outcomes)
- Outcomes cause long-term results (Impact)

Though it may at first seem paradoxical, you create this chain by starting on the right side of this diagram and working left. So, through discussion, the community

- decides on a long term goal (Impact)
- decides what mid-term changes (Outcomes) would need to occur for this Impact to happen
- decides what short-term changes (Outputs) would need to occur for the Outcomes to happen
- decides what Activities would need to be done to produce the Outputs
- decides what human, physical, and financial resources (Inputs) they would need to perform the Activities.

The table on the next page shows a small portion of such an arts-related results chain.[119]

---

119 In literature in the United States, the word "Deaf" is often capitalized. "This is the form used in reference to a specific, self-defined cultural group in the United States, with a common history and language" (Mariana Portolano, http://endora.wide.msu.edu/7.1/coverweb/porto-lano/deaf.htm). This capitalization is a strong marker of identity and respect for many in the U.S. Other global deaf communities do not follow this convention, so we have retained the lower-case form.

PREFACE

PREPARE

STEP 1

STEP 2

STEP 3

STEP 4

STEP 5

STEP 6

STEP 7

CLOSING

PREFACE

PREPARE

STEP 1

STEP 2

STEP 3

STEP 4

STEP 5

STEP 6

STEP 7

CLOSING

How?		What we want		Why?
Inputs	Activities	Outputs	Outcomes	Impact
Willing [1]deaf and hearing members in the church Connections with local deaf community Deaf to spoken language translators, and vice versa Funds, designer	Hold a series of church meetings in which deaf and hearing members learn to know each other well. Emphasis should be on the hearing learning from the deaf Form small groups of deaf and hearing church members who minister to each other and involve themselves in activities in the city's deaf community Create a space in the church building that meets the needs of deaf people to perform, worship, and fellowship Hold a series of workshops in which deaf artists create poetry, visual arts, and other forms on Christian and other themes Hold regular coffee-house type events where deaf artists can perform, display, and discuss their work	Deaf and hearing members of the church are growing together and learning from each other Deaf community members feel comfortable in the church's performance and worship space designed for the deaf	Deaf people in a city make relationships with deaf and hearing people in the church, based on the love they witness in the church	Deaf people are being drawn to Christ by the love and understanding of a church in their city

RBM has been developed into an effective, complex system of planning, management, and measuring results. Other resources are available if you'd like to learn more.[120]

UNDERSTAND MORE ABOUT HOW CONTINUITY WORKS

Though this section isn't essential to a community's cocreative success, reflecting on the underlying dynamics of sustainability will help everyone make wiser choices. Here are a few principles.

GOOD CREATIVITY SPAWNS MORE CREATIVITY
The more something satisfying happens, the more it's likely to happen again. Good begets good. So do lots of good things.

RECURRING EVENTS HELP
It's hard to break a habit. So keep working until enough people have the habit of creating and enjoying new arts that it would take more energy to stop it. These habits become the stable infrastructure on which people can lean when improvising. See "Cultural Dynamism" (**Step 4, Part C**) for more.

ARTISTRY NEEDS TO FILL FOUR CONDITIONS TO BE SUSTAINABLE[121]
Underneath our cocreative cycle lie four strong social dynamics, each of which is necessary for the ongoing life of an art form.

1. **Function**: concerns solidifying or creating social uses for artistic activity. The more positive uses an art form has, the higher status it enjoys. Without status, no one will want to make or experience an art form.
2. **Acquisition**: consists of the ways that the skills, competencies, and knowledge associated with an art form are passed on to others. Without acquisition, no one new will ever learn to create in the form, and it will die.
3. **Motivation:** determines why people choose to use certain arts for social functions.
4. **Environment**: affects how the surrounding society supports the use of an art form or not.

---

120   See, for example, http://www.undg.org/index.cfm?P=224, materials published by the United Nations Development Group.
121   Paul Lewis and Gary Simons, organizers, "Ecological Perspectives on Language Endangerment: Applying the Sustainable Use Model for Language Development," (a colloquium presented at the annual conference of the American Association for Applied Linguistics Chicago, 2011).

PREFACE

PREPARE

STEP 1

STEP 2

STEP 3

STEP 4

STEP 5

STEP 6

STEP 7

CLOSING

I am an ethnomusicologist who lived among and performed research with speakers of the Alamblak language in Papua New Guinea from 2003 through 2006. One of the instruments I documented was the *nrwit* (*garamut* in Tok Pisin): a hollowed length of tree trunk, between 4 and 6 feet long, and between 2 and 4 feet tall, with a long, thin opening in the top. The nrwit player holds a beater stick, 3–4 feet long, and strikes a nodule at the edge of the slit with the blunt end of the beater. The deep, resonant sound from the nrwit carries over a great distance and can be used to send messages within or beyond the village. An individual nuclear family might own one nrwit, which rests on the ground just outside the family home, sheltered from the weather by the overhanging eaves of the roof. Alamblak people stated that previous generations used the nrwit to say anything that people could say, although the signaling system is not sonically imitative of the spoken language. By the time of my fieldwork, the system had fallen into disuse, and only a few older men were able to play the signals. Other people said that they could understand some signals when they heard them but could not themselves produce nrwit communication. Today the primary use of the nrwit is announcing the death of a village resident.

Signaling on the nrwit has been reduced to an identity reminder for the Alamblak ethnic community. No one has more than symbolic proficiency. Recordings and documentation exist, but people are not using the signal system. Kondak, the acknowledged expert who taught me the nrwit patterns, died in 2010. People could, if they choose, re-learn the nrwit patterns, likely in an adapted form rather than the exact traditional system; at this point, it seems unlikely. As mobile phones become a larger part of communication in Papua New Guinea, people will have the option to send text messages, similar to the nrwit signals. But when I asked an Alamblak friend about this, he pointed out an important difference: the nrwit sends one message to entire villages at once, but text messages go only to one individual. Community involvement is a Melanesian ideal that is not well-suited to mobile phone communication.

The nrwit tradition is on the verge of extinction, which affects me personally: I have concern for my Alamblak friends and have hopes for the very best for their lives. They've lost something of great value. – *Neil Coulter*

ARTISTIC SUSTAINABILITY CAN BE GRADED ON A HOPEFUL TO HOPELESS SCALE

Linguists have tried to understand the rapid rate of language death in the world today, thereby developing models that can be applied to artistic communication. The following list describes eight possible states of an artistic genre's vitality:[122]

---

122   Slightly revised text from Neil Coulter, "Assessing Music Shift: Adapting EGIDS for a Papua New Guinea Community," *Language Documentation and Description* 10 (2011): 61–81. See also Robin Harris, "Sitting '*Under the Mouth*': Decline and Revitalization in the Sakha Epic Tradition *Olonkho*," (PhD diss., University of Georgia, 2012); Catherine Fiona Grant, "Strengthening the Vitality and Viability of Endangered Music Genres: The Potential of Language Maintenance to Inform Approaches to Music Sustainability," (PhD diss., Griffith University, 2012).

1. **International**: An art form reaches this level when an international "community of practice" forms around it.
2. **National or regional**: The art's reputation grows beyond the home community. Community members may receive financial or other support from the regional or national level.
3. **Vigorous**: This is the pivotal level for artistic vitality. In this level, oral transmission and largely traditional contexts of education are intact and functioning. People have sufficient opportunities for performance, and young people are learning by observation, participation, and appropriate educational contexts. An art can exist comfortably at this level without needing to move higher.
4. **Threatened**: The first level that hints at downward movement, toward endangerment. An art is still performed/produced, but changes are becoming noticeable: diminishing performance contexts, more time given to more recent introductions, more rural-urban movement.
5. **Locked**: The art is known by more people than just the grandparent generation, but its performance is restricted to tourist shows or other contexts that are not integrated into the everyday life of the community. The performance repertoire is fixed and nothing new is being added to it. Participation and creative energy decline noticeably.
6. **Shifting**: The grandparent generation is proficient in this art, but fewer contexts exist for passing it on to younger people. Possibly the younger people do not express interest (or are perceived that way by their parents and grandparents). The art is not dead or endangered at this level, and can be revitalized, but signs point to downward movement and likely endangerment.
7. **Dormant**: Functional contexts for performance are gone, but recordings and other ethnographic description exist. A community could reacquaint itself with the art, but its rebirth would likely be something different than what it was.
8. **Extinct**: No one in the community is capable of creating or performing in this art. Probably no performance has occurred in the lifetime of anyone currently living. No documentation exists. This is rarer, as most arts grow into other styles, or stylistic elements are perpetuated in related styles.

If you can identify the state of vitality of the art in which the community is interested, then you can target cocreative activities more wisely. The closer it is to state eight (extinct), the more energy it would require to spark creativity.

PREFACE

PREPARE

STEP 1

STEP 2

STEP 3

STEP 4

STEP 5

STEP 6

STEP 7

CLOSING

PREFACE

PREPARE

STEP 1

STEP 2

STEP 3

STEP 4

STEP 5

STEP 6

STEP 7

CLOSING

KNOW WHEN TO LET GO

We believe that the precarious situation of many artists in the world requires us to seriously consider becoming their advocates. But each of us needs to know whom God is calling us to serve, and act accordingly. If you know who these people are, then stubbornly act on their behalf—even when it's not easy.

But also remember that ultimately all we do is about God, not what he created. So take Sabbath rests. Let things go when they no longer make sense. God is running the universe.

QUICK REFERENCE

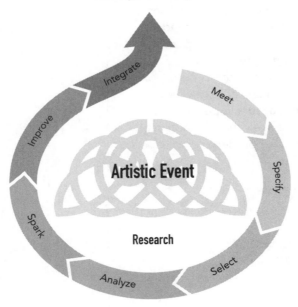

Figure 1: Create Local Arts Together

1. <u>**Meet**</u> **a Community and Its Arts.** Explore artistic and social resources that exist in the community. Performing **Step 1** allows you to build relationships, to participate with and understand the people, and to discover the hidden treasures of the community.

PREFACE

PREPARE

STEP 1

STEP 2

STEP 3

STEP 4

STEP 5

STEP 6

STEP 7

CLOSING

2. <u>Specify</u> **Kingdom Goals.** Discover the kingdom goals that the community wants to work toward. Performing **Step 2** ensures that you are helping the community work toward aims that they have agreed on together.

3. <u>Select</u> **Effects, Content, Genre, and Events.** Choose an artistic genre that can help the community meet its goals, and activities that can result in purposeful creativity in this genre. Performing **Step 3** reveals the mechanisms that relate certain kinds of artistic activity to its effects, so that the activities performed have a high chance of succeeding.

4. <u>Analyze</u> **an Event Containing the Chosen Genre.** Describe the event and its genre(s) as a whole, and its artistic forms as arts and in relationship to broader cultural context. Performing **Step 4** results in detailed knowledge of the art forms that is crucial to sparking creativity, improving what is produced, and integrating it into the community.

5. <u>Spark</u> **Creativity.** Implement activities the community has chosen to spark creativity within the genre they have chosen. Performing **Step 5** actually produces new artistic works for events.

6. <u>Improve</u> **New Works.** Evaluate results of the sparking activities and make them better. Performing **Step 6** makes sure that the new artistry exhibits the aesthetic qualities, produces the impacts, and communicates the intended messages at a level of quality appropriate to its purposes.

7. <u>Integrate and Celebrate for Continuity</u>. Plan and implement ways that this new kind of creativity can continue into the future. Identify more contexts where the new and old arts can be displayed and performed. Performing **Step 7** makes it more likely that a community will keep making its arts in ways that produce good effects long into the future.

SAMPLE COMMUNITY ARTS PROFILE (CAP) OUTLINE

We've created a file that provides spaces to describe and capture the results of activities you and a community do related to the manual. Essentially, it restates many of the manual's sections so you know where to include results of activities you perform. In the file, you will replace the capitalized words with words appropriate to your context. For example, COMMUNITY NAME would be substituted with the name of the community you're working with, such as Sakha, the Bach clan, or *l'Eglise Catholique de Tchinga*. You are free to modify the structure, categories, and content of your CAP however you'd like. What follows is an example of the table of contents of a CAP yet to be filled in.

<COMMUNITY NAME>

Name of arts advocate(s):
Dates of work represented by this document:

SUMMARIZE PLANS, ACTIVITIES, RESULTS

- "Create Local Arts Together" Cycles Completed (to any degree)
- List of Events and Genres Researched (to any degree)

PREFACE

PREPARE

STEP 1

STEP 2

STEP 3

STEP 4

STEP 5

STEP 6

STEP 7

CLOSING

CREATE LOCAL ARTS TOGETHER CYCLE: <NUMBER>, FOR <KINGDOM GOAL(S)>

Step 1: Meet COMMUNITY and its Arts
- Take a first glance at a community
- Take a first glance at a community's arts
- Take a first glance at a community's goals
- Start exploring a community's social and conceptual life
- Summarize results and challenges of this step

Step 2: Specify Kingdom Goals
- Help a Community Discover its Kingdom Goals
- Describe the one or two goals to focus on now
- Summarize results and challenges of this step

Step 3: Select Effects, Content, Genre, and Events
- Describe the process of the discussion of Effects, Content, Genre, and Events
- List the Effects, Content, Genre, and Event chosen
- Summarize results and challenges of this step

Step 4: Analyze an Event Containing the Chosen Genre
- Decide what research you will perform
- Perform research, entering results in "Descriptions of Artistic Genres"
- Summarize results and challenges of this step

Step 5: Spark Creativity
- Describe familiar methods of composition
- Identify opportunities to exploit and barriers to overcome
- Decide on the type of activity
- Design a new or modify an existing activity that helps communities reach their goals
- Perform the activity
- Summarize results and challenges of this step

Step 6: Improve New Works
- Choose and modify an approach to evaluation and improvement
- Perform the approach to evaluation and improvement
- Summarize results and challenges of this step

Step 7: Integrate and Celebrate for Continuity
- Choose what to integrate and celebrate
- Plan actions to keep good things going
- Summarize results and challenges of this step

DESCRIPTIONS OF ARTISTIC GENRES:
\<GENRE NAME\>

A: Event Analysis: EVENT NAME
- Brief description
- First glance at the event
- Performance lenses on an event

B: Artistic Aspects of an Event
- Music
- Drama
- Dance
- Oral verbal arts
- Visual arts
- Interrelationships between formal elements of the event

C: Broader Cultural Context of an Event
- Artists
- Creativity
- Language
- Transmission and change
- Cultural dynamism
- Identity and power
- Aesthetics
- Time
- Emotions
- Subject matter
- Community values shown
- Communal investment

D: Explore how a Christian community relates artistically to its Broader church and cultural context: CHURCH NAME
- Discover a Christian community's arts
- Compare a Christian community's use of arts with that of its surrounding communities
- Evaluate how arts currently fulfill a Christian community's purposes
- Apply a heart arts questionnaire to a Christian community
- Evaluate worship meetings using biblical principles
- Evaluate a Christian community using the worship wheel
- Assess a multicultural Christian community's art
- Interpret Scripture well

PREFACE
PREPARE
STEP 1
STEP 2
STEP 3
STEP 4
STEP 5
STEP 6
STEP 7
CLOSING

PREFACE

PREPARE

STEP 1

STEP 2

STEP 3

STEP 4

STEP 5

STEP 6

STEP 7

CLOSING

GLOSSARY

Agency: The ability of a group or an individual to exert power, usually in terms of making decisions.

Analytical performance: Presentation designed by a researcher in order to isolate features of artistic production.

Artistic communication: An act of conveying messages marked by heightened attention to form and visceral and emotional impact.

Artistic domain: A category of special communication determined by the nature of its production. In the manual, we use this term to refer to Euro-American categories, including music, dance, drama, oratory, and visual arts. Other communities organize their thoughts and words about arts differently.

Artistic event: Something that occurs in a particular place and time, related to larger sociocultural patterns of a community, containing at least one enactment of an artistic genre. It is divisible into shorter time segments. Examples: festival, church service, birthday party, rite of passage.

Artistic genre: A community's category of artistic communication characterized by a unique set of formal characteristics, performance practices, and social meanings. It can draw on multiple Euro-American artistic domains.

Arts: A general term that refers to forms of communication marked by patterns that differ from a community's everyday communication.

Arts advocate: Anyone who advocates the use of local arts for a community's benefit. Also sometimes referred to as an ethnoarts advocate.

Arts consultant (Christian): A specialist who researches and encourages Scripture-infused creativity in local artistic forms

PREFACE

PREPARE

STEP 1

STEP 2

STEP 3

STEP 4

STEP 5

STEP 6

STEP 7

CLOSING

of communities around the world. Sometimes referred to as an ethnoarts consultant, ethnoarts specialist, or ethnoarts worker.

Catalyst: Someone or something that starts an action that keeps going on its own.

CLAT: The acronym for the Create Local Arts Together process.

Cocreation: A synonym for the Create Local Arts Together (CLAT) process. It emphasizes the fact that purposeful artistic production requires people filling more than one role.

Community: A social group of any size whose members share a story, identity, and ongoing patterns of interaction, and whose identity and social practices are constantly in flux.

Contextualization: Adapting an outside cultural form or idea into a society or culture. Often used in terms of the adoption of Christianity.

Cultural domain: A broad category of cultural meanings or phenomena that includes smaller categories.

Cultural theme: Any principle that recurs in several cultural domains and defines relationships among sets of cultural meanings.

Distilled forms: Genres whose enactments are relatively short and inflexible. Examples include proverbs, riddles, aphorisms, sayings, greetings, clichés (melodic, rhythmic, movement, etc.). They are often woven or inserted into larger communication contexts like court proceedings, games, or informal conversation.

Emic: A viewpoint from inside a culture being studied.

Ethnoarts: Study of the artistic communication in a group which strongly identifies itself as an ethnolinguistic community.

Ethnocentrism: An attitude in which one evaluates aspects of a different culture based on values and assumptions from his/her own.

Ethnography: A description of a community based on observation of and interaction with living people over a prolonged period of time. A **performance ethnography** relates how sounds, movements, dramatizations, and other artistic products are conceived, made, appreciated and influence other individuals, groups, and social and artistic processes.[123]

Ethnomusicology: The study of music in and as culture.

Etic: A viewpoint from outside a culture being studied.

Gatekeeper: A person who exerts significant influence on whether a community accepts an innovation or not, who has a personal or social stake in its success or failure.

Genre: A community's category of communication characterized by a unique set of formal characteristics, performance practices, and social meanings. Examples of genre: *olonkho* (Siberia), Broadway musical (New York City), *kanoon* (Cameroon), *huayno* (Peru), *haiku* (Japan), praise and worship (Euro-America), *qawwali* (South Asia). See **Artistic genre, Genre enactment**.

---

123   Inspired by Anthony Seeger, "Ethnography of Music," in *Ethnomusicology: An Introduction*, ed. Helen Myers, (New York: W. W. Norton, 1993), 88–109.

Genre enactment: an instantiation of an artistic genre during an event; artistry that people produce from within a genre. Sometimes we refer to a genre enactment as artistry, or bits of artistry.

Integral performance context: An environment that has many social and artistic components that are familiar to the performers.

Kingdom goals: Objectives that are consistent with the kingdom of God as described in the New Testament. They are incomplete manifestations of heaven on earth.

Labanotation: A system for transcribing dance movements.

Language development: The series of ongoing, planned actions that a language community takes to ensure that their language continues to serve their changing social, cultural, political, economic, and spiritual needs and goals.

Local art: An artistic form of communication that a community can create, perform, teach, and understand from within, including its forms, meanings, language, and social context.

Meristem: the region in a plant in which new cells are created; the growth point.

Music: Humanly organized and heightened sound.

Orality: The way of accessing and passing on information by nonliterate means.

Orature: A body of works communicated orally, such as stories, myths, and folklore.

Organology: The study of musical instruments.

Participant observation: An investigative practice used in ethnographic researcher in which the researcher engages in life activities with the participants of the study.

Performance event: An enactment of a genre at a particular place and time.

Polysemy: The ability of one form or symbol to hold multiple meanings.

Qualitative research: An approach in which the researcher collects open-ended, emerging, and evolving data with the primary intent of developing themes from the data. The results tend to focus on meanings and experiences.

Quantitative research: An approach that focuses on specific variables and the testing of specific hypotheses, that employs strategies such as experiments and surveys, and that yields statistical data. The results tend to focus on numbers and frequencies.

Reflexivity: The acknowledgment that representations of reality are constructions of the researcher and informed by his/her own choices and viewpoints.

Revitalization / Cultural revitalization: Bringing something back to life again, through research, creation, and use of indigenous resources.

Rule of thirds: In photography, a frame can be divided into three vertical and three horizontal sections. Many people believe that

PREFACE

PREPARE

STEP 1

STEP 2

STEP 3

STEP 4

STEP 5

STEP 6

STEP 7

CLOSING

an object becomes more prominent if it is not in the center of the frame.

Scripture engagement: A process where Scripture translated in the language of the users is intentionally integrated in their individual and community life.

Sparking: anything anybody does that results in the creation of new artistry. A catalyst.

Sustainability: Usually used for development projects, a desired characteristic where what is initiated in a community will be continued or further developed.

Syncretism: Combining Christian beliefs with those of another religion or worldview that leads people away from the truth.

Tacit knowledge: Information held by culture-bearers (cultural insiders) that is not easily expressed.

Taxonomy: A set of categories organized on the basis of a single semantic relationship which shows the relationships of all the terms in a domain.

Transcription: Graphic representation of aspects of artistic communication.

BIBLIOGRAPHY

The Annanberg Project. *The Art of Teaching the Arts* video series. Produced by Lavine Production Group, in collaboration with EDC's Center for Children and Technology and the Southeast Center for Education in the Arts, 2005.

Apel, Willi. *Harvard Dictionary of Music*. Cambridge, MA: Belknap Press of Harvard University Press, 1972.

Ball, William. *A Sense of Direction: Some Observations on the Art of Directing*. New York: Drama Publishers, 1984.

Barz, Gregory. *Singing for Life: HIV/AIDS and Music in Uganda*. New York: Routledge, 2006.

———, *Performing Religion: Negotiating Past and Present in Kwaya Music of Tanzania*. Amsterdam: Rodopi, 2003.

Barber, Karin, John Collins, and Alain Ricard. *West African Popular Theatre*. Indiana University Press, 1997.

Bauman, Richard, ed. *Folklore, Cultural Performances, and Popular Entertainments*. Oxford: Oxford University Press, 1992.

Bernardi, Philip. *Improvisation Starters*. Cincinnati: BetterWay Books, 1992.

Biswas, Ranjita. "Dancing Away the Pain." *Guardian Weekly*. October 12, 2010. http://www.guardian.co.uk/world/2010/oct/12/kolkata-women-trafficking-dance-therapy.

Boal, Augusto. *The Rainbow of Desire: The Boal Method of Theatre and Therapy*. London: Routledge, 1995.

Bogart, Anne, and Tina Landau. *The Viewpoints Book: A Practical Guide to Viewpoints and Composition*. New York: Theatre Communications Group, 2005.

Calhoun, Adele Ahlberg. *Spiritual Disciplines Handbook: Practices that Transform Us*. Downers Grove, IL: InterVarsity Press, 2005.

Chenoweth, Vida. *Melodic Perception and Analysis*. Ukarumpa, Papua New Guinea: Summer Institute of Linguistics, 1972.

Colgate, Jack. "Relational Bible Story Telling Part 1." *International Journal of Frontier Missions* 25(3):135-142. http://www.ijfm.org/PDFs_IJFM/25_3_PDFs/colgate.pdf.

Coulter, Neil. "Assessing Music Shift: Adapting EGIDS for a Papua New Guinea Community." *Language Documentation and Description* 10 (2011): 61-81.

Csikszentmihalyi, Mihalyi. *Creativity: Flow and the Psychology of Discovery and Invention*. New York: HarperCollins, 1996.

Davis, Matthew. "Health through Song: Outreach Workers in Benin and Guatemala Use Lyrics to Promote Health." *Harvard Medical Alumni Bulletin* 73 (1999): 36–41.

Dooley, Robert A., and Stephen H. Levinsohn. *Analyzing Discourse: A Manual of Basic Concepts*. Dallas: SIL International, 2000.

Duvall, J. Scott, and J. Daniel Hays. *Grasping God's Word*. Grand Rapids: Zondervan, 2001.

Edge, John T. Twitter post. February 12, 2010, 6:49 a.m. http://twitter.com/johntedge/status/9009036481.

Feld, Steven. "Sound Structure as Social Structure." *Ethnomusicology* 28, no. 3 (1984): 383–409.

Feldman, Edmund B. *Varieties of Visual Experience*, 4th ed. New York: Adams, 1992.

Ferraro, Gary, and Susan Andreatta. *Cultural Anthropology: An Applied Perspective*, 9th ed. Belmont, CA: Wadsworth, 2011.

Finnegan, Ruth. *Communicating: The Multiple Modes of Human Interconnection*. London: Routledge, 2002.

Fortunato, Frank. *All the World Is Singing: Glorifying God through the Worship Music of the Nations*. With Paul Neeley and Carol Brinneman. Tyrone, GA: Authentic, 2006.

Frakes, Jack. *Acting for Life: A Textbook on Acting*. Colorado Springs: Meriwether, 2005.

Franklin, Karl J. *Loosen Your Tongue: An Introduction to Storytelling*. Dallas: Graduate Institute of Applied Linguistics, 2009.

Giurchescu, Anca, and Eva Kröschlová. "Theory and Method of Dance Form Analysis." In *Dance Structures: Perspectives on the Analysis of Human Movement*, edited by Adrienne Kaeppler and Elsi Evancich Dunin, 21–52. Budapest: Akadémiai Kiadó, 2007.

Goodridge, Janet. *Rhythm and Timing of Movement in Performance: Drama, Dance and Ceremony*. London: Kingsley, 1999.

Gowey, Bill. "Walking Out the Gospel among the People." *Mission Frontiers* (September–October 2010). http://www.missionfrontiers.org/issue/article/walking-out-the-gospel-among-the-people.

Grant, Catherine Fiona. "Strengthening the Vitality and Viability of Endangered Music Genres: The Potential of Language Maintenance to Inform Approaches to Music Sustainability." PhD diss., Griffith University, 2012.

Greenwald, Michael L., Roger Schulz, and Roberto Dario Pomo. *The Longman Anthology of Drama and Theater: A Global Perspective*. New York: Longman, 2001.

Grimes, Joseph E. *The Thread of Discourse: Janua Linguarum*. The Hague: Mouton, 1975.

PREFACE
PREPARE
STEP 1
STEP 2
STEP 3
STEP 4
STEP 5
STEP 6
STEP 7
CLOSING

Haaland, Ane. *Pretesting Communication Materials: With Special Emphasis on Child Health and Nutrition Education: A Manual for Trainers and Supervisors*. Rangoon: UNICEF, 1984.

Hackney, Peggy. *Making Connections: Total Body Integration through Bartenieff Fundamentals*. New York: Routledge, 2000.

Hargrave, Susanne. *Doing Anthropology*. Kangaroo Ground, Australia: South Pacific Summer Institute of Linguistics, 1993.

Harris, Robin. "Contextualization: Exploring the Intersections of Form and Meaning." *Connections* 9, nos. 2 and 3 (2010).

———. "Sitting '*Under the Mouth*': Decline and Revitalization in the Sakha Epic Tradition *Olonkho*." PhD diss., University of Georgia, 2012.

Hatcher, Jeffrey. *The Art and Craft of Playwriting*. Cincinnati: Story Press, 1996.

Hatton, Howard A., and David J. Clark. "From the Harp to the Sitar." *Bible Translator* 26, no. 1 (1975): 132–38.

Hiebert, Paul G. *Anthropological Insights for Missionaries*. Grand Rapids: Baker Book House, 1985.

Hill, Harriet Swannie. *Communicating Context in Bible Translation among the Adioukrou of Côte d'Ivoire*. Ann Arbor, MI: UMI, 2003.

———, Richard Bagge, Pat Miersma, and Margaret Hill. *Healing the Wounds of Trauma*. Nairobi: Paulines Publications Africa, 2004.

———, and Margaret Hill. *Translating the Bible into Action*. Carlisle, UK: Piquant Editions, 2008.

Hood, Mantle. "The Challenge of Bi-Musicality." *Ethnomusicology* 4 (1960): 55–59.

Hughes-Freeland, Felicia. "Dance on Film: Strategy and Serendipity." In *Dance in the Field: Theory, Methods and Issues in Dance Ethnography*, edited by Theresa J. Buckland, 111–21. New York: St. Martin's Press, 1999.

Hutchinson Guest, Ann. *Labanotation: The System of Analyzing and Recording Movement*. New York: Routledge, 2005.

Hutchinson Guest, Ann, and Tina Curran. *Your Move: The Language of Dance Approach to the Study of Movement and Dance*. Abingdon, UK: Taylor & Francis, 2008.

Johnston, Clay, and Carol J. Orwig. "Your Learning Style and Language Learning." In *LinguaLinks 1999*. Dallas: SIL International, 1999.

Jules-Rosette, Bennetta. "Ecstatic Singing: Music and Social Integration in an African Church." In *More than Drumming: Essays on African and Afro-Latin American Music and Musicians*, edited by Irene V. Jackson, 119–44. Westport, CT: Greenwood, 1985.

King, Roberta. *A Time to Sing: A Manual for the African Church*. Nairobi: Evangel Publishing House, 1999.

Kirby, Michael. "On Acting and Not-Acting." *The Drama Review: TDR* 16, No. 1 (1972).

Klem, Herbert V. *Oral Communication of the Scripture: Insights from African Oral Art*. Pasadena: William Carey Library, 1982.

Kohls, Robert L., and Herbert L. Brussow. *Training Know-How for Cross-Cultural and Diversity Trainers*. Duncanville, TX: Adult Learning Systems, 1995.

Lauer, David A., Stephen Pentak. *Design Basics*, 5th ed. Thomson Wadsworth, 2002.

PREFACE

PREPARE

STEP 1

STEP 2

STEP 3

STEP 4

STEP 5

STEP 6

STEP 7

CLOSING

PREFACE

PREPARE

STEP 1

STEP 2

STEP 3

STEP 4

STEP 5

STEP 6

STEP 7

CLOSING

Lester, P.M. *Visual Communication: Images with Messages*, 4th ed. Stamford, CT: Thomson-Wadsworth Publishing Company, 2003.

Lewis, M. Paul, and Gary F. Simons. "Assessing Endangerment: Expanding Fishman's GIDS." *Revue Roumaine de Linguistique* 55, no. 2 (2010): 103–20.

Lipman, Doug. *Story Telling Workshop in a Box*. Tulsa: n.d.

Lipoński, Wojciech. *World Sports Encyclopedia*. St. Paul, MN: MBI, 2003.

Longacre, Robert E. "Discourse Structure, Verb Forms, and Archaism in Psalm 18." *Journal of Translation* 2, no. 1 (2006): 17–30.

———. *The Grammar of Discourse*, 2nd ed. New York: Plenum, 1996.

———, and Shin Ja J. Hwang. *Holistic Discourse Analysis.* Dallas: SIL International, 2012.

———, and Stephen H. Levinsohn. "Field Analysis of Discourse." In *Current Trends in Textlinguistics*, edited by Wolfgang U. Dressler, 103–22. Berlin: Walter de Gruyter, 1978.

Maletic, Vera. *Dance Dynamics: Effort and Phrasing Workbook*. Columbus, OH: Grade A Notes, 2004.

Margolis, Joseph. *The Language of Art and Art Criticism: Analytic Questions in Aesthetics*. Detroit: Wayne State University Press, 1965.

McKee, Robert. *Story: Substance, Structure, Style, and the Principles of Screenwriting*. New York: HarperCollins, 1997.

McKinney, Carol. *Globetrotting in Sandals: Field Guide to Cultural Research*. Dallas: SIL International, 2000.

McLaughlin, Buzz. *The Playwright's Process: Learning the Craft from Today's Leading Dramatists*. New York: Back Stage Books, 1997.

Mda, Zakes. *When People Play People: Development Communication through Theatre*. New Brunswick, NJ: Zed Books, 1993.

Mlama, Penina. "Reinforcing Existing Indigenous Communication Skills: The Use of Dance in Tanzania." In *Women in Grassroots Communication*, edited by Pilar Riaño, 51–64. London: Sage, 1994.

Moseley, Christopher, ed. *Atlas of the World's Languages in Danger*, 3rd ed. Paris: UNESCO Publishing, 2010. http://www.unesco.org/culture/languages-atlas/.

Murdock, George P., et al. *Outline of Cultural Materials*, 5th ed. with modifications. New Haven, CT: Human Relations Area Files, 2004. http://www.yale.edu/hraf/Ocm_xml/newOcm.xml.

Myers, Bryant L. *Walking with the Poor: Principles and Practices of Transformational Development*. Maryknoll, NY: Orbis, 1999.

Myers, Helen. "Fieldwork." In *Ethnomusicology: An Introduction*, edited by Helen Myers, 21–49. New York: Norton, 1992.

Neeley, Paul. "A Case Study: Commissioning Scripture Songs among the Akyode of Ghana." *Research Review* (Legon, Ghana), supplementary issue no. 10 (1997), 118–129.

———. "Reflections of a Gatekeeper." *EM News* 6, no. 1 (1997).

Nettl, Bruno. *Music in Primitive Culture*. Cambridge: Harvard University Press, 1956.

Petersen, Michelle. "Scripture Relevance Dramas." *Ethnodoxology* 4, no. 4 (2010): 22–31.

Reagan, Timothy. *Non-Western Educational Traditions: Alternative Approaches to Educational Thought and Theory*. Mahwah, NJ: Lawrence Erlbaum Associates, 1996.

Renkema, Jan. *Discourse Studies: An Introductory Textbook*. Amsterdam: Benjamins, 1993.

Richards, Paul. "A Quantitative Analysis of the Relationship between Language Tone and Melody in a Hausa Song." *African Language Studies* 13 (1972): 137–61.

Ricoeur, Paul. *Time and Narrative*, vol. 1. Chicago: University of Chicago Press, 1984.

Saurman, Mary Beth. "The Effect of Music on Blood Pressure and Heart Rate." *EM News* 4, no. 3 (1995): 2.

———. "Culturally Relevant Songs: Teaching Tools in Education Programs." Paper presented at the joint conference of the Sixth Symposium of the International Council for Traditional Music Study Group on Music and Minorities and the Second Symposium of the International Council for Traditional Music Study Group on Applied Ethnomusicology, Hanoi, Vietnam, July 19–30, 2010.

Saurman, Mary Beth, and Todd Saurman. "Applied Ethnomusicology: The Benefits of Approaching Music as a Heart Language." *Journal of Language and Culture* 23, no. 2 (2004, Institute of Language and culture for Rural Development, Mahidol University), 15–29.

———. "Song Checking." In *All the World Will Worship: Helps for Developing Indigenous Hymns*, 3rd ed., 179–185. Duncanville, TX: EthnoDoxology/ACT, 2005.

———. "Some Principles for Leading Ethnomusicology Workshops: Encouraging the Development of New Songs in the Lives of Believers." Paper presented at the Global Consultation on Music and Missions, St. Paul, MN, 2006.

Saville-Troike, Muriel. *The Ethnography of Communication: An Introduction*. Malden, MA: Blackwell, 2002.

Schechner, Richard. *Performance Studies: An Introduction*, integrated media ed. New York: Routledge, 2006.

Schiffrin, Deborah, Deborah Tannen, and Heidi E. Hamilton, eds. *The Handbook of Discourse Analysis*. Oxford: Blackwell, 2001.

Schrag, Brian. "How Bamiléké Music-Makers Create Culture in Cameroon." PhD diss., University of California, Los Angeles, 2005.

———, and Paul Neeley, eds. *All the World Will Worship: Helps for Developing Indigenous Hymns*, 3rd ed. Duncanville, TX: EthnoDoxology/ACT, 2005.

Seeger, Anthony. "Ethnography of Music." In *Ethnomusicology: An Introduction*, edited by Helen Myers, 88–109. New York: Norton, 1992.

———. *Why Suyá Sing: A Musical Anthropology of an Amazonian People*. University of Illinois Press, 2004.

———, and Shubha Chaudhuri, editors. *Archives for the Future: Global Perspectives on Audiovisual Archives in the 21st Century*. Calcutta: Seagull Books, 2004.

Shawyer, Richard. "Indigenous Worship." *Evangelical Missions Quarterly* 38, no. 3 (2002): 326–334.

Shelemay, Kay Kauffman. *Soundscapes: Exploring Music in a Changing World*. New York: Norton, 2001.

Shetler, Joanne. "Communicating the New Information of Scripture When It Clashes with Traditional Assumptions." Paper presented at the Evangelical Missiological Society Southeast Regional Meeting, Conyers, GA, 2011.

PREFACE

PREPARE

STEP 1

STEP 2

STEP 3

STEP 4

STEP 5

STEP 6

STEP 7

CLOSING

Simons, Gary, and Paul Lewis, organizers. "Ecological Perspectives on Language Endangerment: Applying the Sustainable Use Model for Language Development." Colloquium presented at the annual conference of the American Association for Applied Linguistics, Chicago, 2011.

Society for Ethnomusicology. *A Manual for Documentation, Fieldwork and Preservation for Ethnomusicologists*, 2nd ed. Bloomington, IN: The Society for Ethnomusicology, 2001.

Spradley, James. *Participant Observation*. New York: Holt, Rinehart & Winston, 1980.

Stone, Ruth. "Communication and Interaction Processes in Music Events among the Kpelle of Liberia." PhD diss., Indiana University, 1979.

Tickle, Phyllis. *The Divine Hours*, pocket ed. Oxford: Oxford University Press, 2007.

Tillis, Steve. *Rethinking Folk Drama*. Westport, CT/London: Greenwood Press, 1999.

Unseth, Peter. "Collecting, Using, and Enjoying Proverbs." SIL Forum for Language Fieldwork 2008-002, September 2008.

———. "Receptor Language Proverb Forms in Translation (Part 2: Application)." *Bible Translator* 57, no. 4 (2006): 161–70.

———. "Using Local Proverbs in Christian Ministry." Prepublication draft, 2010.

Wedekind, Klaus. "The Praise Singers." *Bible Translator* 26, no. 2 (1975): 245–47.

West, Amy. "Equipping Urban Believers to Meet Traditional Pressures." Paper presented at the Evangelical Missiological Society Southeast Regional Meeting, Conyers, GA, 2011.

PREFACE
PREPARE
STEP 1
STEP 2
STEP 3
STEP 4
STEP 5
STEP 6
STEP 7
CLOSING

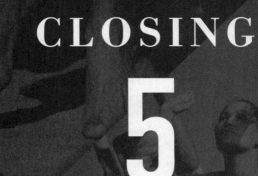

CLOSING

5

INDEX OF ARTISTIC DOMAIN RESEARCH ACTIVITIES

MUSIC IN AN EVENT

DRAMA IN AN EVENT

PREFACE   PREPARE   STEP 1   STEP 2   STEP 3   STEP 4   STEP 5   STEP 6   STEP 7   CLOSING

DANCE IN AN EVENT

ORAL VERBAL ARTS IN AN EVENT

PREFACE

PREPARE

STEP 1

STEP 2

STEP 3

STEP 4

STEP 5

STEP 6

STEP 7

CLOSING

PREFACE

PREPARE

STEP 1

STEP 2

STEP 3

STEP 4

STEP 5

STEP 6

STEP 7

CLOSING

VISUAL ARTS IN AN EVENT

INDEX OF SAMPLE SPARKING ACTIVITIES

IDENTITY AND SUSTAINABILITY

SHALOM

JUSTICE

PREFACE
PREPARE
STEP 1
STEP 2
STEP 3
STEP 4
STEP 5
STEP 6
STEP 7
CLOSING

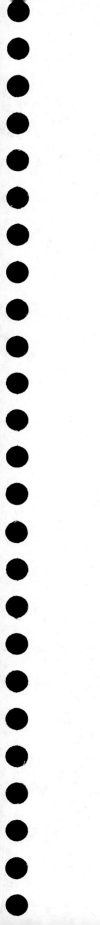